ıs
ɘ ı·
ate,

2

The
Trio

The Trio

THREE WAR CORRESPONDENTS OF WORLD WAR TWO

Richard Knott

For Suzie

'There were three of them, and they stood for three great
London dailies.'

Sir Arthur Conan Doyle in *The Three Correspondents*

'One is rarely seen without the other – we are known as the
three inseparables.'

Alexandre Dumas in *The Three Musketeers*

'The war correspondent has his stake – his life – in his own
hands. And he can put it back in his pocket at the very last
minute.'

Robert Capa in *Slightly Out of Focus* and quoted by
Susana Fortes in *Waiting for Robert Capa*

First published 2015

The History Press
The Mill, Brimscombe Port
Stroud, Gloucestershire, GL5 2QG
www.thehistorypress.co.uk

© Richard Knott, 2015

The right of Richard Knott to be identified as the
of this work has been asserted in accordance with
Copyright, Designs and Patents Act 1988.

British Library Cataloguing in Publication Data.
A catalogue record for this book is available from the British Library.

ISBN 978 0 7509 5593 5

Typesetting and origination by The History Press
Printed in Great Britain

Contents

PART 3 – The Trio is Broken: 'No One Can See Very Clearly'

PART 1

The Duo: 'Follow Clifford! Follow Moorehead!'

1. 'Monty's Blue-Eyed Boys'

In the middle of August 1943, a small group of war correspondents arrived in the hilltop town of Taormina on the island of Sicily. There were three of them – Christopher Buckley, Alexander Clifford and Alan Moorehead – and they worked for three London newspapers: *The Daily Telegraph*, the *Daily Express* and the *Daily Mail*. They had been drawn together by the shared demands of a dangerous job, the familiarity of living cheek-by-jowl in the open air of the North African desert, and the recognition that each of them would be the lesser without the other two. They had not known each other long – a few eventful years – but, in a world of guns, bombs and frantic movement, their friendship had been accelerated to the point where it bordered on love. They were known as 'The Trio'.

On that hot summer's day they approached Taormina by way of a tree-lined road which passed through shaded verges where wild geraniums grew. It was a cautious progress prompted by the fact that the Germans had planted scores of mines in the road. A young peasant woman appeared, clutching a jug of wine and glasses, and offered them a drink. So began the pleasures of Taormina. The town was captured 'in the old style', the *Daily Mail*'s Alexander Clifford wrote home to his mother, declaring it to be 'the most lovely place in the world'.[1] On that Saturday afternoon the three men slowly climbed 'the precipitous goat-track' which led up into the town, watched by the 'townspeople leaning over the ramparts'.[2] On one side, far below the red cliffs and rocks, lay the Mediterranean and, in the distance across the strait, the pale outline of the Italian mainland. To the north-west was 'the great black lava bulk of Mount Etna'.[3] It felt like walking into paradise. By the time the Trio reached the top of the winding path, they were panting for breath and desperately hot, scarcely ready for what greeted them, an excited, enthusiastic mob, and an Italian officer with a fine sense of occasion and a Shakespearian turn of phrase. 'My lords,' he said, 'we have waited too long for you!'[4]

'It felt like walking into paradise': Taormina and 'the great lava bulk of Mount Etna'.
(Author's collection)

*　*　*　*

Buckley, Clifford and Moorehead were called the 'Trio', the 'Inside Set', or
'Monty's blue-eyed boys',[5] often with a hint of envy or resentment by those who
worked outside the privileged circle. Each brought a distinctive quality to this
unique friendship. Buckley was the historian, the military thinker who knew his
Clausewitz and could talk the strategic talk. Clifford was the linguist, able to make
himself understood across Europe, the cook with a flair for improvised cooking
in the most unpromising of situations. Moorehead was perhaps the truest 'writer'
amongst them, a correspondent with the sharpest of eyes for pictorial detail. In
their day, they were famous; their dispatches from distant war zones were breakfast
reading in millions of British households. Then, once the war was over, each of
them had to confront the daunting prospect of forging a new reputation in a
much changed world. It is probably fair to say that only Alan Moorehead's name
is still widely known so many decades after the end of the Second World War. All
three deserve to be remembered, and each was silenced cruelly and too soon.

　　The three of them shared a love of words, an eye for news and great resilience.
Physically, Buckley and Clifford towered over the diminutive Moorehead.

Christopher Buckley was tall, gentle, erudite and donnish, a reluctant schoolmaster who had become an elder statesman to his fellow newsmen. He regularly told people that 'he always wanted to be a bishop because of the peace it would bring him, and also because he fancied himself in gaiters'.[6] Known as 'The General', he could be brusque, even rude at times, and he had little patience with those he thought to be fools. In his military uniform he looked decidedly uncomfortable. He loved cricket, architecture and the novels of Anthony Trollope and, while he was frightened of both heights and depths, he was invariably fearless in the face of gunfire. Alexander Clifford was 'square-shouldered, cool, reserved, with uncompromising eyes'.[7] He was the Trio's translator, chef and source of information. He loved cats and music and was a talented sportsman, excelling at golf and tennis. Gifted and intelligent, he rather drifted into journalism. Alan Moorehead, by contrast, was 'a short neat compact man like a coiled spring'. He had left his native Australia in the mid 1930s, sensing that it was 'a land where nothing happened',[8] and his accent had become emphatically English. His career, writing and life were all profoundly affected by his friendship with Alexander Clifford.

* * * *

The friendship between Moorehead and Clifford had had a fractious beginning in a truculent exchange between the two reporters in a bar in southern France during the Spanish Civil War. However, by the time the two of them and Buckley were holed up in Taormina in 1943 – reading, writing and occasionally staring over the straits of Messina towards the Italian mainland – the relationship was characterised by a shared camaraderie, affection, mutual regard and trust, integrity and an unstinting determination to see the war through, from Cairo to its sombre conclusion at Lüneburg Heath. It was a journey which involved passing encounters with a series of the great and good – and not so good – whose lives came into the Trio's extended circle and who figure in this book: the spy Kim Philby, Ernest Hemingway, field marshals Montgomery, Wavell and Auchinleck, Eve Curie, Randolph Churchill, Lord Beaverbrook, Richard Dimbleby and many others. The principal focus of this book, however, is the Trio and the stories of its individual members. In recounting those stories there is much to be revealed about the role of 'war correspondent': the extent to which they were censored, were unwitting or conscious propagandists, were 'used' by the intelligence services, or suffered from what we would now call post-traumatic stress disorder.

    In October 1944 the magazine *Picture Post* published a piece entitled 'The Men Who Send the Front Line News'. Written by Macdonald Hastings, Buckley, Clifford and Moorehead were among the most important correspondents described; Hastings reckoned that there were 180 front-line correspondents, but of those just twenty-five were responsible for most of the first-hand news of the fighting. 'For nearly five years,' he wrote, 'men like Moorehead, Clifford [and] Buckley … have lent us their eyes. Every day for years, they've followed the fighting. Every day for years, they've sat at field conferences and sweated over their maps to decide where the fighting was hottest.' Hastings described the strain as 'fearful' in an atmosphere which was 'hysterical'. Moreover, 'week in, week out, the war correspondents never get away from it'.[9] By late 1944, when Hastings' piece appeared, Buckley, Clifford and Moorehead had been doggedly pursuing the ebb and flow of wartime front lines for so long that a profound tiredness had eroded the zest of the previous decade. They had, after all, been 'wounded, blown up, lost, hungry, filthy, dirty, frightened and exhausted' for too long. And then, once the war was over, there was the challenge of acclimatising to peacetime, when each member of the Trio went in a sharply different direction. The story begins, however, in Spain, in an earlier war.

NOTES

1   Clifford papers (16727), Imperial War Museum (IWM), file AGC/2/1/7; letter from Alexander Clifford to his mother, 28 July 1943.
2   *Road to Rome* by Christopher Buckley, p.131.
3   *Daily Express*, 17 August 1943.
4   Buckley, p.136.
5   *War Correspondent* by Michael Moynihan, p.131.
6   According to the war correspondent Eric Lloyd Williams.
7   *Magic Mistress* by Doon Campbell, p.73.
8   *Alan Moorehead: A Rediscovery* by Ann Moyal, p.4.
9   *Picture Post*, vol. 25, no. 3, 14 October 1944.

2. The Road to War

I t is the last day of 1937. Under cover of darkness, five cars drive slowly out of the Spanish city of Saragossa, heading for the front at Teruel, a bleak, walled town, high on an exposed plateau. Teruel – 'a mountain stronghold of great strategic significance'[1] – lies besieged by the Republican army in cruel weather: bitterly cold, with driving snow blown about by a piercing wind. At −18°C, it is cold enough for men to freeze to death. Vehicle engines have seized up and frostbite amongst the troops is widespread. Spain's civil war is about to enter its third year, a war characterised by brutal, unforgiving fighting from the outset, when General Franco's Nationalist army had rebelled against the country's

An ambulance unit on the Teruel Front, 1938: 'cold enough for men to freeze to death'. (IWM, HU 33075)

elected government. The war has attracted the world's interest, this rehearsal for the Second World War, and that is why these five dark saloons are leaving Saragossa in the pre-dawn of an unpromising New Year's Eve. They are carrying a posse of war correspondents, each of them muffled up against the cold, their typewriters on their knees, all of them coughing in the collective fug of cigarette smoke.

The road to the front was familiar since they had travelled this way just the day before. The day of 30 December had been one of bright glittering frost, and as the light had finally begun to fade, a Nationalist officer had exhorted them to return early the following morning. 'If you're here in good time tomorrow you'll have something really interesting to write about' – so Colonel Sagardia, his hair lightened by years of Moroccan sun, had put it. The journey was a penance to be endured, however, the road rutted, stony and uneven. *The Daily Telegraph's* correspondent Karl Robson later wrote: 'If you want to test your patience, try typing at dusk in the back of a car on a primitive country track, making two carbon copies; the original for the telegraph office, one copy for the censor, and one for yourself.'[2]

Robson was accompanied by Kim Philby of *The Times*, H.R. (Richard) Sheepshanks of the Reuters news agency, an American photographer, Bradish Johnson, and Edward Neil of Associated Press. It was noon by the time the correspondents' cars rolled into Caudé, some 8 miles from Teruel. They pulled up close to a barn and got out, ears immediately assaulted by the cold and the guns from a nearby battery. The noise, the bitter temperature and the need to consult a map of the front soon prompted Robson to get back into the car, and the others quickly followed. Suddenly they heard the roar of an incoming shell which rocked the car and showered stones and shattered bricks on its roof. Moments later Philby appeared – he had been in the car directly behind Robson's – with blood trickling down his face and soaking into his clothes. He had been lucky: the shell had exploded close to the car's left wheel with sickening results: 'three figures, with grotesquely blackened faces, lolling motionless in their seats'.[3] Johnson had a hole in his back. Philby had survived, but Johnson, Neil and Richard Sheepshanks were either dead or close to it.

To Robson, Kim Philby appeared to be 'a serious, slightly stodgy, young English journalist, rather taken with his own importance, who wrote reports about the Franco side in which his objectivity did not quite conceal his fascist sympathies'.[4] It was a misjudgement, albeit an understandable one shared by many. In fact he was working undercover for the Russians as an intelligence officer. Philby was based in the Basque city of Bilbao where he masqueraded as an archetypal right-wing aesthete by taking an exotic mistress, the Canadian-born divorced actress, Frances ('Bunny') Doble, Lady Lindsey-Hogg. Wounded, and after treatment in a field hospital, Philby was driven back to Saragossa. Once there he headed straight for a bar where the customers stared at his bizarre appearance since 'the blast had destroyed most of his clothes', leaving him clad in 'a pair of old sandals and a woman's pale blue coat with a moth-eaten fur collar'.[5] After one of the waiters, who knew something of the circumstances, had brought him a large drink, he was fêted as a hero. He would continue his double life unsuspected, his credibility helped by his wounds at Caudé.

Philby's luck was not shared by Richard Sheepshanks of Reuters, who was destined never to leave Caudé alive. 'Badly wounded in the head and face, (with) an eye missing', he died later that evening.[6] His replacement was the 28-year-old Alexander Clifford. Born in Eltham, Kent in April 1909, Clifford was a gifted musician (aged 5, he could already play the piano), and a natural linguist, speaking nine languages, six of them fluently. At Charterhouse, one fellow student, the cartoonist Osbert Lancaster, remembered 'the sight of Alex marching purposefully and in time to early school as seen by laggard Lancaster far in the rear'. There was something 'of the air of the cat who walked by himself', Lancaster thought, a characteristic which Clifford never lost.[7] With his brother Henry (known as Tony), he walked and bicycled around Europe during the 1930s and, after taking a degree at Oxford (Oriel College), he joined the Reuters agency in 1931. 'The rest of his career,' his brother thought, 'was like surf riding.'[8]

Clifford knew that following Sheepshanks would not be easy, and indeed his difficulties began the moment he tried to cross the Spanish border. It was early January 1938. 'I had to reveal my grandma's maiden name,' he wrote to his brother, going on to describe the two lots of fingerprinting, the photographs, the weighing and searching of his baggage, and the way he was shunted from one military HQ to another.[9] Once he had finally crossed the border, he checked into San Sebastian's Maria Cristina Hotel, a palatial establishment set alongside a malodorous river, with windows giving a salt-misted view of the white-capped Atlantic. The hotel's old-fashioned charm did not compensate for the fact that the war had already moved on from the city, and Clifford was soon keen to seek out action further west. He needed to be closer to the front – and the difficulties in obtaining dinner before ten at night only made him more restless. Drifting idly from bar to bar, seeking sustenance in prawns and sherry, did not seem fitting somehow for a correspondent at large in a war zone.

So, on 12 January 1938, Alex Clifford set out west on the road to Bilbao and soon came close to the harsh reality of the war. He found himself watching in awe as harassed surgeons treated an Italian officer whose forehead had been shot away. 'His brain was sticking out,' Clifford wrote later, describing how the operation had given the Italian a new forehead, grafted from part of his thigh. He visited the Basque town of Guernica, which the German Luftwaffe had pounded with bombs the year before, and was shocked by the devastation. 'I never imagined a place could be so completely destroyed,' he wrote. Eventually he reached Saragossa, just 7 miles from the fighting. He walked across a section

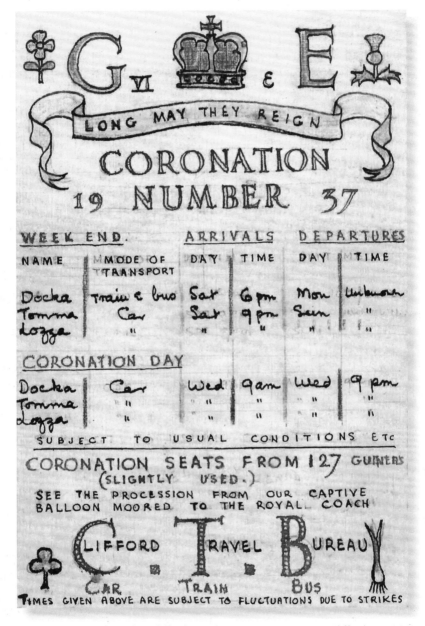

A postcard home from the 'Clifford Travel Bureau', 1937. (IWM, Clifford Papers)

of recently abandoned battlefield looking at the debris and discarded military hardware, bemused both by their scale and occasional quirkiness – a discarded golf putter, for example, lying abandoned in the dust. For a short while he shared accommodation with Karl Robson before moving on to Madrid, travelling via Burgos and Toledo, its ruined, fire-blackened Alcazar somehow symbolising Spain's burning, bitter struggle. At one point he was handed a rifle by some of Franco's soldiers who encouraged him to shoot towards the Republican trenches. It discomfited him enough to warn his brother in a letter that he should keep the story quiet. He spent an evening in trenches which the Republicans had recently abandoned: there were still peas cooking, warm coffee in a pot and an unfinished game of draughts missing its two players. He visited the front at Teruel (where his predecessor had died) and, on 22 February, he and Karl Robson were with the Nationalist infantry when they marched into the town, its buildings heavily damaged by gunfire. Bizarrely, the insurgents had taken to wearing a variety of outlandish hats, and Clifford 'saw one Moor wearing a top hat and carrying a bassoon and a sewing machine'.[10] Of the 9,500 troops defending Teruel, all were now dead or prisoners. Years later, he would be reminded of the surrounding rugged landscape when deep in the Libyan Desert.

Although he was reporting from the Nationalist lines, Clifford was not beyond helping those on the other side of the conflict. For example, he 'was able to render a service for the wife of a British volunteer, Mr Clive Branson, recently captured by General Franco's forces'. Branson was an artist and a Communist; Clifford helped locate his whereabouts in Spain.[11]

For a young man still in his 20s, Spain was a series of vivid initiations: Alex caught a flea in a cheap cinema and was a passenger on a train which derailed as he was travelling to Salamanca (thereby avoiding an air raid). He had his photograph taken with Kim Philby and lunched in Pamplona at a wonderful restaurant run by nine beautiful sisters where the cooking could not be faulted, even by someone with Clifford's cautious appetite. He also interviewed the Nationalist leader, General Franco, at some length, under conditions of the greatest secrecy, and pausing at one point because of an air raid warning. He found the Fascist leader 'very charming'; deploying his Spanish in such circumstances and at considerable length was more of a concern to Clifford than the general's politics. He was more unsettled by Franco's entourage, not least a brooding German presence. He wrote to his sister Liz that he was 'a little entangled with the German secret police and sometimes I am genuinely frightened,'[12] and his fear was evident in his insistence that Liz should tell no one. When he and Kim Philby were photographed in the company of the head of the German secret police, he declared in a letter to his brother that he dared not reveal the German's name.

Clifford liked Saragossa, partly because there were relatively few war correspondents there. It could be unpleasantly hot – 112°F in the shade – and the

Alexander Clifford's 'Salvoconducto' – his 'safe-conduct' when working in Spain.
(IWM, Clifford Papers)

city's 'puritanical mayor' insisted that coats must be worn in public. Fleas were a persistent problem. Just as irritating was the close observation by Franco's secret state. The scrutiny was enough to provoke Clifford into an act of minor rebellion: at the end of one letter to his sister, he added a sentence for prying eyes: 'Oh I must protest in the strongest possible terms against this indiscriminate opening of my letters.'[13] His hand-to-mouth existence was not easy: he developed an 'orticario', a stress-induced red rash all over his body. He was constantly on the move; at one point he complained that his luggage was scattered far and wide across Spain. For the most part he was based in the lands north of Madrid – a month in Burgos, for example – and there were frequent return visits to San Sebastian. The Basque town's hotels were full of well-heeled refugees from Madrid and Barcelona, escaping what they saw as the Red hordes, and the presence of so many exiled fascist sympathisers could prove hazardous. On one occasion, Robson and Clifford were in the lounge of the Maria Cristina Hotel when the Spanish national anthem suddenly boomed out from the radio. They both stood, a gesture insufficiently patriotic for a tipsy young Francoist who demanded why they had not given the Fascist salute, and who refused to accept their Englishness as a legitimate reason. Despite being known in the hotel, Clifford and Robson were asked to leave by the Italian manager: 'No, gentlemen, no, you have caused this disturbance. You have offended my guests. You must go at once.' Their luggage was hurriedly produced and they were compelled to leave immediately. There were apologies forthcoming in the coming days, but it did little to compensate for the indignity of being hustled unceremoniously down the hotel's steps and out into the street, with their luggage scattered over the pavement.

There was more to life in Spain than war reporting; there were affairs of the heart too and gossip about Alex's private life, something which evidently pleased him. He confessed to his sister – no doubt smiling as he wrote it – that there was a rumour he was 'trifling with the affections of two ladies, one a widow and the other a married marquesa with three children'. Evidently the relationship with the marquesa was a serious entanglement: a year or so later she sent Alex a postcard when he was back in London: 'This is Velasquez's view of Zaragoza I used to tell you about. Also our bridge and the place we used to walk in. How far away all this seems! Only last year! … Where are you? I am longing to hear from you.'[14] Clifford's flourishing career as a war correspondent might well have been prematurely cut short: the marquesa's husband was only prevented from seeking satisfaction in a duel by being unable to leave the front line.

*   *   *   *

Alexander Clifford first met Alan Moorehead in the spring of 1938, at the Bar Basque in Saint-Jean-de-Luz, just over the border from Spain in southern France. Moorehead was working as a 'stringer' for the *Daily Express*, on £5 per week plus some expenses, reporting from the border town of Hendaye on the continuing air raids on Barcelona and, more generally, on the campaign in the field. There was nightly gunfire as would-be refugees tried to cross the River Bidasoa between France and Spain. He had arrived in Saint-Jean-de-Luz on the overnight train from Paris and he headed straight for the bar from the station, passing a line of horse-drawn cabs before pushing through the bar's door. Inside there were 'Basque murals on the walls, scenes of pelota players and peasants dancing the *jota*, and the decor was rustic walnut and red plush,'[15] while behind the bar lurked Otto, 'the omniscient Sud-Tiroler barman.' This meeting between Clifford and Moorehead was a significant moment in both men's lives – they would, through the war years, frequently hark back to their shared memories of the Bar Basque's roast duck, dancing, Thursday night cabaret, wine and *Fleurs d'Hendaye*, the local liqueur, as if to a golden age. The bar had the reputation of being at the heart of European intrigue, the haunt of reporters, diplomats, agents and the clandestine in general. The weather had been appalling and this first meeting between the two war correspondents was distinctly chilly too. Otto pointed Robson and Clifford out to the new arrival, and walking uneasily over to them, Moorehead observed that Robson 'had an air of extreme gentleness' as well as being remarkably handsome, reminding him of El Greco. Nothing about Clifford appealed, however. Indeed he looked forbidding, peering 'in an uncompromising way through his glasses' and disconcerting Moorehead with his 'round head, a broad cerebral brow and a

The Bar Basque, Saint-Jean-de-Luz. (Ana and Kino Bardaji)

The Bar Basque in 2014. (Ana and Kino Bardaji)

tight looking mouth'. To cap it all, Clifford seemed irritated at being interrupted, Moorehead thought, and it was Robson who finally deigned to speak. Piqued and confused, the Australian picked up his luggage and stalked out of the bar. He and Clifford would not meet again for two years.

*　*　*　*

Alan Moorehead was born in Melbourne, Australia, in July 1910, and came to England in 1935. Two years later, working for the *Daily Express*, he was in Gibraltar attempting to report on Spain's civil war from across the border. It proved a difficult assignment: 'the war in Spain might have been a thousand miles away for all the information we were able to get about it in Gibraltar.'[16] The days settled into an 'aimless and listless routine': Moorehead dutifully pointed his binoculars at Spain, saw nothing of note and, bored and frustrated, found himself too often drinking coffee in one of a series of bars, reading the *Gibraltar Gazette* while waiting for something to happen. From his balcony at the Rock Hotel, he could see the coast of Africa, but Spain itself was 'mysterious and forbidden'. He went to the cinema, played tennis and swam. His 'mind reeled with boredom'. It was illuminating to realise, amidst the tedium, that the Royal Navy's officers 'almost to a man were supporters of General Franco'.[17] Then, just when it seemed that nothing would ever disturb Gibraltar's peace, a real story broke: in fading light, the German battleship *Deutschland* steamed slowly into the harbour, its deck lined with coffins draped in Nazi flags. The ship had been attacked by Republican aircraft – flown by Russians – off the coast of Ibiza, and thirty-one crew members had been killed. Moorehead felt 'a moment of ghoulish release'[18] at this unexpected gift of news.

For all that, Gibraltar seemed to be a backwater, too far from the action on which a foreign correspondent feeds, and six months stranded on the Rock proved enough for Moorehead. He decided to travel: first to Algiers by Italian liner, then by German freighter to Istanbul, before boarding an oil tanker full of Rumanian petrol bound for Valencia in Spain. It would prove an eventful voyage, though not initially. The tanker headed west through a Mediterranean calm, in sultry heat, while the sea's 'warm water flopped back from the bows like blue jelly being sliced open with a knife'.[19] The first hint of trouble came from the drunken advances of the lascivious Russian skipper who showed an unhealthy interest in Moorehead's underwear: 'He picked up a pair of blue silk underpants and waved them at me chuckling and nodding.'[20] Later, the ship faced a different kind of danger: as they approached the Spanish coast, there was a resounding storm whose dark intensity at least hid their whereabouts. In clear light, an air attack on a ship heavy with highly inflammable fuel was something to be feared.

Once in Valencia, Moorehead warmed to the spirit of its people – their generosity and their mutual respect. Tipping, for example, was frowned upon. Moorehead attributed this 'to the civil war, or rather by the belief on the Republican side that all men are equal'.[21] To his disappointment he could never extend his stays in Spain (older, more experienced reporters had priority). It became a 'place of forbidden exhilaration' and, invariably, his flying visits always found him longing for something to happen to keep him there.

*   *   *   *

Christopher Buckley, the third member of the Trio, had been a schoolmaster at St Christopher's School, Letchworth before deciding to go to Spain, initially as a volunteer for the Friends' Ambulance Unit. In appearance and background it would be hard to find a starker contrast with Alan Moorehead. Buckley was tall, with sandy-coloured hair and a slight stoop. He wore glasses which gave him a professorial look, without ever seeming as if he could see very well. He loved poetry, books and cricket: 'If there was anything of which he was inordinately proud, it was the row of Wisdens' that he collected through his lifetime.[22] After his experience with the Ambulance Unit, he hitch-hiked around Republican Spain, periodically sending back reports to the *Christian Science Monitor* in America, despite having had no Fleet Street training at all. In the summer of 1938 he visited one of the relief camps set up to look after Catalan children whose lives had been scarred by the fighting. This was the Torre Inglaterra, situated in the picturesque mountain town of Puigcerdá on the border with France. Buckley had taught there the preceding summer for a month, stirred by the children's desperate eagerness to learn, despite having just 'half a dozen pencils among a class of 30'. As a freelance reporter, he lived a hand-to-mouth existence, learning, for example, 'the technique of eating whenever an opportunity for a meal presented itself'. The wise war correspondent never turned down a chance to eat, a principle which would prove invaluable in the years ahead.

All three members of the Trio would hold Spain dear in their minds for the rest of their lives: Buckley, for example, would remember the voracious bites of the mosquitoes in Alicante in August 1938 when he was living under canvas in an olive grove on Sicily five years later. He never lost the deep empathy he had for the army of the Spanish Republic, believing that 'of the shames of my life none lies heavier than that I had denied the final proof of my fellowship to the Republic'.[23] Moorehead's view of Spain changed over time. Early on, he had readily left the country for the greater attractions of Paris where 'we were as much engrossed in watching Josephine Baker dancing in her girdle of bananas as we had been in the civil war'.[24] Later he fell in love with the Spanish landscape and felt great sympathy for its people as the Civil War destroyed or changed lives for ever. Early in 1939

Moorehead headed south for a week in the Pyrenees through a chain of mountains that 'makes you wonder why you waste your time living in any other place'.[25] It was the first time he had been able to watch the Spanish Civil War at close quarters and he was deeply troubled by the flood of refugees trying to escape from Franco's aircraft: 'black bombers come down when the men below are helpless'.[26] The refugees, in groups of twenty or more, stumbled down from the snowline, traversing a mountain ridge. The rocks were coated with ice and occasionally someone would lose their footing and tumble down into the valley. Moorehead counted the bodies of eighteen men and women who had fallen far below into the ravine.[27] He met Dolores Ibárruri, 'La Pasionaria', the Spanish Republic's impassioned and articulate voice; Moorehead had been encouraged 'to offer her untold sums of Beaverbrook's gold', presumably for some unworthy scheme dreamed up to sell even greater numbers of newspapers. At all events, Moorehead was enormously impressed by her. But, above all, he was haunted by the images of thousands of Spanish refugees struggling to reach safety as the Republican cause collapsed and died.

Clifford, too, held Spain in his heart, its landscape in particular having a powerful and enduring influence on him. Driving through a desert landscape in Libya years later, he would suddenly recall crossing a similar barren waste in Spain during the civil war. He was not to see the sad end of things in Spain, however. In June 1938 he wrote to his mother from Saragossa, telling her that he had 'just finished a hard spell of work capturing Castellon', but soon after that he moved into the uncertain, trembling territory of the war yet to come. By November 1938 he was in Berlin as Reuters' chief correspondent for Germany. He stayed there for some ten months, observing the drift towards war while caught up in a frantic social whirl of opera, concerts, lunches, hangovers, cinema, cocktail parties, exhibitions, visits to the zoo, and theatre and tennis matches (the Davis Cup). There were also trips abroad, to Venice, for example, and Yugoslavia. Despite all this he found himself homesick for Spain. In a letter to his sister he coyly revealed that he had become 'rather involved' with a 'fantastically lovely Russian princess,' but that didn't stop him meeting his Spanish marquesa in Copenhagen for an illicit and happy weekend together, thoughts of husband and Hitler largely put aside. There were idyllic days still – 'I floated down the Autobahn in a lovely golden evening' – but there was unquestionably a growing sense of menace in Berlin. On 14 February 1939 he got up early and caught the 6.56 a.m. train to Hamburg, arriving in time to see Hitler launching a new 35,000-ton battleship, the *Bismarck*. A few months later, on 1 May, he stood watching 'a terrible torchlight tattoo, where Goering spoke', while, on 22 May, he was present at the signing of the German/Italian alliance – the Pact of Steel.

Towards the end of August the British embassy advised Clifford to leave the country and he duly flew out on 1 September, a circuitous route via Sweden and

Amsterdam, before finally landing at Shoreham on the English south coast. The next day he caught the boat train via Dover and Ostend to Brussels, arriving at the city's Grand Hotel in the early hours. He found himself staring at the walls of a bare, featureless room and worrying about the chaos of his personal affairs back in England, unresolved as a result of his employer's insistence that he leave forthwith for the Continent. Later, he bumped into an old acquaintance, a fellow guest at the hotel. A month ago, perhaps, this would have been a pleasure, but the erstwhile friend worked for a German news agency. They carefully avoided eye contact as they passed in the hotel corridors. In these uncertain times, Clifford did not sleep well in Brussels, his nights often punctuated by nightmares.

The same day Clifford was flying out of Berlin, Christopher Buckley was in Warsaw 'wondering whether (he) should get out of Poland alive'. That Friday afternoon, the 1st, he saw eighteen bombers flying over the city and took shelter under an archway in company with some thirty or forty other people. Occasionally the ground shook as the bombs fell nearby. Warsaw, he thought, was unprepared for the inevitable, 'without a single trench for civilian defence against aviation'.[28] Moreover, there were no deep shelters and gas masks were a rarity. The mood initially was fearful, but this was soon matched by an 'irritation at (the) continued interruptions in the business of the day'. There were queues for most things – for money exchange and for work permits, for example – while Buckley's last meal in Warsaw was 'unduly prolonged by the impossibility of leaving the restaurant during an air raid'. With no little anxiety he found himself remembering the previous summer's raids on Alicante in Spain. Air raid sirens howled periodically. Once, he was in a large department store in the city when he heard, after the ninth round of sirens, an unprecedented announcement over the radio in English, pleading that the bombing raids should be reported to the British parliament. It was only a matter of hours before the British prime minister took to the airwaves himself, his bleak, exhausted voice declaring war on the German aggressor. His reluctant acceptance that appeasement had failed left Buckley unimpressed. He thought the guarantee to Poland 'was the best that could be done in the appalling circumstances into which our Government and that of the French had allowed things to drift'. As for the prime minister: 'the less said about Mr Chamberlain, except to echo Byron's epitaph on Lord Castlereagh, the better!'[29]

*   *   *   *

Alan Moorehead took 'almost the last train out of France before the war', bound for Italy.[30] To the north of the Alps it was cold, but in northern Italy the train rattled through a landscape still in high summer. The *Express*'s editor Arthur Christiansen – 'sometimes genial, most often irascible'[31] – was deploying his writers far and wide, ready for the anticipated outbreak of fighting. Moorehead's home for the foreseeable future was to be Rome, and he took a flat next to the house where John Keats had died in the Piazza di Spagna. The Italian capital was bathed in a 'flickering autumnal light' and the talk was all of war.

In the months leading up to the outbreak of war, Alan had been based in Paris working for the *Express* from its office in Rue du Louvre. His immediate boss was Geoffrey Cox, and the relationship between the two was somewhat edgy, Cox believing that they were 'too alike in appearance let alone anything else' for them to work comfortably together. Cox saw himself as 'a descriptive writer and I jolly well wasn't going to let Moorehead do the descriptive stories'.[32] As for Alan, he had other things on his mind, not least the *Express*'s women's editor, Lucy Milner.

The Mooreheads' flat in the Piazza di Spagna in Rome. (Author's Collection)

Alan and Lucy Moorehead on their wedding day in Rome. (National Library of Australia)

The cartoonist Osbert Lancaster remembered her 'being sent off to Paris to cover the dress shows with her customary but unconvincing air of long-suffering'.[33] According to Mary Welsh, the fourth Mrs Hemingway, when Moorehead had bought her a drink at a bar on the Champs-Élysées he had confided that 'he hadn't found a Parisian girl who suited his taste for long'.[34] The bachelor life was palling; Welsh reminded him about Lucy Milner – 'wise, witty and lovely'. The next day Moorehead was in the London office and stopped off at Lucy's desk on the editorial floor and, a month after the war broke out, Alan and Lucy were married in Rome.

* * * *

Alexander Clifford had left London for France on 19 September 1939, having been appointed to submit reports under the byline of 'Eyewitness', 'a pseudonym which he loathed'.[35] He was to provide basic coverage of the war in France 'while (other correspondents) were being vetted to weed out potential spies'.[36] The War Council had picked him as the 'legman representing the whole world's press on the western front'. Still relatively junior ('no ace reporter'), he had been 'picked to avoid jealousy among great-name newswriters'.[37] As September drifted into October, Clifford grew increasingly impatient – nothing much was happening, and when it did the army censors proved intractable, while senior officers were determined that any localised detail should be taboo: General Gamelin, for example, warned correspondents, 'You are going to describe only anonymous landscapes'.[38] The military historian Basil Liddell Hart for one was disturbed by the heavy hand of censorship: 'The Press ought to be renamed the Suppress', he wrote,[39] while Clifford told the BBC's Charles Gardner that on one occasion an 'army censor had taken out a story referring to the moon having shone'.

By early January 1940 Clifford was based in Amsterdam, still wondering when the 'phoney war' would end. It was a nervy, unsettling interlude made worse for Clifford since Amsterdam was full of former colleagues from Berlin. There was both a news drought and a strong sense of competition, and what news there was must be filtered by the censors. By 19 March the struggle between the army's higher powers and the press was so serious that 'the correspondents ... declared a strike against censorship measures', a protest which continued for a week.

* * * *

It was two years after the ill-fated meeting in the Bar Basque that Moorehead and Clifford met again. In May 1940, Moorehead had headed for Greece and checked into the Grande Bretagne Hotel in Athens. In the lift he came face to face with someone he 'disliked, distrusted and feared' – who else but Alexander Clifford? That 'almost Prussian head'; that 'air of superiority and pernickety indifference'.

Initially, Moorehead's opinion of Clifford was unchanged: he remained affronted by the Englishman's apparent disdain in the Bar Basque. But a few drinks changed everything; now the two men talked for hours at a 'rickety wooden table drinking ouzo, turning away the bootblacks, the sellers of pistachio nuts and lottery tickets', while the dust and heat of the city subsided and the air acquired 'the clear and buoyant colour of a rock pool in the tropics'.[40] Alan hadn't talked so well with anyone for years. By the end of the evening, they 'had agreed to continue our travels together'. The practicalities were discussed – should they enlist? – but Moorehead recognised the cool logic of Clifford's view that 'the thing to do was to become a war correspondent'. Soon they were making plans to get sent to Cairo together, anticipating the strategic importance of Egypt once Italy came into the war, as seemed certain. Clifford duly wired the *Daily Mail* in London, for whom he had been working since 1 May: 'Moorehead of the *Express* proceeding to Cairo stop shall I follow.' Moorehead sent a similar query to his own office. The telegrammed responses from London were perfect: 'Follow Clifford' and 'Follow Moorehead'.

*   *   *   *

Following the story of Clifford and Moorehead so many years after is relatively straightforward: there are letters, diaries, documents and, particularly in Moorehead's case, a substantial body of work. Christopher Buckley, however, is in many ways a more shadowy figure, his past sometimes hidden, a fact made worse by the existence of a modern namesake sprawling over Google. In addition, there are, it seems, no papers, notebooks or diaries extant, other than in the collected archives of others. How then to pursue a shadow, this third member of the Trio? The evidence is that all his papers were destroyed on his death, a conclusion reached after a lengthy investigation via his marriage and death certificates, his will and probate documents, his wife's death certificate, and members of his extended family who remembered him. These family members were sure that his wife would have had little compunction after his death about discarding the papers he had left behind, despite her evident love for him. Businesslike and unsentimental, she just wasn't the kind of person to hoard such things.

So it is that the early years of the Trio's story focuses largely on just two of the three men. Buckley's journey to the villa in Taormina, via Greece and Cairo, remains only partially revealed. If we are to follow Moorehead and Clifford on their exuberant way to North Africa, then spare a thought for the third member of the Trio, Christopher Buckley, destined to fall in with the other two remarkable pressmen, but only once the tide of war had begun to turn, and for now, pursuing a lone furrow somewhere in Europe.

NOTES

1   *Ten Years to Alamein* by Matthew Halton, p.34.
2   *Foreign Correspondent* ed. Wilfrid Hindle, p.257.
3   Ibid., p.259.
4   *Philby KGB Masterspy* by Phillip Knightley, p.56.
5   Ibid., p.58.
6   Ibid.
7   Moorehead papers, National Library of Australia (NLA), MS 5654: letter to Lucy Moorehead (undated, but *c.* 1971). The comparison with the cat was from a review of Alan Moorehead's *A Late Education* in *The Sunday Times*, 20 December 1970.
8   Letter to Alan and Lucy Moorehead from Henry Dalton (Tony) Clifford, 23 October 1970. Moorehead papers, NLA, MS 5654.
9   Clifford papers (16727), IWM, file AGC/2/3.
10   *Evening Standard*, 23 February 1938. Clifford papers (16727), IWM, AGC/5/4.
11   *Reuters Review*, Clifford papers (16727), IWM, AGC/5/1.
12   Undated letter, Clifford papers (16727), IWM, file AGC/2/2.
13   Letter of 27 August 1938. Clifford papers (16727), IWM, file AGC/2/2.
14   Dated 14 October 1939. Clifford papers (16727), IWM, AGC/5/1.
15   *A Late Education* by Alan Moorehead, p.2.
16   Ibid., p.65.
17   Ibid., p.66.
18   Ibid., p.71.
19   Ibid., p.83.
20   Ibid., p.85.
21   Ibid., p.95.
22   Walter Oakeshott in an article for *Time and Tide* entitled 'Journalism and Truth', 9 September 1950.
23   Buckley, p.22.
24   *A Late Education*, op. cit., p.44.
25   Ibid., p.112.
26   *Alan Moorehead* by Tom Pocock, p.44. Pocock is quoting from a letter to Lucy Moorehead.
27   See Moorehead's report in the *Daily Express* for 2 April 1938.
28   *Christian Science Monitor*, 19 September 1939.
29   Byron wrote: 'Posterity will ne'er survey / A nobler grave than this: / Here lie the bones of Castlereagh: / Stop, traveller, and piss.' Quoted from a letter to Basil Liddell Hart, dated 15 May 1944. Liddell Hart Papers, LH1/125/1.
30   *Mediterranean Front* by Alan Moorehead, p.11.
31   *Fighting Words* by Richard Collier, p.9.

32   Interview, IWM Sound Archives, 26937.

33   *With an Eye to the Future* by Osbert Lancaster, p.153.

34   *How It Was* by Mary Welsh Hemingway, p.42.

35   *A.A.S.F.* by Charles Gardner, p.19.

36   *The Violent Decade* by Frank Gervasi, p.204.

37   *Time*, 2 October 1939.

38   Collier, p.13.

39   Liddell Hart papers, LH11/1939/118.

40   *A Late Education*, op. cit., p.5.

3. Cairo and Beyond – the Nomadic Life

The flying boat to Cairo came down on Crete's Suda Bay and Clifford and Moorehead, emphatically not 'following' each other but in companionable cahoots, stripped off and stepped straight into the sea from the aircraft's open door. Once they reached Cairo, however, all semblance of tranquillity disappeared. It was, for a start, unbearably hot – a brutal 106° – and the city assailed them, as it did others who flew in from the grey of northern Europe: its frantic noise, chaotic traffic, the 'starved and beaten cabhorses, mangy dogs, rabies, venereal disease, and dysentery'.[1] Fastidious Europeans complained of the smell: 'The all-pervading, never failing smell. Sweat, and garlic and the musty hangover of a thousand years of smell.'[2] But it had a bewitching quality too, such that the BBC's Richard Dimbleby could describe the city as both 'unbelievably corrupt and, sometimes, incredibly beautiful'.

Clifford and Moorehead settled into Cairene life, bathing in the Nile, watching cricket at the Gezira Sporting Club, where they would sometimes eat lunch together on the balcony, the cold buffet being 'a bargain meal much appreciated by GHQ secretaries'.[3] The two correspondents bought uniforms which were embellished with bright green and gold tabs which Moorehead disliked since they 'gave one the feeling of being a delegate at a Rotary convention'.[4] For their part, the military looked on the war correspondents with a blend of loathing and puzzlement. Accommodation was at the Carlton Hotel which was cheaper than the famous Shepheards; Clifford's room was on the seventh floor with a view down to an open-air cinema. The nights were punctuated by the clatter of dominoes and backgammon pieces, as well as cinematic gunfire.

Alex liked the climate, wore shorts and drove a handsome, substantial Ford V8 motor car. In these early days, it was possible to enjoy a life of partying and polo since the war seen from Cairo was 'merely a noise on the radio'. The threat of bombing was minimal, it seemed, and indeed one Cairo inhabitant remarked that 'the roads are much more dangerous than air raids'.[5] At one point Alex drove the Ford out to the pyramids, but he was not impressed, writing home that it was nothing more than a 'huge heap of rubble' which he thought might have some potential value as air raid shelters, but little else. He climbed one of them, while Moorehead declined the opportunity, only too aware of his vertigo. Coincidentally, Christopher Buckley felt much the same, although when the war correspondent Clare Hollingworth asked him to retrieve her notebook which she had left at the top of the Great Pyramid, Buckley's gallantry prevailed and he trudged back up without looking down.

Arrangements for the correspondents were embryonic and frequently chaotic, a situation exacerbated by the army's deep, visceral suspicion of the press. Middle East Command treated reporters 'at best as irrelevant and at worst as fifth columnists'.[6] Moorehead would remember how the elderly colonels and 'polo-playing messes' regarded correspondents with 'astonishment and abhorrence'. The relationship was one of resentment and distrust, a situation made worse by the issue of censorship. It was essential that each news story had to be scrutinised and approved before it could be dispatched, and that process was made more problematic because there were three distinct censors' offices set 15 miles apart. Worse, the required censor might well be away from his desk, poised to drive off at the first tee.

By June 1940, Moorehead had received his official war correspondents' accreditation, the documentation bound in a hard, blue cover. Soon he, Clifford and the handful of correspondents in the city were clamouring for permission to leave Cairo and head west into the desert. They got vaccinated against typhoid and waited impatiently for a visit to the front to be given official approval. In the event, Clifford's first significant journey away from Cairo was in the opposite direction, to Jerusalem. How different from home! In Britain, invasion fever was beginning to gather, while here he could bathe in the Dead Sea without a care in the world, under the bluest of skies. It was a brief trip, however, and soon both he and Moorehead got their wish and were driving out of Cairo towards the front, heading past Alexandria and Mersa Matruh, carrying with them the food and water they would need. They knew that war correspondents must be self-sufficient and they had duly equipped themselves with suede desert boots, knee-high khaki socks, sun helmets, water bottles, gas masks, a revolver each, mosquito nets, camp beds, sleeping bags and canvas washing buckets, and so they headed into the desert for the first time. It stretched away, seemingly limitless, beige in colour, a world of undulating, empty scrubland, mile after mile of hard, bare sand. Plumes of dust hung in the air and the landscape reminded Clifford of the bleak countryside around Teruel in Spain. Initially, the road was a good one, straight and true, keeping faithful company with a single-track railway. On one

Alexander Clifford of the *Daily Mail*. (Getty Images)

Alan Moorehead of the *Daily Express*. (John Moorehead)

side, there was a glaring white beach and 'a sea tinted the wonderful shades of a butterfly's wing'.[7] When they stopped the car, the silence was profound.

As they were approaching Mersa Matruh a sandstorm blew up – a *khamseen* – and, within minutes, they could not see beyond a few yards. The car's interior became gritty with sand as they edged forward into the opaque heart of the storm. Eventually they reached HQ, which was 'inexpressibly dreary'. Moorehead slept that night with his sleeping bag zipped over his head. He lay there, reflecting that war in the desert was similar to war at sea, the same empty horizon, long spells of isolation, navigational challenges and the absence of people or landmarks. The road that day had stretched ahead for mile after mile, its surface a black ribbon glinting in the sun, while the light had been a strange, almost eerie, yellow. This was, Alan thought, the landscape of Lawrence of Arabia. Encountering people might be a novelty, but there was no escaping the fact that the desert was alive – with gazelle, hares, vipers, rats, tarantulas and ticks. Just occasionally, the Bedouin appeared, a stark reminder that there was some human activity in the wilderness.

They drove on, past Sidi Barrani, its white buildings shimmering in the sun. Soon after, the road petered out, and instead of the reassuring hum of tyres on the blacktop, they wallowed and bounced over the waves and hollows of loose sand. Alan hung on to the side of the car, cursing the desert. At Advanced HQ, on a plateau above Halfaya Pass, they set up camp. They stayed a week, periodically taking trips deep into Libya, while at night they slept in slit trenches uncomfortably reminiscent of the grave. They woke to find blankets heavy with dew, saw desert foxes, and survived on a diet of raspberry jam and biscuits, bully beef and canned vegetables. They were glad to return to the worldly comforts of Cairo.

* * * *

Soon after, Clifford succeeded in getting official approval to join a submarine-hunting mission: no war correspondent had yet managed to take part in an operational flight with the RAF. It meant a ten-hour trip in a Sunderland flying boat, flying from Malta, taking 'breakfast off Syracuse', enjoying a mid-morning snack in the Bay of Cephalonia, surrounded by its wall of mountains, followed by lunch in the shadow of Etna, then 'tea off Corfu' before returning to Malta 'in time to strip off all our clothes and dive straight off the machine into the bay'.[8] It wasn't all lotus-eating pleasure, however. He was obliged to spend 'hours raking the sea with field glasses for traces of enemy shipping',[9] seeing nothing for the most part except distant mountains, sea and sky. The war in the Mediterranean had become a cat and mouse affair: previous submarine losses had made the Italians wary and very reluctant to be seen, while Italian aircraft were scouring the skies for the RAF – hence the need for disciplined, watchful eyes.

The reality of the danger was brought home at the end of the month when Clifford's Sunderland was attacked near Augusta, Sicily. All thoughts of a Sunday morning picnic lunch were dispelled when rounds of machine-gun fire perforated the fuselage, breaking glasses and sending smoke billowing through the aircraft. The second pilot emerged from the cockpit wreathed in smoke. He was stiff-upper-lip and to the point: 'Oh, Clifford, this thing's on fire. We've got to abandon her. Get ready will you?'[10] In the event, after a desperate struggle to extinguish the fire, they stayed on board, but the situation remained perilous: two of the gunners had been wounded and the aircraft's rudder was destroyed. This was no time for journalistic codes of conduct and Clifford duly clambered into the rear turret, easing his tall frame in behind the guns, opening fire with his heart thumping and the sweat misting his glasses. He was drenched in petrol, the smell thick in the narrow confines of the turret. Eventually the damaged Sunderland made it back to Malta, its crew fully expecting it to sink once they touched down. It stayed afloat, however, and Clifford stepped down into the waiting dinghy, glad that he lived by his typewriter, not a tail gunner's Browning machine gun.

Next came an insight into the Royal Navy aboard the battleship HMS *Ramillies*, accompanied by the Paramount News photographer Ted Genock. The ship steamed steadily along the Egyptian coast, while Clifford, poleaxed by the unbearable heat, lay naked with a fan trained on his stomach. *Ramillies* bombarded the coastal town of Bardia, the thunderous noise sending cockroaches scurrying wildly below decks. There was considerable human unease on board too: one officer complained loudly about the continued absence of air protection. Later, they were bombed by Italian aircraft and Clifford's typewriter crashed to the deck from where it had been perched on his knee. Twice now in the space of a few weeks he had come under intense fire from the air. He had felt alone too, since 'everyone else seems to have got themselves stranded in the Sudan'.[11]

* * * *

Alan Moorehead set out for the Sudan in the middle of July 1940, accompanied by a group of other correspondents, including the BBC's Richard Dimbleby. They travelled south aboard the Egyptian State Railway's night train, passing Luxor and the Valley of the Kings at dawn. At Shellal, they embarked on a flat-bottomed steamer from which they could look back at 'the long white train with its sleepers and restaurant car parked in the broiling sun alongside the rickety jetty'.[12] It was well over 120°F without a breath of wind and the loading of the boat was painfully unhurried – nothing less than 'slow torture', Moorehead thought. He was stripped to the waist and killing time by reading *The River War*, Winston Churchill's account of the war in the Sudan forty years before. Dimbleby, meanwhile, was coming down with diphtheria and had 'found a chaise-longue and a grass fan' in a forlorn attempt to keep cool,[13] while steadily slipping into delirium.

By the time they reached Khartoum, Dimbleby's condition had worsened and he sweated and coughed through a press briefing conducted by General Platt in a cool, airy room in the Sudan War Office. He collapsed as he left the meeting and was immediately taken to hospital. Moorehead, meanwhile, set out by train for the front at Kassala. It proved a sociable occasion, courtesy of the officer in charge of the train whose suite on board boasted a bath and who encouraged its use for leisurely soaks, followed by glasses of warm whisky. Not everything was quite so civilised: for example, divisional HQ was established at Gedaref, 'a malarial spot where one sleeps beneath netting, and it is wise to wear long trousers and poke the turn-ups under your socks'.[14] In this mosquito-plagued hothouse, officers defiantly tucked into bacon and eggs and marmalade for breakfast and read *Bystander* and *Tatler* as if they were in a club in Piccadilly. Later, at Khashm el Girba, they dined in the open air, dive-bombed by clouds of insects and 'listening to the BBC intoning from a set perched in a thorn bush'.[15]

The insects proved more bothersome than the Italian army. With the battlefront quiet, there was little to report, so Moorehead decided to return to Khartoum. From there, he and the *Daily Herald*'s Ronald Matthews flew to the base at Erkowit, four and a half hours away, travelling 'in a rattling Valencia' and contemplating an operational flight with a bomber crew in a day or so. That meant a 5.30 a.m. start. It promised to be a run-of-the-mill trip, but Moorehead had little difficulty in imagining the worst – a forced landing, perhaps, and a subsequent attack by tribesmen. He was shown a 'goolie chit' which aircrew routinely carried with them in a forlorn attempt at self-preservation. Written in Amharic and English, it proclaimed the bearer to be a British officer requiring assistance. Aircrew had little confidence in its value, 'since,' as one airman put it, 'the bastards can't read'. Moreover, Moorehead's pilot added, 'some of the tribesmen will slice you up in the usual way and start asking questions afterwards'.[16]

Three Blenheims flew in close formation on a ninety-minute trip to the target, a sprawl of railway yards. The pilot was relatively young, perhaps 23, and he had been the life and soul of those gathered in the mess the night before. There had been some banter about reporters' ill-advised use of the word 'intrepid', a word which the fliers thought deserved gentle mockery. These men, Moorehead recognised, 'felt tired or exhilarated, or worried or hungry and occasionally afraid. But never brave. Certainly never intrepid.' In the early morning, over Kassala, they dropped their bombs and looked out over smoke and tracer fire, before heading back to RAF Erkowit, with Moorehead dozing, lulled by the engine's monotone. Getting out of the Blenheim and stepping on to the wing back at base, he caught his foot in a piece of splintered fuselage and fell flat on his face.

It was an embarrassing return, but there was nothing quite like terra firma for Moorehead and, when he gathered himself, he was glad that he wasn't staring at an angry tribesman's knife.

With the Blenheim raid over, Moorehead was unsure where he would go next. Aden was a possibility, while he had requested to be sent to Durban, since his wife Lucy was on her way to Egypt, flying via the South African port. In fact it proved to be Cairo again, albeit briefly. In August 1940, he sailed from Alexandria at dawn aboard HMS *Warspite* where he found himself enduring an air raid, an experience which proved alarming, with his typewriter sent spinning and the ship's deck littered with fragments of shrapnel.

∗   ∗   ∗   ∗

By the time Lucy arrived in Cairo, Moorehead and Clifford had lived together longer than she and Alan had. The two men knew that her arrival would inevitably disturb their easy routine: 'their friendship had become so close that both were aware that it would be disrupted'.[17] It was a friendship of opposites: Moorehead diminutive and lean, feisty, bubbling with enthusiasm, aggressive and erratic; Clifford, towering over the Australian and 'podgy, testy and supercilious'.[18] They lunched together, bickered over money, talked shop, itemised shopping lists of desert essentials, played billiards and bridge. They both liked women, but Clifford was less tactile, arguably more demonstrative with cats than women. Clifford was a non-smoker and a near-vegetarian, while Moorehead regarded cigarettes as a necessity. Clifford was cautious about spending money and resented the Australian's taste for expensive cuts of meat. Clifford could be arrogant and overbearing; other people's stupidity was liable to provoke in him a rush of quiet anger. He could also be shy, logical and precise. Unlike Moorehead, his expectation was that if things could go wrong, they would. An air of disillusion hung over him and Alan regarded him as consistently unlucky. He was more right wing than the Australian (after all, he regarded General Franco as having some virtue). He had a sharp intellect and Moorehead regarded him as 'The Walking Dictionary'. So what drew these two disparate beings together? It was, above all, the war – the spartan life in the desert, the danger; the shared enterprise. 'We were,' Moorehead thought, 'like two strangers who cling together in a shipwreck.'[19]

Lucy Moorehead's flying boat journey to Cairo was both exhausting and expensive. Clifford later told his sister that 'Moorehead spent all of £300 in getting his wife' to Cairo.[20] It was an arduous trip at the best of times and Lucy was seven months pregnant. She arrived in unforgiving August heat and found Cairo baking hot, insect-plagued and noisy. At lunch in the Carlton Hotel 'the cold sliced meat on the luncheon table was beginning to curl up at the edges, and the buffalo butter had melted into an amber pool'.[21] When she and Clifford met for the first time, the chemistry seemed unpromisingly lukewarm – listless and perfunctory – but they soon settled down into a comfortable *ménage á trois*. The Mooreheads' Cairo flat became, for some, a welcome haven, an escape from the whirling, gritty sand and voracious fleas of the desert. When the Mooreheads' first child – John – was born on 2 December 1940, Clifford was made godfather. A week later, on 9 December, there was a breakfast-time phone call summoning the correspondents to General Wavell's headquarters.

NOTES

1   *The Frontiers Are Green* by Richard Dimbleby, p.21.
2   *Gullible's Travels* by Richard Busvine, p.223.
3   Collier, p.45.
4   *A Late Education*, op. cit., p.8.
5   Letter from Freya Stark to Stewart Perowne, 2 October 1940. See *Freya Stark Letters vol. 4*, ed. Lucy Moorehead, p.98.
6   *Richard Dimbleby* by Jonathan Dimbleby, p.147.
7   *Mediterranean Front*, op. cit., p.28.
8   *Three Against Rommel* by Alexander Clifford, p.18.
9   *Daily Mail*, 5 August 1940.
10   Clifford, p.19.
11   Clifford papers (16727), IWM, file AGC/2/1/4; letter written to his mother, 7 August 1940.
12   (Richard) Dimbleby, p.41.
13   *Mediterranean Front*, op. cit., p.51.
14   Ibid., p.61.
15   Ibid., p.64.
16   Ibid., p.66.
17   Pocock, p.89.
18   Collier, p.46.
19   *A Late Education*, op. cit., p.35.
20   Letter from Alexander Clifford, dated 9 March 1941. Clifford papers (16727), IWM, file AGC/2/2.
21   *A Late Education*, op. cit., p.124.

4. 'We Have Attacked in the Western Desert'

Two days before that surprise phone call from General Wavell's office, on the Saturday (7 December 1940), the British Commander-in-Chief (Middle East) could be seen at a race meeting at the Gezira Club, accompanied by his wife and daughters. That same evening he hosted a dinner party at the Turf Club – all very low-key and leisurely. It was, however, a premeditated demonstration of 'military sangfroid',[1] designed to divert attention from an imminent initiative. A naturally shy man – he might be 'lucid on paper' but was 'exceptionally tongue-tied'[2] – Wavell would no doubt have spent the weekend mentally rehearsing his planned press briefing. At nine o'clock on that bright blue Monday morning, the general, informal in shirtsleeves, hands in his pockets, and leaning back on his desk, confronted seven correspondents looking quizzically back at him. The low numbers were indicative of the level of editorial interest in this apparent backwater of the war.[3] To those stationed in Cairo, the Middle East felt isolated, a self-contained world cut off from London and where MEF (Middle East Forces) stood for 'Men England Forget'.

Wavell smiled uneasily, then announced, 'Gentlemen, I have asked you to come here this morning to let you know that we have attacked in the Western Desert.'[4] As if he was embarrassed by such a confident assertion, he went on to play down the importance of the moment: not so much an offensive, perhaps, more an important raid. The assembled journalists knew better – a C-in-C's Monday morning briefing implied something more than a minor skirmish. Wavell was pleased to learn that, in this city of gossip, not a glimmer of his secret had been revealed. The pressmen were all genuinely taken by surprise, and this in a city 'where no secret is a secret for longer than a few hours' and where it was 'a war correspondent's job to know them all'.[5]

Until that day, the correspondents had largely been kept out of the desert, partly by GHQ's insistence that no correspondent was permitted to spend the

General Sir Archibald Wavell, Commander-in-Chief (Middle East), at his desk, 15 August 1940. (IWM, E450)

night there. Now all that changed, and the day after Wavell's announcement, there was a frantic dash west, leaving just after dawn. The seven correspondents – Moorehead, Clifford, Christopher Lumby (*The Times*), Ed Kennedy (Associated Press), George Laycock (*Christian Science Monitor*), Gordon Young (BBC) and Alec Tozer (a cameraman with Movietone News) – set out for the front in high spirits in five clapped-out Ford station wagons. Two conducting officers accompanied them, charged with keeping the pressmen in check. On the outskirts of Cairo as they headed west, the pyramids were coloured a soft pink in the early morning sun.

It proved to be a chaotic expedition: vehicles broke down with broken half-shafts or punctures, or both; messages were sent but never arrived; obtaining food was a persistent problem; there were sandstorms which sent yellow dust whistling through the slightest gap in their tents and made the desert 'look something like London in a pea soup fog'.[6] It was, all in all, a comfortless existence. 'We travelled,' Clifford wrote, 'with just enough blankets to keep alive as we lay on the hard cold desert at night, a basic iron ration of food, and our typewriters.'[7] On the night of the 10th they pitched camp 'halfway between an aerodrome and a bomb dump'.[8] By the 12th their complement of transport had been reduced to just two cars and they were obliged to abandon their beds and much of their camping paraphernalia, not to mention 'half our food … and all the beer'.[9] They bounced and bumped over desert tracks, or wallowed over no tracks at all; then, once the desert darkness fell, they slept in the cars, 'except for two or three heroic ones who have dug themselves holes in the ground'.[10] It was very cold, even for those huddled in the cars.

They reached the front at Nibeiwa on 13 December, and the sight that met their eyes was unforgettable. There were bodies of Italian troops being buried in the slit trenches criss-crossing the site, while the Italian general's tunic was fluttering sadly in the wind on the back of a chair. The general himself lay dead in a nearby tent. To the east, landmines littered the ground, forcing the correspondents to skirt round the fort to the south-west and follow the tanks in through the rear door. Inside was a scene of grim desolation: corpses propped up by their guns, others twisted and crippled close to their dugouts, some just sprawled, contorted and bloodied, in the desert sand. As startling was the evident luxury enjoyed by the defeated Italians. The evidence was everywhere – scent and pomade, individual coffee percolators, clean sheets, silver-backed hair brushes, packing cases of macaroni, 'barrels of Chianti so large that they could only be moved in heavy lorries'.[11] It had more the air of a branch of John Lewis than a desert battlefield: indeed Clifford remarked it was 'like picking through the wreckage of some popular department store after an earthquake'.[12] The wind gusted letters and other papers this way and that across the sand. There were vast stores of food too: all sorts of vegetables, frozen hams and anchovies, brandy, Parmesan cheese, the best mineral water, bottled cherries and greengages. Already the sand was beginning to swallow this unexpected bounty. A barrel of Italian wine was hoisted on to the roof of one of the correspondents' cars. In a tented battlefield hospital, Moorehead 'drank wine with a soldier who had fought over the places I knew in the Spanish war',[13] while Clifford talked to another Italian prisoner, a medical officer in the civil war with whom he was able to reminisce about Spain. The two writers were prevailed upon to share ham, bread and wine with him. There was something odd in a situation where the defeated played generous host to the shabby, hungry and exhausted victors. It was a strange phenomenon that the Italians regarded it as important to be well dressed and fed to fight a battle. High-quality pasta and good wine were not enough though; the

Italians' military equipment was inferior, and it was clear that many of their troops were unenthusiastic about the campaign. The letters home, now blowing in the wind, revealed a widespread resentment, a sad loneliness. It was, in a way, 'the soul of a nation laid bare in the sand'.[14] You could feel too sorry for them, though; Moorehead noted how profoundly fascist many of the Italian officers were.

They drove north through clouds of dust, past neat caches of abandoned ammunition, and by late afternoon had reached Sidi Barrani, in ruins now but previously the thriving home of the Italian army's mobile brothels. Exhausted, they pitched camp by the sea, avoiding the flies and the rubbish further inland, and contemplated white sand, blue sea – and three dead bodies. Next day they saw long lines of Italian prisoners shambling across the desert. The weather had turned, sun replaced by light rain and a cutting wind. The correspondents' food and petrol supplies were dwindling and the nights were cold enough for six of them to sleep huddled up together for warmth in one car. Associated Press's Edward Kennedy lost his voice, while Clifford became ill with a potent mix of sand-fly fever and catarrhal jaundice. He had succumbed to sand-fly fever before, in October, when his symptoms – headache, a high temperature, fatigue and nausea – had been worsened by an incorrectly made-up prescription. This time the attack was more serious and Clifford felt like death. Reluctantly, Moorehead 'left him one day huddled in blankets in the lee of a sand dune by the sea'[15] while he spent the day pursuing news in the desert – and then struggled to find him when he returned. On top of such physical discomfort, there were evening air raids, the enemy dive-bombing the nearby road as Clifford lay awake watching the flames from the planes' exhausts as they swooped in before at the last minute struggling upwards, straining for height, with their bombs gone.

Clifford lived on orange juice for three days, unable to stomach the rich spaghetti stew the others concocted from ingredients looted from the Italians: tomatoes, bully beef, Parmesan cheese, a feast washed down with Italian mineral water. One night they watched the RAF bombing Bardia, the sky alive with searchlights, tracer and flame. Clifford was proving slow to recover, and with Christmas drawing near, the correspondents decided to return to Cairo. In a pre-festive spirit, they ate a plum pudding and drank whisky, sitting around a fire in the night, nestling in a wadi near Halfaya – 'Hellfire' – Pass while Italian aircraft cruised overhead in the darkness. The bombing was, at best, half-hearted, making a show of belligerence, nothing more.

That winter Moorehead enjoyed one of the best Christmases he could remember, cheered that Lucy had come out of hospital the day before Christmas Eve. Clifford meanwhile was convalescing, confined to bed, or sometimes shivering in front of the fire, cocooned in an eiderdown. He had lost weight, having eaten very little for three weeks, and his doctor insisted that he was too unwell to join Moorehead when the latter left for the desert early in January 1941.

Italian prisoners-of-war 'shambling across the desert' at Sidi Barrani. (IWM, E1378)

Lucy, it was clear, was troubled by her husband's determination to set out for the front so soon after their baby's recovery from illness, an improvement which Clifford, in a letter to his mother, attributed to Lucy stopping breastfeeding.

Alex Clifford was a diligent correspondent to his mother. 'Dearest mama,' he would invariably begin his letters, usually signing off with his family nickname of 'Dick'. He worried about the impact of the war on the family home in Lindfield, Sussex, enthused about progress in the garden ('I only hope it won't be ravaged by the enemy'), detailed the domestic arrangements in the Gezira flat ('fairly nice but very badly furnished'), described the weather ('I haven't seen a drop of rain for three months'), and itemised the whimsical behaviour of the servants ('completely cuckoo'). He was, in effect, part of two families now, and the lives of the Sussex-based Cliffords were soon entangled with the doings of the Cairo

Mooreheads. The fact that Alan and Lucy 'have got to be married before they register the child, otherwise it will be both illegitimate and Egyptian'[16] must have caused a flutter around the Lindfield breakfast table, partly allayed no doubt by Alex's explanation that the pre-war marriage ceremony in Rome was not recognised by the British authorities in Egypt.

* * * *

At three o'clock on the morning of 4 January 1941, Moorehead set out west from Mersa Matruh and drove towards Derna, a lurching, bumpy journey in an army truck. With him were Patrick Crosse (Reuters), Richard Capell (*The Daily Telegraph*), Richard McMillan (BUP) and Richard Dimbleby (BBC), with a Squadron Leader Houghton acting as Conducting Officer. Dimbleby was at the wheel. They crawled slowly up 'Hellfire' Pass in whirling clouds of icy dust, crossed the dilapidated border fence and stared at the lines of demoralised Italian prisoners, guarded at bayonet point. Dimbleby's 'four travelling companions were lying on top of the luggage, pressing themselves into the soft rolls of bedding whenever a shell burst particularly near'.[17] Later, as the light began to die, they explored the smoking, grey town of Bardia.[18] Fires were still burning, flames licking the white stone houses, but the noise of battle had stopped; indeed, it was eerily quiet. The fall of Bardia was big news and the story needed to be revealed to the world as quickly as possible, not least because for once it was a British success at a time when the nation was starved of such things. So they decided to head back to Mersa that same evening despite the bitterly cold weather. They left at 10 p.m. with Richard Dimbleby again at the wheel since the regular driver was dozing. The truck had no windscreen and the cold was extreme, scarcely tempered by hats, mufflers and gloves. Moreover, Dimbleby was heavy with sleep himself, finding it hard to keep his eyes open as the night closed in. Finally he fell asleep momentarily, waking just in time to see the parapet of a bridge looming straight ahead. There was little time to yell a warning before the lorry slammed through the tar barrels marking the edge of the road and toppled over the side. There was a loud, reverberating crash, a splintering of wood and, finally, the truck came to rest in the gully below. While the vehicle was a write-off, the correspondents were unhurt, though somewhat shaken. Moments later, with the brick dust settling and the truck's wheels still turning, a figure emerged in the darkness. He was one of the engineers who had finished the construction of the bridge that very day. 'I've been working for a solid month in this bloody hole,' he said. After a further barrage of blame, he calmed a little and muttered: 'I was just putting up a nice little memorial to say "Bridge begun by the 21st Company of Engineers, December 1940. Completed 1941."' There was no avoiding the bitter note in his voice when he proposed adding: 'Destroyed by War Correspondents, January 1941.'[19]

* * * *

Most days had a simple routine to them based around driving in dust-choked daylight, followed by writing urgent dispatches under hurricane lamps at night. Danger, however, was always just a momentary turn of the steering wheel away. The risks might be real enough, or somewhat exaggerated for the readership back home. The American correspondent Edward Kennedy observed a penchant among his colleagues for 'War Correspondents to write hair-raising stories on "How I Almost Got Killed Today"'.[20] But sometimes death did come very near indeed. Moorehead was never to forget one such occasion; indeed he later claimed never to have fully recovered from it. He, Clifford and Captain Geoffrey Keating, their conducting officer, were some 12km from Barce, driving in a Morris truck along the southern road at about 5.30 p.m. Turning a corner, they found themselves facing a group of green-uniformed Italian soldiers laying mines. An intense firefight quickly followed and Clifford was shot (it would happen twice in the war and both times it was in his backside).[21] Geoffrey Keating was soon shot too – in both his wrist and leg. A bullet sliced through the arm of Moorehead's greatcoat without causing any harm, although in the immediate aftermath he expected to feel intense pain. Clifford later reported in the *Mail* that 'Alan Moorehead, *Daily Express* war correspondent got off scot free.' Their Welsh driver was badly wounded in the upper part of his left arm. It was a terrifying ordeal which could have killed them all.

Cars blazed by the roadside and, with gunfire continuing over their heads, Moorehead and Clifford tried some elementary first aid – a ham-fisted confusion of bloodied bandages, curses and scrabbling in the dust – before making an undignified retreat to an advanced dressing station some miles away. Once there, Clifford was able to inspect the damage, flinching at the long gash in the back of his thigh, as well as the welter of caked blood. In addition, his precious typewriter had been wounded too – terminally in fact – while lying accusingly in the typewriter case was a lump of shrapnel the size of an egg. Decidedly shaken, Moorehead and Clifford passed an uncomfortable night on stretchers after a meagre supper of water and cold Italian tunny fish. Their sole topic of conversation was why on earth they had not done the sensible thing and surrendered.

The next day they cautiously returned to the site of the ambush. It was a chaotic scene of destruction, with bullet-riddled typewriters and shattered cameras, while the captured Parmesan cheese had been shot through with bullet holes and was now 'pitted like a Gruyere'.[22] They gazed forlornly at the debris, realising that the skirmish had, in a moment, turned them into beggars. Bedding, typewriters, clothes, food – nothing remained, and Benghazi was still 100 miles away. They slept in a deserted railway station and woke to a landscape of slushy red mud and a cold, bitter rain, occasionally pocked by bursts of hail. Both men felt bereft,

Clifford and Moorehead prepare to move on after spending another night in the desert. (IWM, E13368)

almost like castaways, their gloom not helped by the heaviness of the grey cloud and the intensity of the rain. Their progress towards Benghazi had little of the steely determination and energy of the advancing Australian troops sweeping the Italians before them like so much trash. For Clifford and Moorehead this was perhaps the moment when a heightened sense of realism was born and a kind of disillusion began to take hold.

NOTES

1   *Destiny in the Desert* by Jonathan Dimbleby, p.32.
2   Liddell Hart's opinion of Wavell; see Liddell Hart papers LH 11/1940/41.
3   In December 1940 there were just seven war correspondents in Cairo; by June 1941, there were 92. See Collier, pp.69–70.
4   *Mediterranean Front*, op. cit., p.109.
5   Clifford, p.36.
6   *Outposts of War* by Gordon Young, p.172.
7   Clifford, p.37.
8   Young, p.172.
9   Ibid., p.173.
10 Ibid., p.174.
11 Ibid., p.177.
12 Clifford, p.42.
13 *Mediterranean Front*, op. cit., p.115.
14 Collier, p.66.
15 *Mediterranean Front*, op. cit., p.128.
16 Clifford papers (16727), IWM, file AGC/2/1/4. Letter dated 22 December 1940.
17 (Richard) Dimbleby, p.103.
18 '25,000 prisoners had been taken … (while) our total of 400 casualties was extraordinarily small.' War Cabinet minutes, 6 January 1941, The National Archives, CAB/65/17/2.
19 *Mediterranean Front*, op. cit., p.144.
20 *Ed Kennedy's War*, ed. Julia Kennedy Cochran, p.93.
21 Both Clifford and Moorehead described the wound as a 'grazed thigh' in their reports; see *Daily Express* and *Daily Mail*, 11 February 1941.
22 *Mediterranean Front*, op. cit., p.177.

5. The Cheese and the Mousetrap

Clifford's family, it seems, were not *Daily Mail* readers, preferring perhaps the more staid *Daily Telegraph* with its recently recruited war correspondent Christopher Buckley. 'No one in my own family,' Clifford complained, 'is sufficiently interested to take my own paper.'[1] He frequently grumbled about this perceived slight in his letters home. As if to reinforce his resentment he made sure his mother was fully aware of the great risks he was running. In mid-February 1941, for example, he reported that he was 'still alive – though only thanks to a miracle' – this after the ambush on the Barce road. He hadn't written for a while, he said, because he had been 'busy capturing Benghazi'. Unaided, he and Moorehead had 'captured an important place with two forts and a waterworks', while the 'last shots fired in defence of Benghazi were fired at me personally'.[2]

When they drove in triumph into Benghazi, Clifford was obliged to wear his bloodstained trousers and sweater, a legacy of the ambush. Approaching the city, the prevailing images were of a barren countryside lashed into a glutinous bog by persistent downpours and the cleansing effect of that same rain on the 'façades of the white villas and blocks of flats'. It had also 'washed the dust off the leaves of the trees'.[3] At the Hotel d'Italia there were beds with clean sheets and hot meals too, which greatly pleased Moorehead since someone else was doing the cooking and the meals weren't prepared in a roadside ditch. For once, Clifford found himself admiring the resilience of the Italians – not their fighting qualities, but their determination that life would, in short order, return to something approaching normality – 'they still had shops to open, hotels to manage, profits to make',[4] despite being blown away on the battlefield. In the more peaceful arena of the hotel dining room, amidst the white-clothed tables, there was a reversal of fortunes: victorious, brash, battle-scarred Australians meekly tipping the Italian waiters. As for Graziani's troops, they had hurriedly withdrawn to the south, leaving Benghazi contemplating peace and Clifford and Moorehead with time on their hands. They wandered through the city's Arab quarter like tourists, and

'haggled for eggs and yellow leather slippers and cheap tinware'.[5] Such indolence
soon lost its charm and they began to wonder what news was being made out of
sight beyond the horizon.

✻   ✻   ✻   ✻

Life in the desert was like no other battleground: those slow, relentless convoys
stirring dust, tanks forging through the sand like naval destroyers on the high seas,
brutal contrasts of temperature, sandstorms fierce enough to uproot telegraph
poles, the unparalleled emptiness, the voracious fleas and clouds of flies, the sand,
scrub and far horizons, mirages, wide arcs of sky and legions of stars at night. The
sand-flies were ever-present, small enough to insinuate themselves through the
mosquito netting; mosquitoes, fleas and scorpions flourished; tracks and paths
were rudimentary or worse. 'To those who knew it the desert was a fortress,' one
British general, 'Strafer' Gott, said, 'to those who did not, (it was) a grave.'[6] Sound
carried for miles – 'occasionally a faint rumbling was borne on the night breeze
to remind me of the battle being fought sixty or seventy miles away'.[7] Landmarks
were few and far between; getting lost was all too easy. The fighting resembled a
chaotic game of chess, but a game fought in blindfolds. The war correspondents
endured all of this, and, beyond that, had to tolerate the edgy wariness of British
commanders towards them. Some thought the war correspondents were 'a bunch
of lazy, overfed, over-drinking, good-for-nothing tramps'.[8] It was a view with
a long history: in his story of the Second Sudan War fought more than four
decades before, Sir Arthur Conan Doyle referred to 'newspaper correspondents
and travelling gentlemen and all that tribe of useless drones'.[9] In the early days
of this war, it was not unusual for Moorehead and Clifford to be given a frosty,
unfriendly reception on arriving at some key position. They might be told that
they had no business being there; that they were supernumeraries, no more than
that; that there was no accommodation available and certainly no transport.

Writing at least seemed easier in the desert, maybe because there were so few
distractions. It was, Moorehead thought, 'a wonderful place for clarifying the mind'.[10]
Looking back on it two years later, it was the silence that he would remember as
being the thing he treasured most about the desert. It was also an attractively simple
existence. Preoccupations comprised sleep and food, keeping warm on cold desert
nights, chasing news, fading memories of women. Undeniably too the desert had a
strange beauty, a brilliant clarity of light, and an ability to bewitch. Moorehead felt
that there was 'never a place which so moved one to composition' – that 'arching
sky and flat desert stretching away on every side'. Sometimes they swam naked
in the 'transparent sea'.[11] Buckley, when he was with them later on, would keep
buttoned-up and dry – he couldn't swim – but the other two members of the Trio
needed little encouragement to fling off their kit and gallop into the waves.

Since they had no proper military status, correspondents were obliged to fend for themselves. So they regularly came face-to-face with the desert's dark side, not least the food which was ghastly, usually unimaginative permutations of bully beef and biscuits, bread and margarine. Drinking was not usually excessive, perhaps gin, lime and water, or nightcaps of whisky in the darkness. Each member of the Trio knew the other's needs: 'When turning in, Moorehead knew that Clifford's priority was a special pneumatic pillow; Clifford knew that, as a dedicated chain smoker, Moorehead's was an ample supply of cigarettes.'[12] Buckley needed books: as well as his 'never without' Clausewitz, he read unstintingly, literature rather than the lightweight: Arnold Bennett, Wilde, Hemingway.

There could be no fires once night fell, a hindrance to Buckley's reading. Correspondents perforce slept longer in the desert, shivering awake when the morning came. Sleeping arrangements could be primitive: nights were often cold, and when they slept on camp beds in the open air, they woke covered in dew. Alternatives to those damp shocks of an al fresco dawn were always welcome: on one occasion Clifford and Moorehead were glad to sleep on a broken-down billiard table. Sex was replaced by an 'enforced monasticism' – indeed 'it was nearly impossible to commit any of the deadly sins'[13] – but it provided a rich source of conversation. The journalist Clare Hollingworth remembered overhearing the Trio exchanging confidences about it as they lay trussed up in their sleeping bags in the desert, a neat 10 yards apart.

Despite everything, at times it felt like paradise, often on those occasions when, out of the blue, there was an unexpected break from the routine. It might be the sudden acquisition of an alternative to the damp tent and rickety camp bed: for example, when they moved into a sumptuous villa nestling on the coast. It had just been vacated in a hurry by the Italian General Graziani, and was surrounded by vivid bougainvillaea and shaded lawns, with good wine in the cellar, an open fire, and – oh such luxury – a bath!

Early on in the campaign 'some correspondents had amused themselves by rounding up willing prisoners in batches of fifty or a hundred … Soon though it was wiser to shoo them away.'[14] Food, sleep, transport were what mattered – and of course news; correspondents were perpetually anxious lest something of great significance was happening somewhere where they weren't, or if dispatches they had written failed to reach Cairo, let alone London or New York. After a while Moorehead began to worry that he was beginning to lose his sense of what constituted 'news'; the solution, he realised, was to write exactly what he saw and felt, no more, no less. Correspondents typed away on the backs of lorries, on beaches, in deserted houses, leaning against gun emplacements, under the awnings and flapping canvas of tents, typewriters resting on sunburnt knees. The light to write by came from guttering candles or smoky oil lamps; only the thunder of bombs or artillery could silence the urgent clatter of sand-encrusted typewriters.

Christopher Buckley of *The Daily Telegraph*. (Getty Images)

It was time to leave Benghazi and return to Cairo, but how to travel a thousand miles without enduring a week-long overland journey? Moorehead and Clifford disconsolately lingered for a day or two, hoping to hitch a flight back east, but without any immediate luck. Eventually, they heard rumours of a Bombay transport plane flying east, and, in a rare case of overt competition between them, they tossed a coin to see who would secure the last remaining seat. Clifford called correctly, but it did him no good since the plane left without him, and with Moorehead perched uncomfortably on piles of luggage. It was no consolation to Clifford that Moorehead's pleasure at leaving Benghazi at last was marred by the fact that the trip proved fearful, 'cold, bumpy and long'. With him on board was a sorry group of captured Italian generals, including General Bergonzoli who had fought in Spain's civil war. Before the aeroplane took off, Clifford had reminisced with him about Spain and the Italian's eyes had briefly lit up. Defeated now, and facing a long captivity, he looked old and broken. He had arrived at the aerodrome on a stretcher and the flight was an ordeal for him: he 'lay there looking ashen grey, not moving or speaking'. How his world had changed in just four years when 'among the Fascist generals, he was certainly the bravest of the lot'.[15]

*   *   *   *

Eventually Alexander Clifford flew back to Cairo too, travelling with the BBC's Edward Ward.[16] But events in Greece – British support for the Greeks against German and Italian aggression – conspired to move him on again rapidly. He chose to go to Athens on his own initiative since, for reasons of military secrecy, he was forbidden, 'to ask my newspaper whether I should go'.[17] Once there, he and Ward were initially confined to the Greek capital since the authorities were concerned that any forays outside the city might alert the Germans that something was afoot.

Christopher Buckley was already in Athens, working for *The Daily Telegraph*, having previously edited a weekly English newspaper in the city. He was much travelled: Poland in the months before the war, then the Balkans, Bucharest and Turkey. He had been witness to the debacle in the Low Countries in 1940 and carried painful memories of the Luftwaffe's Stukas plunging from the skies with their ear-splitting, terrifying sound. In Athens he met up with the war correspondent Clare Hollingworth, sitting next to her at a press conference towards the end of 1940. Like many others, she was impressed by his sound knowledge of history, his academic gravitas and the way fellow reporters deferred to his evident military expertise. These were qualities that Clifford and Moorehead would come to value very highly.

Reluctantly restricted to Athens, Clifford and Eddie Ward spent their days sightseeing and the evenings in the local *tavernas*. Springtime in the city had

a breathtaking beauty, and Clifford felt his spirits lifting, despite the news that
the Germans had just retaken Benghazi – 'the wretched town', Ward wrote,
'changed hands five times!'[18] Not only was the weather delightful, but Churchill's
support for the Greeks meant that British reporters were treated as heroes. 'Had
we accepted all the drinks pressed upon us,' Dimbleby wrote, 'we should have
had to retire again to our bedrooms.'[19] He was none too happy at the prospect
of being hoisted on to the shoulders of the mob and, while he escaped such a
fate by scurrying indoors, Clifford was not so lucky, swept aloft when he went
out to take a dispatch to the censors' office. It was a deeply moving time, with
Greeks marching through the streets of their capital, blue and white flags swirling
in a pure, spring light, singing 'their rude songs about Mussolini'. Clifford found
himself stirred by a 'spirit of friendliness and brotherhood that sometimes made
you want to cry'.[20]

   In an atmosphere of what Alex called 'hysteria', Athens was preparing for the
worst by, for example, pasting strips of white tape and paper across windows
to minimise the impact of the anticipated German air raids. Clifford, David
Woodward (of the *Manchester Guardian*), Richard Busvine, Eddie Ward and others
were all staying at the King George Hotel, an establishment 'being run by three
lunatics known to one and all as Groucho, Chico and Harpo'.[21] The previous
manager had been detained as a fifth columnist and Ward and the other pressmen
were convinced that most of the staff were German agents. At night, from the
hotel's roof, Alex watched the Luftwaffe attacking the shipping in the harbour at
Piraeus with a ferocious intensity. While the Luftwaffe dominated the skies, the
RAF, Ward noted, was nowhere to be seen. Increasingly, it became clear that the
British position was unsustainable; indeed there was every prospect of being cut
off. A New Zealander called MacGregor summed the situation up when he and
Clifford were lying low in a slit trench near the Thermopylae pass. It was like, he
said, being 'a bit of cheese in a military mouse trap'.[22] Over sardines and wine
they gloomily contemplated the prospects of survival amidst yet another debacle.

   It wasn't long before the correspondents decided that it was time to abandon
the King George Hotel, indeed, leave the city altogether – and as soon as possible.
Woodward and Busvine foraged for supplies of food to take with them, spending
£20 on tins, while Clifford and Ward went looking for tents. They set up camp
on the slopes of Mount Hymettus and, as the sun set, swore they would 'see
this show through' and stay together.[23] Predictably, as soon as the bond was
forged, something happened to break it, as was usually the way with plans made
in wartime. It was a Major Alben of Public Relations who, on this occasion,
thwarted them when he gave permission for Ward, Woodward and Clifford to
set out for the front, while Richard Busvine – technically still a civilian – was
denied. Indeed, he was to be evacuated soon after, eventually leaving by ship, after
enduring a two-hour air raid.

There was no escaping the fact that the position was becoming increasingly perilous. At one point the press corps was addressed by a senior staff officer whose attempts at measured briefing went down badly. Leaving the briefing room, Clifford commented, 'All we need now is a rubber boat, a false set of whiskers, and a Bolivian passport,' unaware that the staff officer was within earshot.[24] The British were faced with another ignominious withdrawal: it would be 'Dunkirk all over again', but perhaps without the sense of victory plucked from defeat that characterised that retreat. The mood now was one of chaos and embarrassed humiliation, made worse by the generous attitude of the Greeks: 'Greek women, who might have been bitter and resentful, came to us weeping in the streets and kissed us goodbye.'[25] An old woman said to David Woodward, 'Goodbye. We know you will come back properly next time.'[26]

The exodus gathered pace as the enemy became closer and more dangerous. Ed Kennedy from Associated Press (AP) found himself tumbling 'from his truck to take cover from strafing planes no less than fifty times'.[27] Travelling light was essential, and the correspondents headed south with just a haversack each and a typewriter. Clifford spent a long day hiding in a cornfield, looking up anxiously at German aeroplanes sweeping the skies, dropping bombs indiscriminately. It was a desperate time, with trucks and vehicles set alight, tanks pushed off cliffs, tyres deliberately punctured and troops throwing away virtually everything but their rifles. Orders were issued that the wounded were to be carried only for as long as there was some hope of reaching safety, but that the dead should be abandoned. Eventually Clifford reached the coast and, in the darkness, scrambled aboard a ship bound for Crete from the cobbled quayside. Four thousand men were aboard and each of them was fed hot soup, bread and cheese. Clifford and David Woodward shared the captain's private dining cabin with four Gunner subalterns and, as they were falling into an exhausted sleep, a bottle of gin was surreptitiously slipped through the door.

* * * *

The island of Crete was of critical strategic importance, but difficult to defend: vulnerable to air attack, with just one major road and no railways. On 28 April 1941, Churchill sent an urgent memorandum to Wavell: 'It seems clear from our information that a heavy Air-borne attack by German troops and bombers will be made on Crete (Stop).' The prime minister's orders were clear: 'It ought to be a fine opportunity for killing the parachute troops. (Stop) The island must be stubbornly defended.'[28] Clifford stayed in an empty house in Canea with Woodward, Eddie Ward and Christopher Lumby of *The Times*. Sometimes they slept out 'underneath the olive trees looking up at the tall flat chain of mountains'.[29] In November of the previous year he had been on the island, flying patrols in Sunderlands; he had camped in an olive grove and lived idyllically on the island's 'wine and honey, and oranges and delicious bread.'[30] Six months later this Mediterranean paradise had gone, dispelled by hordes of German paratroopers and an army still demoralised by its hurried departure from Greece. It took a month, but eventually London reluctantly approved the evacuation of Crete, bowing to the inevitable. Troops were encouraged to 'make for Sphakia, the fishing village on the southern coast, by the rough mountain road which provided their only line of retreat'.[31]

*　*　*　*

The Daily Telegraph's newly acquired correspondent, Christopher Buckley, reported on the evacuation while on board an Australian cruiser in the Eastern Mediterranean. Under cover of darkness, he had watched a succession of small boats ferrying men away from the island's beaches, plying 'backwards and forwards, carrying fully 50 a-piece, across glass-smooth waters under a tranquil starry sky'.[32] Some 1,200 men were taken on board Buckley's ship where they were given hot cocoa and biscuits, while Buckley willingly gave up his cabin to two exhausted officers who were thrilled by the sight of sheets on the beds.

Buckley was a brave, inquisitive and independent man. His understanding of the sweep of history put him 'head and shoulders above the other correspondents'.[33] He was, Moorehead thought, 'quite unable to resist a craving to explore anything and everything whether it lay inside enemy territory or not'.[34] Buckley conformed to Richard Dimbleby's assertion that war correspondents needed to be 'habitually careless and casual; they are always moving from country to country, making and breaking friendships as they go. They have no roots.'[35] He did not look like the typical newspaperman – too much of the erstwhile schoolmaster remained – and his donnish glasses and drooping moustache gave him rather a mournful appearance. He was also 'prone to quote Shakespeare or the Lord's Prayer in moments of stress' when the average reporter might have relied on just plain cursing.[36] Before the war he had travelled widely – relying partly on his independent means – and the global conflict merely extended the scope for journeying. In time Christopher Buckley would become the third member of the Trio, that glittering triumvirate of correspondents whose other two members were Alan Moorehead and Alexander Clifford. This was one friendship that would not break. Indeed it would become something more than a friendship, with the three of them gaining a kind of collective authority and strength from being part of such a distinct unit. It also set them apart, earning the envy of those consigned to working alone.

All this lay ahead. In May 1941, the Trio was yet to establish itself and it took the defeat in Crete to begin the process of drawing them together. Thereafter, the three men would spend perhaps 80 per cent of their time in each other's company.

For now, while Clifford and Buckley were caught up in the campaigns in Crete and Greece, Alan Moorehead was many miles away, in East Africa. There had been a moment when it seemed that he too was heading for Athens; indeed there had been a pre-departure drink in the lounge bar of the Hotel Cecil in Alexandria when both Mooreheads, Clifford and Eddie Ward had shared their unease over the probability of a 'new Dunkirk at Salonika'.[37] Then, at the last minute, Moorehead was instructed to head in the opposite direction, for Addis Ababa, in Ethiopia. His attitude to travelling was in sharp contrast to Buckley's – for Moorehead, it was a necessary evil, the inevitable result of needing to be either at the front, or back at headquarters, not wasting time between the two. As he stepped on board the flying boat, the Nile swirling around the vast aircraft's hull, Moorehead wondered whether the long flight into the Horn of Africa would be worth it, or would he be caught in mid journey when the news was being made elsewhere?

A trip by flying boat down the Nile when the weather was calm and still was the only kind of flying Moorehead could tolerate. Nothing for it but to sit back resignedly and chain-smoke through Africa. Later, on the terrace of the Grand Hotel, Khartoum, he watched wild hippos floating on the river and enjoyed the novelty of iced beer for breakfast. Thereafter, the pleasures of the trip diminished rapidly. To begin with, moving on from Khartoum proved difficult, wasting precious time. Eventually he reached Nairobi, but only after a flight to a heat-struck Juba followed by an eight-hour drive. The Kenyan capital was 'a survival from some lost world along the pre-war Riviera'.[38] It was, by turns, glamorous, exotic, dramatic ('elopements and fights and runaway marriages between nobles and chorus girls'); full of men in uniform, and hot with scandal. Initially Moorehead was intrigued by the city's louche atmosphere, but after a week all he wanted was to get away. When he finally negotiated a flight out, he heard that Addis Ababa would soon fall.

The flight to Addis was eventful, the ex-South African Airlines Junkers casting its shadow over burning sand, then being lashed by cold rain as it strained to top the mountains of Abyssinia. It spooked camels and giraffes, then an ostrich which bolted under the aircraft's wheels somewhere in Italian Somaliland. Moorehead became stranded in the dank, walled town of Harar for ten days, still 300 miles from Addis Ababa, and pestered by 'flies innumerable and persistent clustered like blackcurrants upon every living thing'.[39] When he finally reached Addis, the atmosphere was chaotic and wild. The lounge of the Albergo Imperiale was thickly populated by Italians, while outside the rain poured down on a sad, bedraggled city. Moorehead drove up into the mountains above the city, hoping to find some food more appetising than that served by the Imperiale. He stopped at a restaurant full of Italians, intending to order food, wine and coffee. He was refused them all, despite the 'rich smell of onions and frying meat' that wafted across the room.[40] It took a trick learned in Spain to dispel the mood and earn himself stew and Chianti: he passed his cigarette packet around the room. The food came seasoned by a long conversation with a Fascist Italian officer.

Moorehead soon realised that Addis was not the place to be: there was no story there, only confused guerrilla warfare. He should have stayed in Egypt or gone to Greece. Predictably, leaving Addis was as difficult as getting there and he began to feel trapped. He worried that his dispatches seemed tired and lacking substance. It didn't help that he seemed to be on the very edge of things, with Lucy and the baby in Cairo, the Germans advancing in the Western Desert, and Alex reporting on the unfolding disasters in Greece and Crete. Imagine the relief when the pilot of a Blenheim bomber arrived at Jijiga airfield and climbed out of the cockpit with a cheery, 'Is your name Moorehead?' I should bloody well think so![41] He flew to Aden, sitting in the rear-gunner's turret, and looked back at the stifling heat, lumbering transport, voracious flies and glutinous mud of the past few weeks. By contrast, he could contemplate the prospect of a cold beer at the Gezira, his pleasure only marginally diminished by the colourful tales of Greek adventures told by David Woodward, Eddie Ward, Richard McMillan, and, of course, the inimitable Alexander Clifford.

NOTES

1   Clifford papers (16727), IWM, file AGC/2/1/5. Letter of 25 February 1941.
2   Ibid., letter of 17 February 1941.
3   Clifford, p.67.
4   Ibid., p.68.
5   Ibid., p.68.
6   (Richard) Dimbleby, p.31.
7   Ibid., pp.30–1.
8   Busvine, p.227.
9   From Conan Doyle's short story, *The Three Correspondents*, written in 1896.
10   *A Late Education*, op. cit., p.124.
11   Ibid., p.61.
12   Collier, p.106.
13   *A Late Education*, op. cit., p.62.
14   Kennedy Cochran, p.92.
15   *Mediterranean Front*, op. cit., pp.192–3.
16   Eddie Ward had reported on the campaigns in Finland and northern France earlier in the war before being sent to the Middle East to replace Richard Dimbleby.
17   Clifford, p.81.
18   *Number One Boy* by Edward Ward, p.161.

19   (Richard) Dimbleby, p.80.

20   *The Sickle and the Stars* by Alexander Clifford and Jenny Nicholson, p.100.

21   Busvine, p.232.

22   Clifford, p.85.

23   Busvine, p.234.

24   Collier, p.74.

25   Clifford, p.87.

26   *Front Line and Front Page* by David Woodward, p.101.

27   Collier, p.74.

28   The National Archives, PREM/3/109.

29   Woodward, p.104.

30   Clifford, p.35.

31   *Greece and Crete 1941* by Christopher Buckley, p.286.

32   *The Daily Telegraph*, 3 June 1941.

33   *There's a German Just Behind Me* by Clare Hollingworth, p.152.

34   *The End in Africa* by Alan Moorehead, p.175.

35   (Richard) Dimbleby, p.83.

36   Collier, p.70.

37   *Mediterranean Front*, op. cit., p.243.

38   Ibid., p.205.

39   Ibid., p.208.

40   Ibid., p.216.

41   Ibid., p.224.

6. The Trio's Early Days

After the Greek campaign was over, General Wavell wrote to the War Office seeking to explain away the defeat: 'The dice,' he wrote, 'were loaded against us from the start.'[1] Christopher Buckley took a similar view: 'To those of us who were in Greece at the time,' he wrote, 'it looked an exceedingly bleak prospect.'[2] At least by 1941 there was some experience of the art of retreat amongst the correspondents: 'I've been making strategic withdrawals,' the *Daily Mirror*'s David Walker complained, 'all the way across Europe.'[3] The evacuations from Greece and Crete in April and May of 1941 were no mean feat, more challenging in some ways than Dunkirk since the distances involved were far greater (160 miles to Crete compared with the relative narrowness of the English Channel); air cover was less; and there was no armada of little ships. In truth, though, the evacuation from Crete was at best only a partial success: of the '27,550 Imperial Troops on the island at the beginning of the attack, 14,580 were evacuated'.[4] As for Alex Clifford, he had been very pessimistic about his prospects of making it back to Cairo. For his final eight days in Greece he did not sleep in a bed, hunkering down instead on floors, the decks of ships, or in fields. Moreover, he had no opportunity to change his clothes during that time and he recognised that he 'smelt pretty bad' by the time he had returned to Egypt. Once there, he sent a cable home, dated 11 May: 'to Clifford Scampshill Lindfield Sussex. Back safe well Egypt after many adventures lost most of my possessions.'[5]

Being deprived of his possessions was becoming a habit for Clifford in 1941, but at least he was safely back in Cairo. It was a city of pleasure and rumbustious life where, according to Christopher Buckley, happiness came easily. Moreover, for the present at least, there were many miles of empty desert between the city and the Germans. It was 'a city for fun, a colourful mélange of smart hotels like Shepheards, night clubs, belly dancers and tarts, noisy trams and faded monuments, spies and intrigue, smells and disease, the Nile and the pyramids'.[6] As well as 'fleshpots', it also had 'good food, comfortable beds, hot baths and lavatories that work'.[7] For Clifford there was also the comfort of the family whose life he now shared. When the Mooreheads' son, John, was christened at the city's cathedral on 6 May, Alex Clifford was godfather, a role he took very seriously, acting as an additional father; for example, when Lucy and Alan went to Palestine, it was Clifford who gave the baby his bottle and changed him every night.

By the summer of 1941, Moorehead and Clifford had been reporting the war from the Middle East for a year and they both craved a rest. The prospects of that were remote, however, given the likelihood of an 'attack in the Western Desert, in Crete, Syria, Cyprus, Iraq – or in all five places simultaneously'.[8] There was to be no respite. Once Crete had fallen, Moorehead took the train to Jerusalem, hoping for a week's leave 'in the cool air there', but, just as he stepped on to the platform, an American correspondent warned him of an outbreak of fighting away to the north where the Allied forces were advancing. 'There was nothing for it but to get a car and chase after them.'[9] He set off on a headlong drive to Haifa where he exchanged the car for an ambulance, before continuing towards Tyre. Later, he stayed in a hotel on Mount Carmel which he thought both beautiful and well situated – 'never was a war so convenient for the war correspondent'.[10] The views down to the sea were magnificent and he 'could see the fleet steaming out along the Syrian coast'.[11] There was snow on the mountains and, when he wasn't on the trail of the fighting, he could swim in the sea and drink chilled glasses of the local white wine.

By late June, Moorehead was in Damascus, 'the most ancient hotbed of intrigue in the Middle East,' and unexpectedly dusty, noisy and shabby.[12] At night, though, from his window at the Orient Hotel, Moorehead could look out over a city flaunting its lights. It was the first time in a year that he had seen a city which wasn't cloaked in blackout darkness. Exploring a city of light and shadows, in the company of Christopher Lumby of *The Times*, was a rare pleasure. The news from Damascus, however, was soon to be blacked out, erased from the front pages, when, on 22 June 1941, the German army crossed the Russian border. The Nazi invasion of Russia turned events in Syria into a sideshow and so 'Middle East correspondents were not expected to fill the news and keep up a daily stream of messages'.[13] Moorehead received a cable from his editor congratulating him on his magnificent reporting to date, but explaining that from now on, only the most sensational would be given significant coverage in the paper. The war had moved on. This twist in events did not stop Moorehead travelling – after all, 1941 was the year in which he claimed to have travelled some 30,000 miles. He headed north towards Aleppo and the Turkish border, getting as close as he ever would to Russia, before finally deciding to head back to Cairo. Meanwhile, German tanks were rolling east across the Russian steppe, their progress monitored by other war correspondents far from Cairo.

*   *   *   *

Alex Clifford and his godson John Moorehead. (John Moorehead)

Clifford, Moorehead and Geoffrey Keating were all mentioned in dispatches in the summer of 1941 for their distinguished service.[14] But Clifford at least was aware of a growing malaise. On 3 June, writing from near Tobruk, he confided in his mother that he had had 'too much of the desert' and that he felt 'stale'. The novelty had long since faded and it seemed, for example, that they were forever driving up to some remote desert HQ, clustering around an intelligence officer and his map, and being briefed on some impending action that mirrored dozens that had already been conducted.

If there was a glimmer of comfort, it lay in the fact that, back in London, his *Daily Mail* and Moorehead's *Express* 'must think it a bit strange that we always have the same adventures'.[15] Imagine then Clifford's misgivings when, in mid July, he embarked on preparations for yet another trip to the desert front, and without his trusted friend. Lucy Moorehead came with him as he bought tinned food, water bottles, fly netting and the other items which he now knew were essentials in the war correspondent's survival kit. He set off at mid morning on 15 July and by evening was encamped at Smugglers' Cove, near Mersa Matruh, sharing a tent with Richard Capell, a former music critic for the *Daily Mail* and

The Daily Telegraph who had turned war correspondent for the duration. Faced with a furious Italian artillery barrage, all thunder and fire, they enjoyed a 'terrific musical pickover' and chatted 'completely unrestrainedly about our favourite subject'.[16] For the next week, Alex swam, sunbathed and read, 'occasionally skipping through various trashy novels', and slapping away at the legions of flies. As well as the clouds of flies there were 'scorpions and some furry spiders with two mouths looking like tarantulas and sand vipers with horns'.[17] The snakes, vultures and insects lived on the birds lying on the sand, stunned by the heat as they migrated across the desert.

Geoffrey Keating, mentioned in dispatches with Moorehead and Clifford. Alan Moorehead is on his left and Moorehead's daughter, Caroline, is to Keating's right. (John Moorehead)

To make up for the uncomfortable routines of desert life, Clifford had hoped on this occasion to visit Siwa, an oasis near the Libyan border. Permission was refused, however, since there was great concern about the regularity with which German patrols attacked the road and cut off its users from base. There was the compensation of an interview near Sidi Barrani with General William 'Strafer' Gott who, right at the outset, enquired after the well-being of both Moorehead and Captain Geoffrey Keating. Soon after, Cecil Brown of CBS arrived, immediately 'whipping out a note book and a great pen and taking down everything that Gott said'. The general was disconcerted, while Clifford was scathing about the incident that night in his diary: it was, he wrote, 'terrible technique for a journalist'.[18] That night he camped amongst the sand-hills and, after a dinner improved by a tin of Palestinian sauerkraut, he soon fell asleep, although not before looking up at a darkening sky 'full of Hurricanes and Tomahawks' protecting the shipping near the besieged port of Tobruk.

Next morning he avoided breakfast since 'the army out in this desert persists in a diet which would be suitable for Yorkshire in winter'[19] – no doubt about it, 'fried bread, sausage, bacon, fried potatoes, tea' did not appeal. Instead, Clifford spent the time in a concerted effort to relieve his constipation, a frequent consequence of desert life. Later, they set out in a truck along the Via della Vittoria, no longer the smooth autostrada it had once been, its blacktop pitted now with mile after mile of ruts and potholes. The sky was a perfect blue and occasionally they stopped for a naked swim on beaches of dazzling white sand. The desert was at its most beguiling: at one point, past Buqbuq, Clifford was struck by the remarkable colouring of an 'escarpment, which looked like a purplish filling in a sandwich consisting of tawny desert and this blue sky'.[20] They stopped that night in an oasis where figs and grapes grew, a site that seemed idyllic, until Clifford climbed the sand dunes and saw a beach littered with 'rather sinister corpses'.

Enough was enough: two days later he took the train back to Cairo and, while waiting on the station platform at Sidi Inish, he listened to the discordant sounds of many languages, troops talking in Polish, Hindustani, Arabic or English. The journey was grim, one of constant delays and overcrowded carriages thick with heat. Stations along the railway were invariably crowded and at the quaintly named Zagazig, the platform resembled nothing more than a madhouse. But by evening he was back home where he luxuriated in a bath, then dined with Lucy whose husband arrived back soon afterwards (at 1 a.m. on the 22nd). Cairo life resumed. The two correspondents returned to the comforts of bridge or snooker, or dining under the stars in the open air, as well as meeting new arrivals in the city, including the stalwart Christopher Buckley. It was the real beginning of the Trio's existence.

In time, the Trio would become 'committed together', since they had become 'encompassed by the same risks, the same hardships and the same hope'. So wrote Alan Moorehead in *Cooper's Creek* almost twenty-five years after he and Clifford had first glowered at each other so unpromisingly in that bar in Saint-Jean-de-Luz. In fact, the book he was working on then was not about his wartime friendship, but rather about the nineteenth-century explorers of the Australian hinterland, Burke and Wills. But he could have been describing what the Trio would become during the war years. 'They were now building up that intimate network of habits, the knowing of one another's abilities and failings and oddities, and the acceptance of these things, that develops among any group of men who are isolated on a long journey and entirely dependent on one another.'[21]

By the summer of 1941 Christopher Buckley had arrived in Cairo, and the Trio was beginning to form. Alexander Clifford and Buckley were always likely to be friends since they had so much in common – they were alumni of the same Oxford college, for example, and both were lovers of literature and tempted by the academic life. It was always likely that, in time, Moorehead and Buckley would be drawn together too, since 'any friend of Clifford's became a friend of Moorehead's'.[22] Buckley was a natural friend too, with characteristics that revealed a warm heart: he could be moved by architecture, would suddenly begin reciting pastoral poetry and was stirred by landscape. He was troubled by Cairo's poverty, acutely aware of the vast gulf between the relative wealth of war-making incomers and the city's own people. He never forgot certain places – the gardens of St John's College in Oxford, a pre-war wine garden near Heidelberg, sunset on a midsummer's eve at Corfe Castle in Dorset, and looking out from a rocky ridge above Salamis on 15 September 1940, having abandoned Athens, and work, for the day. His influence on Moorehead was of a different order from Clifford's: less intimate and close, more donnish and exemplary. He was a man to be looked up to.

＊　　＊　　＊　　＊

Christopher Buckley's prior knowledge of North Africa helped him acclimatise more quickly than some when he first arrived in Cairo after the hasty exodus from Crete. For many, the city was a profound shock; it assaulted the senses and battered the nerves. The taxi Buckley took when he arrived was not as dirty as some, nor the driver quite so wild (Richard Dimbleby's cabbie when he first arrived was as high as a kite on hashish), but there was no avoiding the evidence that the city was unremittingly chaotic. For a start, the noise was never less than cacophonous – voices hollering, trams rattling, car horns, whistles, street vendors' cries, the grinding gears of army vehicles. At night the symphony of noise changed, but not the volume: that first Cairene night Buckley could hear the familiar, rhythmic clip-clop of horses plodding along the road outside his window, the crack of whips as the gharry-drivers exhorted the weary beasts, and the tinny sounds of the open-air cinemas. The city blazed with light, since there was no blackout. The night air smelt of jasmine and, just before midnight, he heard the strains of 'A Nightingale Sang in Berkeley Square' once again, reminding the exiled of home.

The next day, the traffic was as dense as ever, clouds of blue exhaust vapour thickening the air. Crossing the road was hazardous and it was not a place for the nervous motorist. Rules of the road were there to be ignored, it seemed, while the streets were a constantly shifting battleground with the tide of people flowing in all directions.

Buckley, despite being used to Athenian light, found himself screwing up his eyes against the sun, so bright it hurt. The colour of Greece was gone, replaced by a faded, drained look to buildings and city streets. The wind from the desert blew in clouds of swirling dust which clung to the leaves on the trees and coated everything with a gritty deposit. Some houses looked as if they were made of dust. Walking in the pounding heat, what struck Buckley was the variety of military uniforms, the mix of nationalities and cultures, the vast numbers of people for whom the war meant an adopted way of life with no obvious conclusion. The streets were a riot of red fezzes, pith helmets and turbans, beggars and street peddlers, sunburn and khaki. It was a kind of bedlam. There were things to savour: the occasional cooling wind off the river in the early evening, the sight of pink feluccas, or the Nile barges with their curved sails, the sun setting behind them. Then you could imagine that there was indeed something other than a war to be fought and dispatches from a war zone to be written.

In his early days in the Egyptian capital, Christopher Buckley was involved in an 'apparently chaste relationship' with the war correspondent Clare Hollingworth. Chaste it might have been, but it seems that the romantic Buckley was head over heels in love.[23] Sometimes Buckley could be seen walking hand-in-hand with Hollingworth through the gardens of the Gezira Club, wistfully discussing what they would do once the war was over. The two of them shared a 'chummery', a flat looking out on the Nile to one side and the Gezira Club on the other. The Mooreheads and Clifford shared the view of Gezira: green watered lawns, the new clubhouse, the tennis club and the awnings shading lunchtime diners. The neighbours included a Free French general, the Japanese legation (right above the Mooreheads), and Colonel Philip Astley 'who controlled the war correspondents in the Middle East'.[24]

To Hollingworth, Buckley was 'slim, tall, but with a slight stoop … he wore thick glasses and although he was basically good looking, few women noticed him'. Before the war he had travelled the North African coast from Cairo to Rabat and, as a result, he 'knew North Africa better than any other allied war correspondent'.[25] Later she would surmise that his military knowledge was of great value to both Moorehead and Clifford. Buckley's work routine in Cairo was disciplined: he would wake early, between six and seven, and read some history, perhaps from his edition of Clausewitz which he was never without. Then, at about nine, he would scrutinise the papers, make some phone calls, decide what the day's story should be, then attend a press conference. It all led up to the writing of a piece, negotiating it through the censors and then dispatching to *The Telegraph* desk in London. Each member of the Trio had the same pressure, standing as they did 'for three great London dailies', and the wiring of dispatches – powerful, descriptive, uplifting, 'newsy' – back to battle-hardened editorial desks in London was a recurring priority.

*   *   *   *

That August was blisteringly hot. On airless, sweaty afternoons, Clifford would lie across his bed, his chin resting on the mattress, a book open on the floor. But his reading habits had changed, since, 'when civilisation itself was in jeopardy it was a luxury and an aberration even to read a good book … to indulge in it was to weaken your ability to endure the present.'[26] So, Clifford now read guidebooks or thrillers, or an Arabic grammar. At night, when the heat was beyond endurance, he slept naked on the balcony. Surprisingly, he missed the early indications that Moorehead had embarked on writing a book about the previous year's campaign. Indeed he thought his friend was set on doing as little work as possible and somehow seemed to be successful in not sending very much to the *Express*'s London office. Out of the blue, though, on 5 August, Moorehead sent a detailed and comprehensive round-up of news to his paper, and four days later Clifford found himself reading the book whose existence he had not suspected. He had put his head around the door one morning, provoking a confession at what his friend was up to. Clifford's reaction was a startled 'Good God!' prompted in part by a realisation that the flat would be anything but peaceful for a good while, what with Moorehead's 'incessant type-writing'[27] – he was working ten or twelve hours a day on the book – the baby's teething, and the heat. It only served to increase Clifford's disaffection with the Middle East, the sense that, after nearly two years of war, progress seemed minimal. His teeth were playing up too and he had developed an ulcer which proved tiresome. Eventually he had to have five teeth extracted and was briefly hospitalised.

Occasionally, though, there were breaks in the routine, enough to hint that news might not have dried up entirely. On 10 August, for example, he and Patrick Crosse of Reuters flew as far as the RAF base at Bagush, where the 'revoltingly dirty and comfortless' mess proved dispiriting, despite their amusement at the new CO's ill-fitting wig.[28] Four days in the desert was enough though. Back in Cairo, the prime minister's son, Randolph Churchill, came to lunch. He proved 'quite pleasant', Clifford thought, 'but a terrible Fascist'.[29] (Not everyone was so positive about him: the travel writer Freya Stark for example thought him 'a quite insufferable young man with appalling manners'.[30]) Through that summer of 1941 Clifford grew increasingly uneasy about work, and when Eddie Ward turned up in Cairo, fresh with news of the continuing siege of Tobruk, Clifford found himself feeling guilty about not being there. Outside the window, though, there was a poignant reminder of an English summer, enough to banish thoughts of another trip to the desert. On the Gezira turf they were playing cricket, serious stuff with one team captained by the legendary Wally Hammond.[31] The afternoon drifted by, its peace broken by the crack of willow and leather, sounds infinitely preferable to the thump of artillery, or the roar of aircraft.

NOTES

1   The National Archives, PREM 3/313/2.
2   *Greece and Crete 1941* op. cit., p.117.
3   Collier, p.74.
4   The National Archives, PREM 3/313/2.
5   Clifford papers (16727), IWM, file AGC/2/1/5.
6   *Front Line* by Clare Hollingworth, p.130.
7   Woodward, p.107.
8   *Mediterranean Front*, op. cit., p.252.
9   Ibid., p.275.
10 Ibid., p.276.
11 Ibid., p.278.
12 Ibid., p.286.
13 Ibid., p.292.
14 This appeared in the *London Gazette* for 8 July 1941.
15 Clifford papers (16727), IWM, file AGC/2/1/5.
16 Ibid., file AGC/1/2: diary entry for 15 July 1941.
17 Ibid., file AGC/2/1/5; letter of 21 July 1941.
18 Ibid., file AGC/1/2: diary entry for 17 July 1941.
19 Ibid., diary entry, 18 July 1941.
20 Ibid., diary entry, 18 July 1941.
21 *Cooper's Creek* by Alan Moorehead, p.76.
22 Pocock, p.104.
23 Pocock papers, National Library of Australia, MS 8377; Pocock drew this conclusion from an interview with Cecilia Russell-Smith (formerly Cecilia Buckley).
24 *A Year of Battle* by Alan Moorehead, p.13.
25 *Front Line*, op. cit., p.131.
26 *A Late Education*, op. cit., p.130.

27   Clifford papers (16727), IWM, file AGC/1/2: diary entry for 7 August 1941.

28   Ibid., diary entry for 11 August 1941.

29   Ibid., diary entry for 20 August 1941.

30   Lucy Moorehead, p.136.

31   Hammond was a batsman of the highest class with Gloucestershire and
      England; during the war he was in the RAF and was stationed in Cairo from
      December 1940.

7. The Road to Persia

'Can you fly to Persia at once?'[1] The telegram from Arthur Christiansen, Moorehead's editor at the *Daily Express*, gave no hint as to the reason for the proposed visit. Nor was it entirely clear if this was an instruction or a genuine question. Moorehead's response was to drive across the Nile bridge to the Persian embassy, situated near the pyramids, and meet the ambassador. Ali Akbar Bahman 'sat amid his splendid Tabriz carpets' and passed Moorehead 'a little eggshell cup of sweet Turkish coffee' before confirming that he would grant a thirty-day visa. The ambassador was keen to have Persia exonerated from claims that the country was riddled with German agents. 'Persia (he called it Iran) is pro-British, pro-German, pro-Russian and pro-everybody.'[2] The country's neutrality, Moorehead was assured, was absolute. The interview solved little, other than the obtaining of a visa; it did not clarify why there was a sudden upsurge of interest in the country. Ali Akbar Bahman seemed as much in the dark as anyone. Then, on 24 August, Moorehead was summoned to see the new head of the army's propaganda branch, Randolph Churchill, who was adamant that Moorehead should not travel to Persia alone. 'I have something better arranged for you,' he said, but would not reveal what.[3]

In fact Churchill was keen to see a group of correspondents, rather than a lone operator, entering Persia at much the same time as the planned invasion by Russian and British troops. Moorehead flew from Heliopolis with two conducting officers, Kim Mundy and Geoffrey Keating, as well as correspondents Ed Kennedy, Desmond Tighe of Reuters and Russell Hill of the *New York Herald Tribune*. Clifford was not one of the party, however, and he sensed trouble, fearing that he would get 'a fearful raspberry' if Moorehead was on the case and he wasn't.[4] Working alone, the logistics were problematic and time-consuming: obtaining a movement order, drawing cash from the Field Cashier, and getting formal approval from Colonel Astley. He also cabled the *Mail* which, to his surprise, was unenthusiastic about the trip. Unperturbed, he 'managed to get away before they told me to stay,'[5] and they were never to catch up with him.

Clifford left Cairo by Empire Flying Boat on 26 August, its first port of call being Tiberias on the Sea of Galilee. In trying to move on from there, the aircraft developed engine trouble, flames emerging from two of the engines. Clifford was temporarily stranded and Moorehead extended the distance between them, flying on over a bare and desolate landscape. He played hands of bridge to combat the flight's tedium, using a suitcase as a card table, but bothered by turbulence 'so severe the cards jumped up and hung briefly in the hot atmosphere'.[6] A two-day sandstorm detained him at RAF Habbaniya, a remote airbase north-west of Baghdad. When Clifford arrived there soon after, he found the place distinctly unpleasant. From the air, Lake Habbaniya itself resembled just more rippled sand and, once on land, the heat was extreme. There were clouds of 'revolting sand coloured flies'; the scenery was 'the deadest bore you could ever imagine';[7] and bullet holes in the walls of the RAF mess admitted shafts of intense sunlight and were testimony to recent troubles.

It wasn't just Habbaniya which repelled Clifford. The country as a whole was dispiriting. Basra, he thought, was hot, sticky and shabby – Moorehead concurred, describing it as 'hateful' – while the wine tasted like motor oil. There was a desperate shortage of news too, leaving Clifford feeling uncertain and isolated. He took the night train to Baghdad struck down with melancholy, despite securing a seat in the train's one air-conditioned coach. Baghdad seemed little better than Basra – a squalid, down-at-heel city thick with foul smells, he thought, with none of the exotic mystery he had imagined. It got worse: his fellow correspondent, co-traveller and room-mate, Ray Brock, typed far into the night; then, when Clifford got up at 4 a.m., he promptly cut his foot on a sharp tile. The two correspondents set off in a battered Chevrolet on a three-hour drive across the billiard-table flatness of the Iraqi Desert in the company of four other correspondents, including Patrick Crosse and Richard Busvine, in two more cars not far behind. Dust settled on everything – cameras, typewriters and, worst of all, their precious luncheon baskets.

Nonetheless, just after midday, Clifford ate a refreshing lunch, sitting 'beside a swiftly running stream' in a valley, with his feet soothed by the cooling water while eating pineapple from a tin. Lunch over, they drove on, crossing the Persian frontier and entering a landscape of bare, malformed hills. The road began to climb soon after, up and over a spiralling mountain pass, magnificent and dangerous, with precipitous hairpin bends. Later, the cars had stones thrown at them and their drivers threatened mutiny, citing 'broken springs, faulty brakes, punctured tyres and wrenched steering gears' as evidence that any further driving was unwise.[8] They stopped for the night at Kermanshah in a hotel with a garden of bright flowers, a fountain, birds singing in the poplar trees and music from a two-piece band. The pleasures of the garden were not enough to quell Clifford's distaste for the Persian music or the wine, which he thought unfit to drink, even worse than that in Iraq.

But there was no denying that the landscape had a rare beauty. Sunday 31 August was a glorious day 'with white clouds and bare mountains and rows of poplars and early sunlight'.[9] They struggled on, unconvinced that the army – and any breaking news – were getting closer. The grumbling drivers and their creaking jalopies were a constant source of worry. Russian aircraft roared over at one point, dropping leaflets. The road, such as it was, meandered up and down the hills and they drove through 'villages where they were threshing and winnowing by biblical methods and the air was golden with corn'.[10] The landscape stretched away before them and the light had a remarkable clarity.

Soon after passing through the town of Kazvin, just as the sun was setting, they saw lorries full of troops in field-grey uniforms and steel helmets. These were not Germans, however, but the Red Army. It was a dramatic meeting of east and west, 'both of us staring at one another as though we were something fabulous'[11] – which in a way they were. The Russians were slim, deeply burnt by the sun, with faces caked in dust. Their bayonets were fixed, 'silhouetted in the evening sky'.[12] At a road block the Russian troops, despite appearances, proved friendly and one shook Clifford's hand, smiling as he said in halting English, 'We are brother.' That evening Clifford ate fried eggs and drank too much vodka with the Russians, topping that off with a whisky nightcap. Initially he slept in a wooden bed, but he soon abandoned that for the brick floor of the balcony, having been attacked by legions of bugs. Next morning they made another early start – Clifford calculated that it was the fifth morning out of the past six that he had risen at 4 a.m. Scratching their angry, red insect bites, they drove on towards Teheran, after a brief altercation with a suspicious sentry who had approached them, idly swinging a bomb in his hand. They drove past straggling lines of Iranian soldiers before finally entering the city. It was, Clifford thought, 'a little shoddy and cheapjack',[13] but clean and modern and he immediately preferred it to Baghdad.

*　*　*　*

Moorehead's party also had its mutinous drivers and each time the expedition came to a stop they demanded additional payment. They muttered and grumbled increasingly as they motored on, the cars raising plumes of dust as they entered a landscape of gaunt hills, broken occasionally by slivers of green valley. When one of the drivers realised that there was to be no respite for three more days and nights until they reached Teheran, the mood of sullen mutiny turned to sabotage: 'he decided to wreck his vehicle and that was child's play. He ran it over a monstrous rut and smashed what was left of all four springs.'[14] The repair took two hours, during which the drivers stretched out in the shade and slept. When they were woken up, there was no budging them and their excuses – (petrol? food? broken carburettor?) – multiplied, until one menacing figure produced a knife, stood tall and said, 'Finish. We stop.'

It took Kim Mundy's no-nonsense bravado to resolve the situation. Not for nothing was he known as the 'Flying Tank'.[15] 'You're in the army now,' he said, flourishing his service revolver. 'Come on. Get started.' Scowling, the drivers got back into the cars, spat into the dust, and slowly the caravanserai creaked and jolted back into action. They lunched on Persian beer and (appropriately perhaps) bad eggs, before driving fast through a heat-struck afternoon. Sleep was minimal that night, a few tortured hours in a bug-ridden 'hotel' and, by the following morning, the whole frenetic adventure had begun to pall, although the meeting with the Russian troops was unquestionably memorable – those well-equipped, 'robotic' soldiers! Later, in a hotel dining room in Kazvin, they saw a group of Russian officers and political commissars – 'rough, leathery, sweaty and cheerful'[16] – unsettling the Persian waiters who were nervously setting the tables. One of the commissars stared at Moorehead before remarking that surely they had met in Valencia during the Spanish Civil War? Really? Moorehead could not remember the face, the place or the time but he and his companions were content to join the Russians for a late lunch which turned into an early dinner, leaving Moorehead with a thumping headache, the gift of the fiery Persian vodka.

* * * *

It was Tuesday 2 September when the Moorehead party finally reached Teheran, 'an unreal world of golden domes and shaded verandahs and carriages drawn by mangy horses, jolting over cobbled streets'.[17] Before entering the city they carefully removed their war correspondent badges, thinking it was wise to pass as ordinary civilians for once. Strangely, the city contained both abject poverty and examples of western comforts. 'Never in my life,' Moorehead wrote, 'have I seen so many shops filled with electrical goods as I saw in Teheran. The majority of the people in Persia have no electrical current.'[18] It seemed to make no sense at all. Later that morning he, Russell Hill and Patrick Crosse finally met up with Clifford again and the day became a celebratory blur of vodka, bridge and eventually sleeping al fresco on the terrace of the oil executive Jock Luard's villa in the cool hills above the city.

Three days later, Clifford and Moorehead, together with the cameraman Alec Tozer and Conducting Officer Kim Mundy, drove north heading for the Caspian Sea. They went through glorious country, on a sleek road that flirted with a meandering river, before plunging into a tunnel, some 2 miles long, through the heart of the mountain. Eventually they emerged into even more wonderful country, the road often poised over an alarming precipice and, far below, trees blue with distance. The car ground its way ever upwards, on past 10,000ft, leaving Moorehead 'dizzy with the tremendous spectacle'. At one point, they 'drove into a beech forest dripping with fine rain'.[19] There was a green carpet of thick bushes, willows, oaks and elm trees, lush countryside, tigers and wild boar. When they met a Red Army patrol Clifford spoke Russian and Moorehead smiled, enjoying the fact that his friend was 'able to speak any language he likes after about 10 minutes'.[20]

They reached the Caspian on 5 September 1941. They looked out at a gunmetal grey sea, dotted with Russian destroyers and stretching away to a limitless northern horizon. Driving along the coast road, they looked out on one side at the sombre uniformity of sea and ships, while on the other side of the road, there were streams tumbling down from the regiments of tall trees on the hills high above, the water sweeping under the road before reappearing to sprawl over the Caspian's black beaches. In the middle of nowhere they were brought to a halt by the sight of a sumptuous, isolated hotel. Built on the orders of the Shah, it 'would have been a sensation in Monte Carlo', Clifford thought, with its formal gardens, terraced steps and marble statues. The interior was equally dramatic, coloured deep red and rich gold, with cascades of chandeliers reflecting light, and deep-piled Persian carpets. 'As far as I could see,' Clifford wrote to his mother, 'they mowed the grass with pairs of scissors.'[21] The hotel employed sixty gardeners, while the Swiss hotel manager could have auditioned for a role in the Folies Bergère. Despite the grandeur, the manager admitted that 'he had only two guests – and they would get away if they could'.[22]

On the hotel's steps was the local chief of police, disconcertingly obese and sweaty, and wearing a Prussian helmet. He stood bolt upright, the keys of the town in his clammy hands, evidently convinced that a ceremonial surrender was in order and occupation imminent. He made a long, heartfelt speech and insisted on exchanging one of his uniform buttons with a bemused Moorehead. What followed in this palace in the back of beyond had a dream-like quality, a heady mix of hot baths, 'mounds of caviar and vats of vodka', a sumptuous meal, then more drinking in the hotel lounge with the oleaginous police chief – the vodka now diluted with lemonade. At one point, they were invited to go pig-sticking in the woods the next day, an offer they declined. Eventually Clifford 'reeled to bed and sank into a stupor'.[23]

It was a subdued Moorehead and Clifford who motored back to Teheran·the next day. Once there, they rested up for a day or two, played some bridge and snooker, and wrote. It was the briefest of interludes. Soon, Moorehead, in company with Sam Brewer of the *Chicago Tribune* and others, left the city for Cairo, sensing that something was about to happen in the western desert.

Not everyone left Teheran, however. Clifford decided to stay on, pending instructions from his office, while Richard Dimbleby, accompanied by James Holburn, arrived from Baghdad, unsettled by a midnight ambush in the mountains en route. The ongoing Teheran story was whether the captured Germans in the city should be handed over to the Russians. There was also the possibility of a Russian cavalry regiment entering the city in triumph. On 13 September, Dimbleby and Clifford went to the main railway terminus, an imposing building whose German origins were hinted at by the artfully concealed swastikas. That morning, it was packed with diplomats and press, both Russian and British, and Iranian police gaudy 'in their mauvish uniforms and fin-de-siècle helmets'.[24] Eighty German prisoners were lined up in two rows, wearing 'ersatz suits' and carrying rucksacks, with cases, trunks, bed-rolls and parcels at their feet. They were to be sent away: seventy-two to go south, while an unlucky eight – their fate evident in their anxious faces – were destined to freeze in some distant Russian gulag. Patrolling the ranks of Germans, looking them up and down, Dimbleby thought he had 'never seen such a tatterdemalion crowd of Nazis'. He saw 'little tubby Bavarians in knickerbockers and caps, men of Prussian build and bearing and a few of those detestable sleek, black-haired, bespectacled characters who make the most fanatical Nazis'.[25] Alex also noted 'some pretty sinister looking types' amongst them. Some defiant Germans essayed Nazi salutes, while 'British and Russians got their own back by skirmishing round the Nazi cars outside tooting Vs on our horns'.[26] Then the eight Russia-bound Germans climbed heavily on board their single-coach train; there was a long, forlorn whistle before it slowly eased out of the station. Those on board looked back to a smoke-wreathed platform where the more belligerent had their arms raised in stiff-armed salute. That and the shouted 'Heil Hitlers!' were no compensation for what lay ahead. Five minutes later, a second train pulled out, taking its occupants to captivity in India.

The abdication of the Shah three days later was an even bigger story, and Alex Clifford witnessed the formal announcement, the only correspondent to do so. The speed of events began to accelerate rapidly: lorries took more Germans away; the Swedish flag flew over the German legation, the Russians had almost encircled the city, and a new Shah was sworn in – an occasion for which Clifford had to borrow morning dress from the hotel's head waiter in order to be granted entry. The Iranian soldiers of the bodyguard slaked their thirst after the ceremony

The Mooreheads in Cairo. (John Moorehead)

by drinking from the goldfish ponds. It had been a frantic, unreal day; how better to end it than with a gentle game of bridge with Geoffrey Keating? With the Shah gone and the Germans being flushed from the city, there seemed little point in staying any longer, particularly as Clifford was running short of cash. It was time therefore to return to Egypt. They drove past Red Army sentries in the outskirts, then a column of Russian troops. Dressed in their newly acquired *pushtins* – thick sheepskin jackets with the fur inside and skin outermost – they must have looked an outlandish sight to the men from the Russian steppes. Clifford's was a startling vivid yellow embroidered with orange, while Richard Dimbleby's made him look remarkably suave.

They were travelling for eight days, enduring punctures (and playing three-handed bridge on the roadside while the repair was made), mutinous drivers, broken spectacles (Clifford's), and a cold night sleeping at an Indian Army camp 5,000ft above sea level in a landscape of 'huge valleys and vast skies'.[27] At Hamadan, west of Teheran, they spent a wild evening during which Geoffrey Keating wallowed in the duck pond, splashing and floundering on a duck hunt, and Clifford lost his voice. The original plan had the Russians cast as victims: they were to be invited to drinks which were to have been literally doctored by a medic, over-proof rum spiked with chloroform. Wisely the Russians never turned up. Soon after, Clifford passed through Baghdad and then took the Nairn desert bus to Damascus, in company with Keating, Russell Hill and Dimbleby.[28] The Nairn was 'a miracle of air-conditioning and springing' which took fifteen hours to cross 500 miles of desert non-stop. It boasted 'supper baskets and a lavatory'.[29] After the desert, the journey south from Damascus seemed idyllic – up and over the mountains of Lebanon, the air sharp with the smell of cedars, through Beirut (which Clifford thought delightful), and later stopping for languorous dips in the Mediterranean. Later they rolled through the olive groves of Palestine, and travelled the coast road to Haifa where Clifford found himself 'perpetually talking German, which is not really the thing for British officers to do'.[30] The last leg was by train. Arriving in Cairo station in a flurry of steam, grating wheels and shrieking porters, Alex was delighted to see the Mooreheads waiting steadfastly on the platform to greet their old, dear friend.

Cairo, despite its soaring prices and racketeering, was a blessed relief after the past few weeks on the road. The weather was benign; whisky at the Gezira was cheap and the food at the club was good. There you could dine under a canopy of stars, the restaurant tables subtly lamp-lit, entertained by a cabaret, while waiters slid discreetly between the tables and cut-glass English voices pierced the warm Egyptian night. Such occasions compensated, in part, for the relentless travelling, the arguments with the censors and the press conferences that told you nothing. Clifford often fretted about the evident hardships in England, so cold and drab in comparison to Cairo it seemed, and yet he longed for a holiday at home. He knew too that if he did make it back to England, it was unlikely his newspaper would return him to the Middle East. That troubled him too, since he did not want to miss the final act of the drama in the desert.

NOTES

1   *A Year of Battle*, op. cit., p.26.
2   Ibid., p.26.
3   Ibid., p.26.
4   Clifford papers (16727), IWM, file AGC/1/2: diary entry for 24 August 1941.
5   Ibid., file AGC/2/1/5: letter to his mother, 29 September 1941.
6   *A Year of Battle*, op. cit., p.28.
7   Clifford papers (16727), IWM, file AGC/1/2: diary entry for 28 August 1941.
8   Ibid., diary entry for 31 August 1941.
9   Ibid., diary entry for 24 August 1941.
10 Ibid., diary entry for 31 August 1941.
11 Ibid., file AGC/2/1/5: letter to his mother, 29 September 1941.
12 *Daily Mail*, 2 September 1941.
13 Clifford papers (16727), IWM, file AGC/1/2: diary entry for 1 September 1941.
14 *A Year of Battle*, op. cit., p.35.
15 So called because he had wartime experience with both the Tank Corps and the air force.
16 *A Year of Battle*, op. cit., p.35.
17 Collier, p.89.
18 *A Year of Battle*, op. cit., p.39.
19 Ibid., p.41.
20 Ibid., p.42.
21 Clifford papers (16727), IWM, file AGC/2/1/5: letter to his mother, dated 30 September 1941.
22 *Daily Mail*, 8 September 1941.
23 Clifford papers (16727), IWM, file AGC/1/2: diary entry for 5 September 1941.
24 Ibid., diary entry for 12 September 1941.
25 (Richard) Dimbleby, p.221.
26 Clifford papers (16727), IWM, file AGC/1/2: diary entry for 13 September 1941.

27   Ibid., file AGC/2/1/5. Letter to his mother, dated 31 September 1939; clearly
      Clifford had forgotten the verse which reminds us of the number of days in
      September!
28   Dimbleby had left Teheran on 21 September by train for Baghdad before
      taking the Nairn bus across the desert.
29   (Richard) Dimbleby, p.228.
30   Clifford papers (16727), IWM, file AGC/1/2: diary entry for 26 September
      1941.

8. 'What's the Flap?'

T he alarm clock woke him at four in the morning. Bleary-eyed and still heavy with sleep, Alex Clifford took a cab out to the aerodrome at Heliopolis. He was due to fly into the heart of Africa, piloted by the illustrious Free French pilot, Colonel Lionel de Marmier. The aircraft was 'a crazy looking thing, rather like a big Bombay, but with four engines in two pairs back to back'.[1] It did not inspire confidence, particularly in a man who, in company with Alan Moorehead, had luckily escaped death when a recent flight they had been due to take had crashed, killing everybody on board.

Once aloft, Alex looked down on Africa, the Nile's sinuous turns and the way the colours of the land turned from a fertile green to a dull ochre. Eventually he began to doze, mesmerised by the droning engines and recouping some of the hours stolen by the morning's alarm call. Then, just when the aircraft was beginning its approach to Khartoum, he suddenly realised he had failed to leave the car keys for Moorehead as they had arranged. He could almost hear the little Aussie's fulminating oaths. Too late now! Below Clifford could see Omdurman, 'a sprawl of mud and dung'[2] and a source of fascination to a man who understood its significance in military and imperial history. The rivers, the White and Blue Niles, were in flood, and Khartoum itself was 'laid out on the plan of a Union Jack'.

They stayed overnight at the city's Grand Hotel and in the morning, there was a full English breakfast, designed to fortify the bluff empire-builder, but of a kind to appal the fastidious French: there, in defiance of the early morning African heat, were bowls of prunes, dishes of porridge, plates of fried fish, bacon and eggs, toast and marmalade. Unsuitably sustained, they flew on, ever deeper into the unknown. At El Fasher there was a lion prowling the RAF mess; at Fort Lamy, mosquitoes and huge grasshoppers almost blotted out the lamplight, and Clifford's sleep that night, under a mosquito net in the garden, was much disturbed. He lay there half awake, listening to the eerie shrieks of night birds, the croaking of frogs, and the rumpus of the ongoing war between chickens, hyenas and their human hunters. The glimmer of an enormous moon added to the night's strangeness.

The expedition remained bizarre and exotic. On one occasion Alex was warned to watch out for the local panther who was wont to prowl the garden at dawn. Later, he bought a python's skin, all 16ft of it, for a few shillings, before arriving for dinner with the governor who, when Clifford arrived, was sitting haloed by a cloud of insects in the shadows of his garden. The host's dinner jacket was 'self-designed' and consisted of 'a short white coat and black balloon trousers fastened tightly around the ankles'.[3] The atmosphere might have been magical, but the dinner proved 'atrocious'. Arriving in Brazzaville on 11 October, the hibiscus, jacaranda and red bougainvillea were in bloom. The vivid colours of the vegetation might have been predictable, but Brazzaville also had 'the world's strangest war materials factory'; its only machines were sewing machines, but it equipped and clothed all the Free French troops on the African continent.[4] At sunset, clouds of parrots flew over the river and Clifford saw rain for the first time since he had been in Greece. It was no half-hearted shower either, more like a tornado.

Clifford was in Brazzaville for three days before an eventful return flight: a jar of pickled onions burst in his luggage and soaked his underwear and one night was blighted by the spectacular dive-bombing of huge bats. The conversation at a dinner in Fort Lamy was decidedly unusual: the ex-pat Brits waxed lyrical about 'native flagellation', the trade in human limbs (legs available every Thursday at the market in Leopoldville), 'the tribe which eats human breasts boiled in milk with onions', and what quinine does to one's sex-life.[5] All in all, it had been 'the most intensive bit of travelling I have ever done'.[6]

A few days after Clifford's return to Cairo, it was Alan Moorehead's turn to be on the move. It meant another early start, as he set off in the company of Russell Hill and Alaric Jacob in an army station wagon. Their objective was 8th Army Headquarters and en route they stole a swim at Alamein in a turquoise-coloured sea, floating naked on the water while watching mock dogfights between Tomahawk and Hurricane fighters quartering a clear blue sky. Back on the road, they could hear the fragile shells of white desert snails being crushed by the tyres. They drove 180 miles that first day and camped within 50 miles of Siwa Oasis, where they sat round a campfire in the evening, drinking gin and singing. Next morning, they drove on across a sandy waste that extended to the horizon like the sea. As they approached Siwa, 'running downhill off the desert through rose-pink canyons',[7] they saw signs warning of malaria. Clouds of mosquitoes and flies reinforced the message. Dinner was bully beef, bread and margarine, washed down with gin, lime and water, and they slept in the desert chill draped in mosquito netting. Russell Hill woke in the morning to find his head poking out of the mesh, an invitation to any passing mosquito with an appetite for a correspondent's blood.

While Moorehead was away in the desert, Alex Clifford and Lucy were at home together in the Cairo flat sharing a contented domesticity. They cooked together (a 'delicious cabbage and bacon pie'),[8] and, when Lucy came down with a cold, he made his 'sovereign mixture of hot lemon and honey and cinnamon and rum',[9] then tucked her up in bed. He looked after the baby too, even changing its nappies.

On 22 October, Clifford and others were summoned to a briefing by Brigadier Shearer, Director of Intelligence, Middle East, who proceeded to harangue everyone in the room, accusing them of 'breaches of trust and tendentious reporting'. Shearer was a 'dug out', an officer unearthed from retirement for the duration; pre-war, he had been a senior executive with Fortnum and Mason in London. When Ed Kennedy of Associated Press attempted to defend a piece he had written that was the particular focus of Shearer's anger, he was summarily ordered from the room. Kennedy was no admirer of Shearer, holding him 'responsible for a large part of the misinformation made public from the Middle East'.[10] For example, he had once heard Shearer describe an ambush where the Germans had inflicted heavy losses on the British with the duplicitous words, 'We compelled the enemy to disclose his strength'.[11] Hence Kennedy's fury at the accusation of 'tendentious reporting'. He proceeded to stalk out of the room in protest at Shearer's ill-chosen phrase and had his hand on the door handle when Shearer tried to stop him with an imperious 'Kennedy!' The American didn't respond, prompting Shearer to splutter, 'Well that ends all relationship between us!' For his part, Alex Clifford thought it 'all extremely petty'.[12]

A few days later, on 25 October, Alan Moorehead returned to Cairo after a week away, and the ménage was re-established. Alex was a third parent to John; they cooked and ate en famille; hit Cairo's nightspots together, and engaged in sustained conversation about life and their places within it. There were few secrets and not much left unsaid it seems. One evening, the three of them shared an 'extremely tense conversation about sex relationships (which) finally … developed into a bit of a sentimental swing music session'.[13] Well, it made a change from bridge.

There were changes of a different, more serious, kind ahead. First, at the end of October, Lucy, still struggling with a heavy cold, went to GHQ to finalise arrangements for her new job as personal secretary to General Claude Auchinleck. She started work on Monday 3 November, with 'Alan still fiercely protesting she had been double-crossed'.[14] It worried him that she would be required to work long, exhausting hours, and he could see all too clearly that there was considerable potential for conflicts of both interest and loyalty. In time, his doubts would prove prophetic: the relations between the press corps and the army would never be straightforward and the spat between Kennedy and Shearer was not an isolated incident.

The second tremor which unsettled the status quo was a dawning sense shared by the two correspondents that they needed to return to the desert. It was a familiar, recurring feeling, born of conscience and curiosity. Three days after Lucy started work at GHQ, Moorehead and Clifford, together with Russell Hill and Richard Busvine, flew from Heliopolis to Kabrut to watch parachute manoeuvres. It was interesting enough – fifty parachutists drifting to the ground, white roses of silk against the blue sky – but it was scarcely news. There was the minor compensation of a slap-up picnic lunch, taken on board a Bombay aircraft – those stuffed quails in aspic! – but any sense of well-being was short-lived. As lunch was ending, a Wellington coming in to land crashed on the runway in a burst of flame, the explosion flinging the occupants high into the air after they

Three-handed bridge in the Cairo flat. (IWM, Clifford Papers)

had burst through the fuselage. The correspondents' return to Heliopolis, with the image of the burning bomber all too vivid, proved a sombre one.

Three days later, Clifford was in a convoy of army lorries driving west on the familiar desert road. He had made the most of his last day in Cairo, lunching with friends, writing and then going to the cinema in the evening to see a film starring Marlene Dietrich. The 'terrible too well-known trip to Bagush' was in stark contrast to life in the capital.[15] Once there, he shared a tent with Jimmy Holburn of *The Times*, and, that first evening, won 33 piastres at bridge. The days that followed were strangely idle, essentially a week of waiting for something to happen. 'Photographers were cleaning their lenses, our drivers were cleaning their tommy guns and we our typewriters.'[16] The military authorities discouraged the press from writing very much – which reinforced the sense that something serious was in the wind. Clifford swam every day before lunch, gliding through water that was often warmer than the outside air. He read and tried to be patient.

In the middle of the week, Alan Moorehead turned up and moved into Clifford's tent. The two of them, together with Busvine and Hill, played fiercely competitive games of bridge under the soft light of kerosene hurricane lamps, 'sipping whisky and arguing about conventions. Everyone played a different convention, and Alan was inclined to be against all conventions.' The desert experience was not quite what Russell Hill expected: he was amused to be served hors d'oeuvres and blinked in surprise at the 'white tablecloths, china dinner services, beer glasses, wine glasses, liqueur glasses, coffee cups and other comforts. Dinner ended with a box of cigars being passed as people sipped their coffee and liqueurs.'[17] Someone at HQ knew how to make the best of things.

By the end of the week, it was clear that there would soon be real news to write, for the press censors had turned up, together with the powers-that-be, Randolph Churchill and Colonel Astley ('an aging playboy of finely chiselled face and greying hair' but the man to whom the correspondents must defer).[18] Astley had been married to the actress Madeleine Carroll and was evidently unpopular with some correspondents, the American photo-journalist Croswell Bowen, for example, describing him 'smoking his cigarette in a long ivory holder' and resembling 'an old time London Shakespearean actor who's down to playing tank towns in the United States'.[19] Randolph Churchill was regarded by many as a 'truculent drunken bully, but to the Western desert warcos, from the Marxist Jacob through the vaguely socialist Moorehead to the high-Tory Clifford, he could do no wrong'.[20]

On the evening of Sunday 16 November, General Sir Alan Cunningham, the 8th Army's commander-in-chief, summoned the correspondents to his underground headquarters, a concrete, bombproof construction half-buried in the sand. Finding it was not easy in the darkness, the newsmen were obliged to tread warily, trying to avoid the maze of trenches and hidden tent ropes. It was

Randolph Churchill: a man who 'could do no wrong' according to the desert war correspondents. (IWM, CBM 1585)

9.30 p.m. and very cold, the sand gleaming like snow. There were about twenty reporters and perhaps the same number of photographers who filed down the bunker steps. Once below ground, they sat around a bare trestle table, drinking whisky and listening to the smiling Cunningham who had made a point of shaking each reporter's hand. He was quietly spoken, blue-eyed, and with pink, glowing skin which gave him a cherubic look. Moorehead thought 'he looked more like a successful businessman than a general,'[21] while he reminded at least one of the other journalists of a fox-hunter.

Colonel Philip Astley – 'an aging playboy of finely chiselled face'. (Betsy Connor Bowen)

'Gentlemen,' Cunningham began, 'I am taking you into my confidence. I've called you all together to let you know that zero hour for our planned offensive will be before dawn on Tuesday. We shall advance into Libya at selected points along the whole front.'[22] The impression he gave was of a man untouched by doubt, secure in the RAF's command of the skies and in his superior tank numbers. Reluctantly, he conceded that, perhaps, his troops were slightly fewer in number, but that would not prevent 8th Army driving deep into Libya. There was a certain amount of wary, quizzical glances cast among the press. This was a man who had been successful in East Africa, it was true; indeed he had yet to know failure, but the Libyan Desert was a very different situation, requiring different strategy and ways of waging war. This was a man who 'had never before fought against Germans,' Russell Hill thought. 'He had never before fought against large numbers of tanks. He had never before fought in the open desert.'[23] It did not augur well. As the correspondents stumbled back to their tents, arms outstretched, feeling their way in the darkness, there were anxious sotto voce mutterings about the potential for a comeuppance. Clifford had found Cunningham's sang froid to be 'rather frightening' and both Moorehead and Matt Halton were agreed that a catastrophe was looming.[24]

They made a slow start next morning, despite stowing bedrolls before dawn. Groups of three war correspondents were formed, each with its own conducting officer. The protocol was that the correspondents would agree an itinerary which the conducting officer would then approve, subject to issues of military security. Moorehead, Clifford and Richard Busvine were allocated a Humber staff-car, two 15 cwt. trucks and the services of a diminutive Glaswegian, the 22-year-old Captain McIver, who soon showed that he knew next to nothing about either the desert or warfare. They headed out on the Siwa road, past 'Charing Cross' and 'Piccadilly', with its Eros shaped from 4-gallon petrol tins. All seemed well, with the RAF clearly dominating the skies. The air smelled early morning clean, and despite the previous night's misgivings, there was a distinct feeling of optimism. Then it slowly dawned on them that there was a problem: McIver had misread his map (he had been 'aiming at the left-hand of the place-name instead of the right-hand end')[25] and they were quite lost. It was a state of play which rarely changed over the ensuing days. Poor McIver was flummoxed by reading a compass, understanding a map, or recognising the lie of the land in terrain which scarcely changed anyway. His war correspondent charges became increasingly disenchanted, even rebellious during that first day and, by the time they blundered into 8th Army HQ, it was dark.

The night sky was bright and they argued at first as to whether it was caused by intense shellfire or bolts of lightning, but it soon became clear that it was a violent thunderstorm on the coast. The rain rapidly filled the wadis and churned up the desert tracks. Richard Busvine woke next morning to find a pool of rainwater in the middle of his sleeping bag. When the rain stopped, they hung their soaked bedding out to dry, but it soon became evident that the storm signalled a marked decline in the weather. It became much colder and with a cloud-base low enough for the RAF to curtail its patrols.

McIver and his unhappy flock continued to blunder around, hopelessly lost in the desert wilderness. Around them, the army convoys resembled great naval fleets patrolling the oceans, evidently navigating this barren landscape with calm assurance. Not so the witless McIver. Typically, after much aimless wandering, they would eventually pin down a location, only to find that everyone else had long since moved on. Then MacIver would begin 'another of these ridiculous stampedings about, asking questions, following convoys, taking bearings, and never getting anywhere'.[26] The mismatch between the correspondents' impatience and the little Glaswegian's self-importance grew steadily. At one point, much to Clifford's fury, McIver refused to let the correspondents have lunch. It was a relief when they finally found some action and they stood, tin-hatted, on the car's roof to watch the sweeps and turns of tank manoeuvres in the sand. They came under intense machine-gun fire from two Messerschmitts, before, in fading light and having chanced on Eddie Ward and others, they settled down for the night like pioneers in the wild west, in close leaguer, their vehicles in a nose-to-tail circle and protected by a second ring of armoured cars and tanks. It was a bitterly cold night, partly fended off by a hot bully beef stew. As they ate, wary eyes scoured the skies for night bombers.

It was raining hard when, at a bleak 4.30 a.m., a volley of Bren-gun fire served as an alarm call. After some stumbling around in the pre-dawn shadows, the correspondents settled down to hammer out their early morning dispatches, pausing every so often to swear about bloody McIver who, predictably, 'had made a balls of things'.[27] German dive-bombers flew over and Clifford flung himself to the ground, trying to bury himself deep into the earth. He found his nose 'was resting on a complete fossilised jelly fish'.[28] Moments later, the bombers' thunder was already fading in the distance and Clifford gingerly stood up, brushing sand from his knees, aware that he had survived another close encounter with death. There would be another later that day when some thirty-five Stukas attacked and one stricken aircraft looked certain to plough straight into them as it careered towards the earth.

MacIver's stock continued to fall, symbolised by his ham-fisted breaking of Richard Busvine's camp-bed. The Scot was not the only one to attract disaster; the man at the top, cheery General Cunningham, was similarly cursed, to the extent that, by 22 November, his much-heralded advance into Libya was beginning to unravel. Instead of an inexorable drive west, there were the signs of imminent retreat, with army trucks driving fast in the opposite direction, in increasing numbers. Worse, 7th Brigade, it appeared, had suffered heavy losses with only four tanks remaining of its original 150. That night, a beautiful one, the three correspondents showed commendable calm as things threatened to fall apart. Instead of soul-searching and gloom, they indulged in 'a long and rather undergraduate discussion on poetry and art and things'.[29]

Next morning there was time for Clifford to savour a rare desert pleasure, a leisurely washing of his feet, but it soon became clear that there was trouble brewing. Once again it was heralded by vehicles racing through the camp, all heading away from the enemy. It felt significantly more frantic and serious than the panic of the previous day. Clifford looked round for Moorehead and then remembered that he had seen him wandering off purposefully with a spade and a roll of toilet paper. The Australian soon realised that this was not a time to be caught with his trousers down and he raced back to the camp. He found Clifford and Busvine flinging bedding, cooking pots and clothes into the back of the trucks as fast as they could. There was no doubting in their minds that this was the real thing, a genuine retreat, but not everyone was so concerned. An officer with soap lathering his face waved his shaving brush nonchalantly and smiled in a studied attempt at worldly bravado: 'What's the flap?' he said. He got an answer soon enough and he too joined the desperate rush to the east, following the dust clouds as Cunningham's troops ran headlong for Egypt. By the afternoon, the retreat became something more reprehensible when 'some British planes caused a really disgraceful panic'.[30] For nine hours there was no stopping this undignified exodus from Libya.

That night was one of the coldest they had yet endured. They ate stew and drank whisky in the lorry's cab before deciding to bed down for the night. Busvine and Moorehead slept in the car while Clifford chose to sleep outdoors, unrolling his bedding alongside the car and hunkering down to make himself as warm a nest as he could find. He slept well, but Moorehead and Busvine shivered throughout the night. In the morning, they drove on, eventually finding HQ where they were greeted with relief by an anxious Colonel Astley who was increasingly worried about his flock of correspondents. While Jimmy Holburn, Dick Mowrer and Russell Hill had turned up, a number of others including Alaric Jacob and Sam Brewer were still missing.

There were, however, a large number of correspondents at headquarters, including the unlikely pairing of Randolph Churchill and Eve Curie. Curie – daughter of Marie, the discoverer of radium – was a correspondent for the *New York Herald Tribune*. She typed away under a bright sun, elegantly dressed in slacks and snood, oblivious to the bewilderment of the rest of the camp, for whom this manifestation of chic and demure elegance was a reminder of a life now far away in time and space. That faint drift of French perfume could not have been more different from the stench of diesel, sweat, burnt cooking and cordite which usually prevailed. For Russell Hill, who also worked for the *Tribune*, there was a double shock: the incongruity of seeing a woman in this desolate landscape (such exoticism!) and the more mundane fact that he and Curie apparently shared the same employer and, until then, he had been blissfully unaware of her existence. The greater shock though was that Eve Curie was the only woman for some 300 miles in each direction, only there because the solicitous Randolph had seen fit to escort her into the depths of Libya. Women war correspondents, after all, were regarded with great suspicion: 'The British War Office … regarded women in the field as bad luck, bad business and something to be scotched vigorously.'[31] As if to reinforce such prejudice, it was deemed necessary to drive Miss Curie to an empty patch of desert 4 miles away when she needed to answer the call of nature. Randolph Churchill did the decent thing of course and turned his broad back on the crouching goddess, choosing to stare resolutely into a hazy middle distance.

The flap was over, for the present at least. Instead of Germans, it was the weather that made life difficult, a dust storm howling through the camp, blowing grit and sand everywhere and making the tents flap like sails. The other constant menace was Captain McIver, in his way as irritating as the fiercest *khamseen*. In recent days he had 'surpassed himself in villainy' by deciding 'to lock up the water and dole it out'.[32] Enough was enough!

Clifford and the others contemplated going on strike to get him replaced, but in the event Kim Mundy was deputed to replace him and, while they waited for him to arrive from Syria, Major Churchill was assigned as their conducting officer. It was an improvement, although Churchill had his faults too, being, for example, 'even more wildly optimistic and tendentious than his father'. With Churchill too you got his batman and driver – Clifford thought one was idle and the other 'an idiot … who was never allowed to drive because he couldn't'.[33]

With Churchill fussing over his charges, they set out together for Libya, back the way they had so recently come and proceeding with considerable uncertainty. McIver-less, they still suffered a series of mishaps. Clifford offended Churchill by insisting that he preferred army biscuits to the latter's offering of stale white Egyptian bread. Later Churchill's motor car collided head-on with the only other vehicle in an otherwise empty desert. There was disturbing news too: the BBC's Eddie Ward had been taken prisoner with a number of other correspondents, overrun by German tanks as they took refuge lying low in a series of slit trenches. Ward had seen the tanks drawing near, recognising their tell-tale black crosses and horrified at the sight of a German tank commander, with a machine pistol in his hand, heading straight towards him. Ward 'sat bolt upright' with his hands aloft 'and then lay down quickly'. He held his breath, waiting for a volley of gunfire, but instead the tank swerved to avoid him and the German shouted, in English, 'Hands up! Surrender!'[34] That same morning, Clifford received a letter from the Inland Revenue demanding £423 in back tax. At least, Ward's capture put that in perspective.

Next morning was achingly cold and the tanks were streaked with an icy dew. Churchill took them to meet Brigadier Alec Gatehouse who, after days of intense fighting, was dressed piratically 'in a Hebron sheepskin coat and a brown rug strapped around his waist'.[35] The correspondents watched the action and, in periodic lulls in the fighting, they played bridge, Busvine losing badly and not always with good grace. Throughout the day, tanks were sweeping across the sand, turning this way and that in the churned-up dust, with no thought it seemed for the extent of territory over which the fighting spread. Clifford for one was confused about who exactly was winning and scared by the confusion and uncertainty. It was a feeling not helped when the RAF inadvertently bombed them.

In the far distance there were petrol and oil dumps ablaze, while for a distance of some 50 miles inland from the coast, there was incessant gunfire. The front line was non-existent, shifting like the wind; tank losses on both sides were considerable; and so too were the numbers of prisoners and casualties. They heard rumours that General Cunningham had been sacked, just a few days into his vaunted offensive. In an extended lull, Churchill, like a magician, produced some fresh eggs from Cairo which they hard-boiled and ate. The rapid consumption of a bottle of whisky and the arrival of Kim Mundy hotfoot from Syria added to the sense of well-being. They had, after all, survived a dangerous day. Mundy sat smiling on the end of one of the cots, in every way an improvement on the banished MacIver. Thinking over what had happened that day, Clifford found himself smiling, noting, not for the first time, one of Alan Moorehead's greatest qualities, the Australian's 'favourite principle of making the most of what he happens to have at the moment'.[36] On days like this, it made him the very best of companions. The smile faded when Clifford realised that Moorehead was still writing about the battle long after he had finished his own story. They were the closest of friends, staunch comrades, but there was a competitive edge to the relationship nonetheless. Nothing for it, Clifford thought, but to write another piece, which he duly did, giving it a different dateline – but worrying that it wasn't good enough once the typewriter had fallen silent after the final full stop.

* * * *

On the first day of December 1941, the Duo's paths separated for a while: Clifford was offered \$500 to write a piece for *Life* magazine and so he packed rapidly and hitched a flight in a Lockheed back to Cairo. Lucky man, Clifford thought, back to a world of good food and bath tubs. It was enough to prompt him into the luxury of an all-over wash: it was rare that desert life permitted such things. Now was as good a time as any. He undressed in the dubious privacy of a slit trench, blanching at the murkiness of the water when he had finished. It was the colour and texture of a thick pea soup. He was still contemplating the squalor of it, and standing naked and doubly exposed, when two German aircraft flew over, low and fast, leaving a shuddering Clifford to contemplate the ignominy of being shot while the Luftwaffe crews flew on, laughing at the tall Englishman's pink innocence.

Clifford and Busvine left for Cairo the following day. It was a gloomy flight, with more sour weather – cold stinging rain at Bagush – and bouts of turbulence which made Clifford airsick for the first time. But Cairo was wonderfully reviving: sunny and warm, and his greeting at the flat from baby John – whose birthday it was – was nothing less than ecstatic. Moreover there was no more rough sleeping for a while, no more bully beef or biscuits, no friendly fire or the smell of burned-out tanks or flesh. Instead, it was a gentle life of clean sheets, hot baths, with time to live a bit – which meant, in practice, claiming expenses, sorting finances, writing, eating and drinking, wearing clean clothes and dancing at Shepheards. It was all very necessary: a reporter could easily become 'stale and write the wrong kind of story',[37] so Russell Hill believed, and there was no doubt that, as 1941 drew to a close, the war's progress was dispiriting. When and how would it all end? For those correspondents who had followed it from the early days, exhaustion and depression were becoming harder to fend off. It wasn't just the press that felt ground down by events, there was a widespread malaise, a feeling not helped by the stark difference between life at the front and that back in Cairo. To Moorehead, 'it seemed that we saw the last fortnight's battle as though reflected in distorting mirrors,' while the city 'was going through all the spasms of despair, hope, exhilaration and back to despair again'.[38] Nothing seemed certain any more, and nothing stayed the same.

NOTES

1 Ibid., file AGC/1/2: diary entry for 7 October 1941.
2 Ibid.
3 Ibid., diary entry for 9 October 1941.
4 *Daily Mail*, 20 October 1941.
5 Clifford papers (16727), IWM, file AGC/1/2, diary entry for 14 October 1941.
6 Ibid., file AGC/2/1/5. Letter of 19 October 1941.
7 *A Traveller's War* by Alaric Jacob, p.92.
8 Clifford papers (16727), IWM, file AGC/1/2: diary entry for 21 October 1941.
9 Ibid., diary entry for 22 October 1941.
10 Kennedy Cochran, p.113.
11 Ibid., p.130.
12 Clifford papers (16727), IWM, file AGC/1/2: diary entry for 22 October 1941.
13 Ibid., diary entry for 29 October 1941.
14 Ibid., diary entry for 3 November 1941.
15 Ibid., diary entry for 9 November 1941.
16 Jacob, p.95.
17 *Desert War* by Russell Hill, p.114.
18 Kennedy Cochran, p.86.
19 *Back From Tobruk* by Croswell Bowen, p.62.
20 Collier, p.107.
21 *A Year of Battle*, op. cit., p.55.
22 Jacob, p.96.
23 Hill, p.116.
24 Clifford papers (16727), IWM, file AGC/1/2: diary entry for 16 November 1941.
25 Ibid., diary entry for 17 November 1941.
26 Ibid., diary entry for 18 November 1941.
27 Ibid., diary entry for 20 November 1941.
28 Clifford, p.141.

29   Clifford papers (16727), IWM, file AGC/1/2: diary entry for 23
      November 1941.
30   Ibid., diary entry for 24 November 1941.
31   *No Woman's World* by Iris Carpenter, p.110.
32   Clifford papers (16727), IWM, file AGC/1/2: diary entry for 27
      November 1941.
33   Ibid., diary entry for 27 November 1941.
34   *Give Me Air* by Edward Ward, p.10.
35   Clifford papers (16727), IWM, file AGC/1/2: diary entry for 29
      November 1941.
36   Ibid., diary entry for 30 November 1941.
37   Hill, p.184.
38   *A Year of Battle*, op. cit., p.74.

9. Cold Christmas in Benghazi

The interlude in Cairo was short-lived: just five days and then it was back to the front. The expedition began badly and soon got worse. The final night's valedictory dinner party proved farcical, the cook producing a quirky meal of pea soup, followed by a pea-filled omelette, served with peas. It was merely irritating to the near-vegetarian Clifford, but Moorehead 'was furious, this being probably the last chance he will have for months of eating fresh meat'.[1] Replete with peas, the two correspondents were due to leave on the half-past-midnight train. Despite the lateness of the hour, the station was chaotic – troops burdened with kit, people running into each other and shouting, porters scurrying to and fro, and a frenzied scramble for seats. A porter swung one of Clifford's bags against an iron pillar and broke a full thermos flask. There was one moment of good fortune when, in company with Preston Grover of Associated Press, they found seats in a first-class carriage, but it was a false moment of hope, being chilly and uncomfortable. Eventually the train pulled out of the station emitting swathes of steam into the darkness, and they were embarked on what Clifford would remember as the most unpleasant journey he ever made.

They woke next morning to learn that the United States had finally entered the war, following the surprise Japanese attack on Pearl Harbor. 'Whatever happens to us in the next few days,' Clifford wrote in his diary, 'it doesn't matter much, the whole interest must be concentrated on the Pacific.'[2] Overnight the return to the desert had lost some of its value; to make matters worse, the journey became increasingly troubled and unpleasant. Already slow and much delayed, the train was eventually derailed and they were forced to spend a 'second and even more uncomfortable night in a brake wagon'.[3] They shivered for hours in a dark and remote siding, remembering rumours of impending air raids aimed at the railway system. They decided to abandon the stationary train, choosing instead to hitch-hike to Bagush where aircraft, buildings and people were all choked by a sandstorm of red dust. Initially it was impossible to get a flight out and there was a long delay until they managed to get on a hospital flight from Mersa Matruh. In the end, the journey from Cairo took three long days (and 'three hell-nights'[4]); Richard Busvine, by contrast, completed the same journey in just three hours. At least they could console themselves by broaching some of the nineteen bottles of whisky in their supplies.

Early December drifted by in familiar fashion, the correspondents waiting for something to turn up. You killed time, tried to ignore physical discomfort, stifled impatience and toyed with potential stories – for example, Moorehead and Clifford talked at length to an Italian pilot, now a prisoner and formerly the mayor of Stresa on Lake Maggiore. Mostly, there was nothing for it but to lie on a bed in a dust-choked tent and read. Then, on 10 December, they cadged a lift in a hospital plane, intent on reaching the recently relieved port of Tobruk. They prepared by dividing up the rations; then Kim Mundy and Clifford cooked, before settling to a rubber of bridge played in the Humber while the car's windows were peppered with dust from yet another sandstorm.

It was a bitterly cold night and, not for the first time, Alex was glad of his reliable waterproof groundsheet which he had 'liberated' from the Germans. They woke late to discover that everyone else had already gone, leaving them behind, alone in the middle of a desolate salt-flat. This stung them into action and they drove fast in an effort to catch up, with Moorehead and Clifford sitting side-by-side in the back of the car loudly debating the merits of Jane Austen, as the car rocked and rolled. Clifford thought Alan's opinions were 'illogical and spattered with irrelevancies'.[5] Moorehead, no doubt, was convinced by the power of his argument. They were soon back in Libya, driving through a lonely landscape, stopping once in a while for a spot of mild looting – petrol cans, newspapers, letters. It was a pastime which never failed to cheer them up, particularly Alex, attracted by the flimsy pages of correspondence blowing in the wind. They passed burned-out tanks, one of which contained 'two neatly roasted bodies and an Edgar Wallace novel'. There were many dead Germans, including 'a young fair-haired hero (who) was sitting at the wheel with his brains piled on the seat beside him'.[6]

They travelled on towards Tobruk, stopping at night in a large camp, placed next to an anti-aircraft gun, where sleep proved precious in a location both noisy and dangerous. Early next morning Moorehead brewed tea while the others, still snug in bed, offered advice on the best tea-making strategies. Once on the road, they found another deserted German camp, evidently looted and largely emptied by local Arabs, and nearby a more profitable cache of booty – forks, goggles, torches, 'long underpants for Alan', mouthwash, foot powder, 'little gadgets and appliances that will prove most welcome to our ménage'.[7] They were on the same road they had travelled twelve months before, reliving the discomforts of that trek west: the stinging sandstorms, the flies, mosquitoes and fleas, the scorpions, bumpy tracks, lack of fresh vegetables and shortage of water. The only difference was the amount of debris which the siege had spawned. Tobruk was surrounded by a landscape of shattered masonry and broken windows, but the Germans had gone. Its capture was a huge fillip to Allied morale, perhaps best summed up by one senior officer: 'Tobruk is relieved but not half as relieved as I am'.[8]

For Clifford, Moorehead and Busvine this was a period of comfortable routine – 'a spell of almost normal war reporting'. In its way, it was a trial run of the Trio, with Busvine playing the Buckley role, while the expedition had acquired 'the intimacy, the self-sufficiency of an expedition to Tibet or the North Pole'.[9] Each of them had their treasured luxuries: Clifford's pillowcase; Busvine's outsize flagon of eau de cologne; Moorehead's cigarettes whose provision demanded sustained and thorough planning to ensure that supplies remained constant. They each had their designated tasks too. Moorehead looked after the blackout, the lighting at night and the seating arrangements in the truck; Clifford cooked; Busvine took on the washing-up which Clifford thought was 'pretty nearly the nastiest domestic chore in the desert'[10] since water was always at a premium and Busvine was obliged to stand over a bowl of greasy plates as night brought a sudden darkness and a desert chill.

'A spell of almost normal war reporting' hints at an easy, settled and comfortable existence, but in truth there was much to make life unpleasant. Fleas, for example, were an ever-present problem. Each morning Clifford scrutinised his sleeping bag, intent on hunting them down, but he would rarely find more than five or six. Sitting naked in bed in the ice-cold early morning, he would search his clothes with painstaking care. You would not believe where the little perishers hid! Given the chance, he would change every item of his clothes in an attempt to fool them. He also helped Moorehead to cope with the same problem: 'I turned Alan's sleeping bag inside out and laid it on a thorn-bush and showed him how to catch the nimble brown fleas that were living in it.'[11]

Then there was the capricious weather. It could be extremely cold, or wet, with lashing rain, or a sandstorm might blow in, creating an impenetrable yellow fog in a matter of moments. A war correspondent, it could be said, was only as good as the transport available, and journeying in the desert could never be taken for granted. Vehicles' springs broke with great regularity; tyres were frequently punctured; engines overheated. The skies brought another hazard: enemy aircraft regularly swept in, firing machine-guns, or dropping bombs.

Writing, the life-blood of correspondents, was never far from their minds, but there were other considerations too: the search for petrol, or supplies of food, or decent water to go with their diminishing supply of whisky. Food – its acquisition, preparation and consumption – was a constant preoccupation. It was never fine dining, but Clifford in particular, with his reputation as a gourmet cook to preserve, worked hard to ensure an acceptable level of cuisine. It might include a mixture of marmalade and honey, or a pleasant cheese wangled from stores. There might be some fresh lemons, perhaps, or a vast can of tomato extract liberated from the enemy, a very good Christmas cake sent to Moorehead from Australia, a comforting dinner of curry, rice and onions followed by Welsh rarebit, or excellent Nazi cheese which came in tubes like toothpaste. Once, they heard lambs bleating and their Welsh driver, Pryce, a butcher in his former life, promised them a mutton treat. Sadly, it never materialised.

*   *   *   *

The year of 1941 was drawing to a melancholy end. One morning, just before Christmas, Clifford was reduced to eating the previous night's stew on toast in the rain. Richard Busvine left them at much the same time, bound for Cairo in the first instance, then the Far East. He bade goodbye to 'two of the most pleasant, helpful and capable companions I have ever had',[12] leaving the two of them wandering disconsolately around Gazala airbase in the rain, looking at the sad ruins of wrecked Nazi aircraft. A few half-hearted artillery exchanges scarcely comprised news, so they resorted to some listless looting which produced a useful find: 500 gallons of pale blue aviation spirit abandoned by the Germans, together with some typing paper (a godsend!) and a newspaper which contained a malevolent news story about Randolph Churchill. More sobering was the Italian newspaper half-buried in the sand with its photograph of war correspondent Harold Denny who had been taken prisoner at the same time as Eddie 'Tweaks' Ward.

The Duo camped by the seashore amongst bleached white sandhills, trusting that the sea air would make for a good night's sleep despite the Luftwaffe's continuing thunder overhead as its aircraft followed the bombers' path to Tobruk. The battlefield had fallen silent; where once the guns had made it necessary to shout to be heard, it was now possible to hear the wind in the trees. The battle's pendulum had swung to the extent that Italian troops were scrambling to discard their uniforms and adopting Arab or civilian clothing in a desperate attempt to avoid capture.

As they drove once again towards Derna, Clifford sat in the back of the car, reliving the same journey of twelve months before, stirred by the clarity of his memory. Moorehead, by contrast, sat in the front seat and talked without cease. The familiar villa at Derna now stood forlorn and empty, but at least it offered the prospect of sleeping indoors for the first time for many days. In fact, when it came to it, the building inhibited sleep – 'a roof somehow bothers me', Clifford thought.[13] The weather was miserable – rain that fell with little respite and a wintry monotone of grey sky and drab landscape. The roads were rutted and slick with mud; a German bomber machine-gunned them briefly but with sufficient accuracy to provoke their driver into slamming the car into neutral and jumping out before he had put the handbrake on. The car zigzagged downhill and it was left to Clifford to stop it careering off the road and into a rock wall.

Rumours that Barce and Benghazi had both fallen offered some comfort, however. Then, on 22 December, there was the cheering sight of Geoffrey Keating and Russell Hill swinging down a hill towards them, instantly recognisable thanks to their exotic fur Persian hats, legacies of the Teheran trip earlier in the year. The headgear had prompted rumours about Russians operating in the region. Rommel's retreat from Tobruk had drawn the press towards Benghazi, and the renewed companionship encouraged a flurry of expansive cooking: Freddie Bayliss, of Paramount News, cooked a tomato omelette insisting that it should include a stomach-binding six eggs per person.

Dawn the next day was crisp and clear, while the desert was white with a frosty dew. A few dirty, mud-spattered British vehicles, their tyres hissing on roads greasy with rain, had captured Benghazi, and the correspondents followed close behind them into the town. The manager of the Albergho d'Italia had donned his best white waistcoat, cleaned the rooms, laid the tables and lit the fires, as if the war was over, or, at worst, postponed for Christmas. For his contribution to the festivities, Clifford had paid 250 lire for two turkeys. On Christmas Day they were on the road early before finally arriving in the blackened ruins of Benghazi. 'The whole world was out looting in the sunshine.'[14] At the hospital they discovered that Eddie Ward had been acting as an interpreter there only a matter of days before, until the Italian retreat.

The correspondents occupied flats near the railway station – Keating, Freddie Bayliss and Hill joining with Moorehead, Clifford and Kim Mundy – and their agreed immediate priority was the cooking of a proper Christmas dinner. The turkeys were fried at the deserted Berenice Hotel, basted in margarine over a fire fuelled with broken furniture. It proved a remarkable meal of mashed potatoes, stuffing, vegetables, a tinned ham, plum pudding blazing in brandy, Chianti, chocolates and raisins. As for the turkeys, they were wonderfully tender and unforgettably flavoursome. German aircraft flew over, on their way to mine the harbour at Tobruk, but the eating went on undisturbed. A tank roared down the street with the crew singing carols and pulling crackers. Then, his entry timed to perfection, Christopher Buckley arrived, to great applause. The Trio and their friends sang and danced until midnight, only stopping when the conscientious Kim Mundy counselled sleep. After all, there was no knowing what the morning would bring.

Desert war correspondents, perhaps contemplating 'a spell of almost normal war reporting'.
(John Moorehead)

NOTES

1 Clifford papers (16727), IWM, file AGC/1/2: diary entry for 7 December 1941.
2 Ibid., diary entry for 7 December 1941.
3 Ibid., file AGC/2/1/5: letter of 18 December 1941.
4 Ibid., file AGC/1/2: diary entry for 10 December 1941.
5 Ibid., diary entry for 11 December 1941.
6 Ibid.
7 Ibid., diary entry for 12 December 1941.
8 Clifford, pp.171–2.
9 Ibid., p.180.
10 Ibid., p.181.
11 Ibid., p.189.
12 Busvine, p.268.
13 Clifford papers (16727), IWM, file AGC/1/2: diary entry for 20 December 1941.
14 Clifford, p.202.

10. Written Out?

Back in London, the powers-that-be at the *Mail* were evidently delighted with their special correspondent: 'Seasonable greeting and congratulations on a grand year's work from editor and entire staff.'[1]

How different were the respective Christmases of editor and correspondent! Nursing 'a pretty shattering hangover', Clifford was soon on the move that Boxing Day morning, heading south towards the township of Agedabia where the Germans were resolutely dug in. Scattered far and wide as they drove were the wrecks of enemy aircraft. For his part, Moorehead had wanted to return to Cairo, but 'if the *Daily Mail* was going to Agedabia, the *Daily Express* would have to go too'.[2] Despite his thumping head, Clifford had prepared an elaborate picnic of ham, tomatoes, cheese and fruit – further evidence, if such were needed, of his resolute persistence.

Towards evening, a broadcasting unit from South Africa turned up and Clifford and Moorehead were prevailed upon to make recordings for subsequent broadcast. Moorehead talked about Eddie Ward, languishing somewhere in a prisoner-of-war camp, while Clifford painted a grim picture of ruined Benghazi. Both pieces were touched by melancholy and Clifford was also bothered by his voice when he heard the playback, thinking it to be 'irritatingly cultured and extremely flat and dull'.[3] In truth, both men were succumbing to a 'desert depression', the symptoms of which were the draining away of the energy and zest they had enjoyed twelve months before and feeling somehow 'written out', struggling with each day's turn of duty at the typewriter. It wasn't helped by the fact that the capture of Benghazi was proving to be just a sideshow; the critical battle was still to come, probably to the south 'in that huge desert area which merges into Tripolitania'.[4]

Perhaps the mood might be lifted by a return to Cairo. Geoffrey Keating and Clifford set off in the former's 'so-called passion-wagon – a utility with the back seat taken out and a bed spring fitted permanently inside'.[5] The passion-wagon rattled and shook as it threaded its way through roads pockmarked by shell damage and bomb craters. Inevitably, it was slow progress, and eventually they drew to a complete halt in the middle of nowhere when the car ran out of oil. They stood on the passion-wagon's roof, sweeping the far horizon with binoculars, but they could see nothing resembling help, or indeed much sign of anything in all that barren emptiness. They drank a few cans of American beer while they contemplated the possibility of rescue. That came in the end from some Indian troops who virtually carried the passion-wagon over a high desert pass. The soldiers laughed and whooped as lumps of red mud flew past them, thrown up by the vehicle's spinning wheels.

Much relieved to be on the move again, Clifford and Keating motored into Barce. At one of the town's hotels, they found a note from Alan Moorehead which encouraged them to drive on further eastwards, despite the failing light. The road took them through countryside that reminded Alex of rural Surrey; it 'was deserted and somehow very chic and orderly with its stunted evergreen bushes bordering the fine metalled road. It might have been somewhere around Hindhead.'[6] They were making good time until the darkness suddenly fell and, while the passion-wagon had bed springs, it didn't stretch to lights. Reluctantly, they decided to stop for the night, coincidentally at a group of farm buildings already identified by Moorehead as an acceptable night-stop. Keating and Clifford stepped out of the passion-wagon in the desert night and felt their way into the building, finally emerging from the darkness into a room filled with firelight and a pungent smell of wood-smoke. Instead of a wary progress through a short-lived twilight, there was hot stew, tea and whisky, camaraderie and animated conversation – 'What kept you?' 'Bloody Geoffrey's bloody passion-wagon, that's what!' – and a few intensely competitive hands of bridge to remind them all of better days.

Clifford broke the Freddie Bayliss egg record the following morning, breaking eighteen to make the breakfast scrambled eggs. It was a grey morning and the day remained sombre and troubled. There were arguments about where to head next, then they failed to find a Cairo-bound aircraft, and when they arrived at Bardia as night was falling, the brigadier at the South African 3rd Brigade Headquarters (for whom newspapermen were anathema) gave them a distinctly frosty reception. Things only began to look up when they were invited to lunch the next day with General de Villiers. They ate in a large tent whose palatial splendour reminded Clifford of the crusades, and de Villiers carefully outlined for them the details of the planned offensive which was due to begin at dawn on New Year's Eve. The artillery barrage began at 4.30 a.m. at the end of a wild and very cold night, so cold that the heavy dew on Clifford's groundsheet had turned to a crisp white frost. The correspondents hurriedly turned out stories huddled in the car, and Moorehead and Alaric Jacob then departed for Cairo, their route taking them in a long sweep around Hellfire Pass and into the teeth of yet another sandstorm through which they drove as fast as they dared. Ah, the thought of a hot bath! It would be Jacob's first for four months, a pleasure enhanced by a large whisky and soda perched on the side of the tub.

An exhausted Clifford decided to remain at the front, despite sensing that he could only tolerate being away from Cairo for a couple of days more. He ignored New Year's Eve since sleep mattered infinitely more than celebrating the uncertainties of the next year of wartime. The new year, 1942, began with torrential rain and a sandstorm. In company with the South African journalist Brian Young and a bottle of brandy, Clifford watched the unfolding battle about which de Villiers had briefed them, the arcs of gunfire strung across the heavens. Their vantage point gave the battle a curiously unreal quality so that it felt more like spectating at a race meeting, or watching a glorious display of lights, than a military action. They wrote up their stories that night, working under the flickering half-light from a candle in a bottle.

It had been a dangerous and exhausting campaign – more so than any of its predecessors – and these final few days around Bardia had been particularly unpleasant. At one point, for example, Clifford walked 'eight miles into no man's land so as to get a close-up view of the Bardia moonlight battle'.[7] But at least a German surrender was imminent, signalled by the long lines of morose prisoners, the burning supply dumps, and, everywhere, abandoned, derelict lorries. Bardia's church lay in blackened ruins, a fitting symbol of both sides' battle fatigue and indeed Clifford's aching weariness. He was desperate to escape the battlefront, having been away from Cairo for twenty-seven consecutive days, and his tiredness was accompanied by the familiar concern about whether his dispatches – written at such personal cost – were even reaching the outside world. It was time to go. The day of departure, 3 January 1942, was another overcast, raw morning. The first thing Clifford did on waking was to tip pools of rainwater off his bed. Then he hurriedly packed, before setting off for the sanctuary of Cairo. Securing a seat on a flight east was no easy task – it involved a heated argument – and when he finally managed it, his name on the passenger list appeared next to a defeated German general, 'a stiff sour-looking bird with cropped hair and watering pale blue eyes'.[8] Then Alex discovered that his 'seat' was in fact a pile of stretchers, and next to him was the general's batman. They began a conversation, but it was soon made clear that such fraternisation was unacceptable and the silenced batman duly succumbed to airsickness.

* * * *

That night both batman and general continued their way to a separate captivity, while Clifford enjoyed a mellow, long drawn-out dinner at Shepheards with the Mooreheads and Kim Mundy. Returning to Cairo was like being reborn. In the desert 'men are reduced from the things that make life worth living to the things that make life possible',[9] while in the Egyptian capital, life had a peculiar intensity to it, an atmosphere of frenzied pleasure; its bars and clubs were packed; so too were the cinemas; there was even a football match every day in Gezira. In comparison to Europe, food was plentiful, although three days a week were designated as meatless. Even the January weather held out some hope, a promise of spring, although there were days chilly enough for an overcoat. It was dry too – Moorehead contended that Cairo never had rain – whereas Benghazi, at the turn of the year, had endured ten days of perpetual rain, leaving aircraft bogged down on runways, lorries struggling through deep furrows of mud, tents dripping, and a pervading sense of despair where 'farmhouses, orchards, cattle, sheep, crops – everything – were abandoned to the rain and the mud and the invader'.[10]

The one thing missing from Cairo life was news. While the ticker machines at the Turf Club continued to chatter away, there was little new, and nothing of substance, in the tapes that emerged. What could be said about a continuing stalemate in the rain? With no action to describe, all that remained were reflections on progress and strategy, a situation where it was tempting to stray into criticism of the way the campaign was being waged. Early in January, Clifford wrote such a piece – extending over seven pages – which was highly critical of the Libyan campaign. The censors didn't like it and passed it up the line to higher authority. Clifford also wrote an article about the captured German general – he of the ice-blue eyes and shaven head – who had shared his flight back to Cairo. It was some consolation that Alan Moorehead's bosses at the *Express* in London were concerned that their man had not covered the same story for whatever reason. Moreover it helped preserve the myth that the two of them were bitter rivals, rather than two trusting friends following the war in tandem.

There was no question that 1942 had begun badly. Two days after Clifford had submitted his damning criticism of the Libyan campaign, he received two unsettling telegrams from the London office. The first was an unprecedented 147 words demanding a leading article contriving to give 'the air force a build-up'[11] – the cable's length stemmed from the fact that it told him precisely what to write. Even more unsettling was the second telegram since it demanded from him exactly the kind of piece which the censors had so disliked. Fuming, he wrote a second version and sent it off, eliciting a warm response from the *Mail*, delighted that the article 'admirably offset the "much trumpeted Moorehead feature"'. The very same day Moorehead received a similarly enthusiastic telegram from *his* employers, who were ecstatic that his piece was 'the talk of the town'. It was a wonderful moment when the two correspondents realised that, notwithstanding their shared life, there was no thought back home that the two men were anything other than fierce rivals. What a hoot! Clifford and Moorehead merely 'laughed like hell', imagining 'the indignation of our respective editors had they seen us exchanging telegrams'.[12] In London, the rivalry of Beaverbrook and Rothermere, the world of scoops and market share, mattered hugely, but in the Middle East, with its mix of danger and desert hardship, exile and constant travelling, what mattered most were the relationships that kept you able to battle on. So it was that the *Mail* and *Express*'s men had become brothers under the skin. For two long years their lives had been so close: they had faced death together, dived for cover into neighbouring ditches, argued and laughed, shared whisky, hangovers and a hundred sad meals of bully beef and biscuits. Quite simply, they had become closer than many husbands and wives.

Although Moorehead and Clifford took great pleasure in the fact that their respective editors believed their two reporters to be cut-throat competitors, there were occasional tensions between them. Once, when they were shaving side by side in the flat's bathroom, a telegram from the *Express* arrived which Moorehead found troubling, upset by the fact that Clifford's strategic analysis was lauded – the *Mail*'s correspondent, it said insidiously, 'informatively takes gravest view'. Moorehead felt criticised and was 'rather upset', while Clifford smiled at the fact that their respective papers 'probably think we are deadly rivals who hardly even speak to one another'.[13] There they were, the two of them, a shared mirror reflecting back their faces, both soaped white with shaving cream, side by side and the most resolute of friends.

Moorehead was all too aware that his editor at the *Express*, Arthur Christiansen, was both demanding and impatient, characteristics evident in the peremptory wording of the cable which had disturbed the Australian's companionable shave with Clifford. In fact Christiansen believed Moorehead to be 'the greatest correspondent of the Second World War', and would later pride himself on spotting and developing his talent, claiming that in the early days he had encouraged him 'to look for detail, to describe the flowers that grew in the desert, oblivious of war, while the big battles raged'.[14] Christiansen also ensured that Moorehead's earnings were commensurate with his value to the paper, putting up his salary 'so fast that by the time he was reporting the German surrender at Lüneburg Heath he was in a higher pay bracket than Field Marshal Montgomery'.[15]

＊　＊　＊　＊

There is an irony that, at a time when Moorehead and Clifford were increasingly aware of war-weariness – both of them fearing that they were 'written out' –

they both decided to write books about the campaign. In the late summer of 1941, Arthur Christiansen approved Moorehead's proposal for what became *Mediterranean Front*: 'as you've been a good boy will give permission to publish book'.[16] It was fortunate that Christiansen did not object since there was keen interest from a number of publishers: both Gollancz and Hutchinson wanted the book, but Alan, supported by his literary agents, opted for Hamish Hamilton whose £150 advance was £50 more generous than either of the other two. On 7 January 1942 a first copy of *Mediterranean Front* arrived in Cairo, impressing Clifford who thought it looked 'very well in print', while Moorehead was 'delighted and spent most of the day reading it'.[17]

Within three weeks, Clifford would embark on his own book, but for now he was preoccupied with fulfilling the *Mail*'s instruction to write a piece presenting the RAF in a good light. He interviewed Air Marshal Tedder, RAF commander-in-chief, Middle East, before writing 2,000 words which went through unaltered; indeed, the censor made a point of telephoning to congratulate him. Clifford thought this 'sinister'; after all, he 'didn't really want to please the RAF too much'.[18] He was uneasy more generally anyway, struggling to come to terms with a way of life in Cairo that seemed unacceptably remote from the war, and troubled that, while he was there, he was enjoying a life of relative comfort. Simply heading off to the front was no solution since he recognised that he had grown to hate every aspect of life in the desert. He combated his growing dissatisfaction by reading (Virgil sitting on the balcony), cooking (that 15-egg omelette embellished with chicken and ham!), and enjoying evenings of conversation and bridge with the Mooreheads. It was frustrating that there *were* significant news stories around – but they could not be written about; he was even unwilling to confide them to his diary since they were 'a good deal too secret to record right now'.[19] Instead, he recorded baby John's first steps, taken on Sunday 18 January 1942. Troubling too in its way was the fact that Clifford could see that Moorehead, for his part, was increasingly absorbed in a number of projects, including a film script. The Australian interviewed 'Strafer' Gott and lunched with General Auchinleck, walking with him through the rose garden, their heads bowed in conversation. It was evident to Clifford that the lunch had gone well, since Moorehead returned to the flat clearly very pleased with himself.[20]

Then suddenly, towards the end of January, the war intruded again, threatening upheaval. An official communiqué was released which announced that on the previous day: '... in conditions of bad visibility, the enemy, in three strong columns disposing between them the bulk of the remaining Axis tanks, made a reconnaissance in force to a depth of about ten miles east of a general line running south of Mersa Brega. Our light forces which had been harassing the enemy since his retirement from Agedabia withdrew ... (while) weather conditions again seriously handicapped the activities of our air forces.'[21] In its way the communiqué was a masterpiece of obfuscation. Official spokesmen had long since mastered the art of disguising setbacks – they had had plenty of practice after all – but the tell-tale clues were there all right, hidden between the lines – the weather had been 'bad'; the enemy was 'strong'; a withdrawal had been necessary. Suspicions were aroused, and so too a willingness to question the status quo. A piece appeared in the *Mail* which suggested that 'Rommel wouldn't be so active now if we had used our tanks the right way'.[22]

Then, on 22 January, the press was summoned to a conference by Sir Walter Monckton, Director General of British Propaganda and Information Services, and Oliver Lyttelton, the Minister of State in the Middle East. It proved an unruly occasion, with the government minister being heckled to such an extent that 'the poor man was driven from corner to corner', so much so that he 'finally left the room in bad shape'.[23] It was yet another retreat. Two years after Moorehead and Clifford had first flown into Egypt, there were still few signs of victory.

* * * *

Three days later, on 25 January 1942, Clifford took his first cautious steps towards writing his own book. On the 23rd he had received an enquiry from a literary agent and that, together with Moorehead's success with *Mediterranean Front*, proved enough of an impetus for him to begin his account of Operation Crusader. He began very tentatively, writing 'just to see if I ever could do it',[24] and, right from the outset, doubtful that he could. The next day he persevered, writing quickly but fearing 'that when I come to read it again I shall dislike it so much that I shall never bear to let it be printed'.[25] Nonetheless, he continued, never sure of the book's merit, but showing typically dogged persistence. The manuscript grew in step with the looming threat of a German advance on Cairo.

As the German advance became ever more serious, the relations between the military authorities in Cairo and the press deteriorated. The Middle East-based war correspondents had long believed that they were deemed vulgar, troublesome mischief-makers by the military. What compounded the problem was that they felt talked down to by the military men and patronised in a particularly irritating way. Trust was noticeable by its absence. When Monckton told them in confidence that Benghazi had been evacuated, Clifford's reaction was to think that the propaganda chief had 'been given the job of keeping the press sweet,'[26] something at which he was entirely unconvincing. Like the British stumbling in the desert confronted by Rommel and his troops, it seemed that Monckton could not hold out against the onslaught of the press. Certainly the military situation was bleak: on 30 January, Clifford wrote an uncompromising piece describing the fall of Benghazi; then Barce fell and it seemed that Derna would be next. Where once these places had seen victories over the well-fed, pomaded Italians, now the story was one of tactical defeat and withdrawal, desert rats smelling disaster.

Uneasily, Moorehead and Clifford continued to file their stories, although in Clifford's case he admitted to doing so simply to ease his conscience. They went to the races and played tennis on a morning made in heaven – this on the last day of January. Clifford had taken Lucy to the cinema the night before, with Moorehead complaining of feeling under the weather and taking to his bed. They began to accompany Lucy as she learned to drive, Moorehead taking her out to the desert near the pyramids for a morning's lesson, driving to and fro in a landscape devoid of hazards. When Clifford went with her, he found the experience 'pretty nerve-wracking' and it was no surprise when she drove 'the car slap into a gate and buckled up the mudguard'.[27] Meanwhile, not so far away in the desert, the German juggernaut was closing in.

By early February Clifford was contemplating – with considerable reluctance – a return to the desert. To his natural distaste for life in the wilderness, however, was added a further complication: the book! By now, it was tightening its grip on him: 'I don't really want to (go) as long as I haven't finished'.[28] That same day the Mooreheads seized the moment, leaving for 'the snowfields of Lebanon' to ski and enjoy a much-needed break far from Egypt and the Libyan Desert. The last time Lucy had skied was in Switzerland long before the war, while Alan had last done so 'at St Cloud during that cold winter in 1938 when all Paris was sheeted with snow.'[29] The staunch Clifford took them to Cairo Central Station to catch the 3.30 p.m. train to Palestine. As ever, the platforms were in chaos, while the Haifa train was slow and scruffy, despite its wagon-lit flaunting 'advertisements for "Hotel Splendide, Ostende"'. Moorehead was amused by how, in the Middle East, the word 'express' might more accurately be defined as a 'train which may or may not stop for half an hour at every station'.[30] It was an uncomfortable journey: hot, flyblown and dusty with the overhead fan effective only in recirculating dust, bugs and heat. It was late afternoon before they reached Haifa. From there it was a three-hour drive into Syria, recently taken by the British and the Free French. Hunger, poverty and a cold winter were all causing problems – and that in a country where intrigue 'festers endlessly'.[31] But there was good snow for skiing on the mountains' upper slopes while the whole Syrian coast lay at their feet. Looking down on the distant sea, they ate oranges and chocolate in the glare of the sunlit snowfields.

In 1942 such moments of tranquillity were rare and usually short-lived. Reality had a way of intruding. While Lucy and Moorehead were gleefully skiing in the high mountains of Lebanon, Singapore fell to the Japanese, and Clifford was planning to head off into the desert: 'God knows why but my conscience is driving me.'[32] It was evidently time for the Mooreheads to come down from the mountains and go back to the heat and dust of Cairo. Moorehead had cabled Arthur Christiansen at the *Express* asking if there was any prospect of him being sent to Australia. The idea appealed, not least because he hadn't been there for six years, and, with the fall of Singapore, Australia had moved much nearer the front line. Moorehead's cable to the London office argued that the Middle East was relatively quiet and, as he had been born and had grown up in Australia, he knew the country well. The suggestion was unceremoniously turned down, however, scotched by foreign editor Charles Foley, who may have sensed that the Middle East had the potential to become front page news again quite soon.

*   *   *   *

Meanwhile Clifford was leaving Cairo for the desert in company with the American reporter Russell Hill. They set off at a leisurely 10 a.m. and were delayed by the Nile bridge opening to let the feluccas through and a puncture on the road to Alexandria. They had arranged to pick up BUP's Richard McMillan there, but 'he turned out to be incapably drunk'.[33] (He would turn up the next day nursing a monumental hangover.) So, they travelled on without him, eventually reaching Bagush in darkness where they bedded down for the night. Next morning, driving slowly towards the township of Maktila, near Sidi Barrani, they witnessed one of the desert's miracles, barren scrubland transformed into a garden by the heavy rain. Clifford surmised that the 'seed may have lain there for years'. The richness of the resulting flora was astonishing, swathes of asphodel, stocks, campanula, antirrhinum and yellow daisies. Smiling, he contemplated sending some gardening notes to the *Daily Mail*. A few days later they 'camped among a great field of dwarf night-scented stock' and, when Clifford walked through them, 'the fragrance as my boots crushed them was almost tangible'.[34] They were sharing a campsite with a group of 'very raw sergeant photographers who had neither petrol, water, food, nor cooking utensils. They apparently just thought they would nip round to the pub for their meals'.[35] The two correspondents rallied round and lent them everything they needed. That night, as Alex was trying to sleep, a large rat started to gnaw on his ankle.

There might be a carpet of flowers colouring the desert, but the mines remained, buried under the same sand and grit. On 21 February, when they had been heading for Tobruk, they found themselves in a 'place stiff with minefields', so that 'it was quite impossible to find a compass course'. They ended up camping in a sliver of land between two sets of mines, the narrow confines of which might have been irksome were it not for an invitation from some Indian sappers to share some drink and listen to their wireless. As the days passed,

Clifford and Hill dutifully made their way from HQ to HQ: Army Advanced Headquarters to Army Battle HQ, to division, brigade – and so on. It could be a frustrating experience, this round of visits: Russell Hill remembered a remark of Moorehead's that 'it was like a game: if you missed one step, you had to go back to the beginning and start over again'.[36]

It was proving another frustrating trip, not least because of continuing problems over getting dispatches away. Uncertainly they continued towards Tobruk, with Clifford, having opened the truck's roof, peering out all day, keeping a sharp eye out for air activity. They interviewed General Gott whose chilly reception Alex put down to disapproval of Hill's flamboyant pushtin and Persian hat. Perhaps Gott was simply distracted, rather than disapproving, since there was considerable expectation of an imminent German attack. The Luftwaffe was very active and there were tanks on the move. By 23 February they had had enough and were intent on returning to Cairo, since 'offensive or no offensive we couldn't send any messages from up here'. A ferocious dust storm whirled through the tent the next morning, reminding Clifford of how much he hated the desert, its discomfort, its emptiness, the way it reduced men to an uncivilised state. 'Sand swept across the roads and tracks, blew into tents, got into beds and clothes and food'.[37]

Eventually, Clifford got back to Cairo, dust-streaked and exhausted, and there were the Mooreheads looking rested and sun-tanned. Before they could all settle back into the familiar, comforting cycle of Gezira, Shepheards, cinema, games of bridge and tennis, there was another of those disruptive cables from London. This one consigned Moorehead to India, vulnerable now because of the Japanese advance through Burma and its own contending movements for independence. Moorehead said a gloomy goodbye to Lucy and boarded an eastbound flying boat, to report on 'the strange case of Stafford Cripps versus the Indian people'.[38]

NOTES

1   Clifford papers (16727), IWM, file AGC/5/1.

2   Hill, p.269.

3   Clifford papers (16727), IWM, file AGC/1/2: diary entry for 26 December 1941.

4   *Daily Mail*, 29 December 1941.

5   Clifford papers (16727), IWM, file AGC/1/2: diary entry for 27 December 1941.

6   Ibid.

7   Ibid., file AGC/2/1/6. Letter of 5 January 1942 to his mother.

8   Ibid., file AGC/1/2: diary entry for 3 January 1942.

9   Clifford, p.230.

10   *A Year of Battle*, op. cit., p.87.

11   Clifford papers (16727), IWM, file AGC/1/2: diary entry for 9 January 1942.

12   Ibid., diary entry for 13 January 1942.

13   Ibid., diary entry for 27 January 1942.

14   *Headlines All My Life* by Arthur Christiansen, p.3.

15   Ibid., p.246.

16   Moorehead papers, NLA, MS5654. Telegram sent on 25 August 1941 to Alan Moorehead c/o the Carlton Hotel, Cairo.

17   Clifford papers (16727), IWM, file AGC/1/2: diary entry for 7 January 1942.

18   Ibid., diary entry for 15 January 1942.

19   Ibid., diary entry for 15 January 1942.

20   Later in the year, Moorehead would be asked to write Auchinleck's biography: 'life of Auchinleck badly needed will you undertake stop War Office approves.' The offer was from Harrap who were also publishing Clifford's book. Cable to Alan Moorehead dated 6 July 1942. See Moorehead papers, NLA, MS 5654.

21   Hill, p.284.

22   Liddell Hart papers, LH 11/1942/1.

23   Clifford papers (16727), IWM, file AGC/1/2: diary entry for 22 January 1942.

24   Ibid., diary entry for 25 January 1942.

25   Ibid., diary entry for 26 January 1942.

26   Ibid., diary entry for 26 January 1942.

27   Ibid., diary entry for 5 February 1942.

28   Ibid., diary entry for 8 February 1942.

29   *A Year of Battle*, op. cit., p.6.

30   Ibid., p.97.

31   Ibid., p.101.

32   Clifford papers (16727), IWM, file AGC/1/2: diary entry for 16 February 1942.

33   Ibid., diary entry for 19 February 1942.

34   Clifford, p.234.

35   Clifford papers (16727), IWM, file AGC/1/2: diary entry for 20 February 1942.

36   Hill, p.298.

37   Hill, p.304.

38   *A Year of Battle*, op. cit., p.108.

11. Foreign Correspondent

With his head resting on the aircraft's window frame, Moorehead looked down on a landscape of 'brown lake, brown rocks, brown fields and brown villages'.[1] Ironically, it had the look of yet another desert landscape. He was not to know it yet, but the next two months in India would take its toll on his health, the climate inflicting on him a succession of minor illnesses. There were some compensations: accommodation was no longer in sand-encrusted tents; there were no lurking desert minefields, or vindictive forays by the Luftwaffe, no more variations of Clifford's bully beef stew. He was no longer required to traverse the war zone in search of yet another tank skirmish, or a general's blustering insights. The story was one of political in-fighting and Moorehead was now operating in the world of the foreign correspondent, war reporting put to one side. It would be no easy task, but it was substantially easier than the mission he was charged to cover: whether Sir Stafford Cripps, the 'single Englishman (who) had come to offer freedom to India', could strike a deal in enough time for the Japanese to be resisted.[2]

The BOAC flying boat journey to India was painfully slow, the result of its usual ponderous speed and the regular stops for refuelling, the aircraft hopping from one convenient sheet of water to the next. When the flying boat finally alighted on a murky brown lake in Gwalior, India looked to be burning under a ferocious sun. In company with the Canadian reporter Matthew Halton, a hot and bothered Moorehead headed into the Gwalior Hotel's lobby where it was explained that there were some unfortunate problems over the rooms. It was so hot that Alan no longer cared one way or the other. Lunch did not improve his mood since the curry was distinctly second-rate. It would prove to be the norm: 'not once in India did I succeed in getting any decent curry'.[3] They took the train to Delhi, travelling first class – something of a misnomer since the shower was only tepid and the 'air-conditioning' fans whirled hot dust around the corridorless carriage. There was no denying that the further they travelled the more fascinating India became. Thanks to the Cripps' mission, Delhi had been invaded by large numbers of press and officials, not least Americans who had, in effect, 'occupied' the newer part of the city and marked their territory by installing traffic lights. Getting a room at the city's Imperial Hotel proved quite impossible until Richard Busvine turned up. He had been in Delhi for a while and in typical Busvine fashion had rapidly got things sorted: room, bath, drinks – the lot. He was just the man to resolve the problem of Moorehead's roomlessness. An extra bed was put in Busvine's room, but not before he had exterminated the creatures he had been sharing it with – the cricket in the fireplace, the birds, the white rabbits on the balcony, the lizards and the cockroaches.

* * * *

Moorehead had left Cairo two days after Cripps had arrived in India, on 22 March 1942, leaving Clifford in the flat with Lucy and the baby. Far from being glad that he was spared the journey east, Clifford was increasingly beset by the tribulations of the Egyptian capital. The battles with the censors, for example, had become even more exasperating, to the extent that a story might all too often be delayed, and involve a protracted wrangle before finally being released when its news value was diminished. In company with other pressmen – the *Manchester Guardian*'s David Woodward for example – Clifford was struggling with a persistent melancholy.

Early in March, he had a heart-to-heart with Woodward, 'even going so far as to be sentimental about the good old days in Amsterdam'[4] – which, thinking about it later, Clifford realised weren't that great anyway. Nevertheless, there was no doubt that Cairo was rapidly losing its attraction. To begin with, it bothered him that the Middle East seemed to have been relegated to a sideshow. 'This is a bad period out here now, with terrible things happening everywhere else and nothing but idleness and comfort here.' Then there was the book, unfinished as yet. Clifford was uncertain about its quality, one minute feeling pleased with progress, the next convinced that it had no merit at all. Moreover, he was often left in sole charge of baby John – 'the brat' as he ungraciously called him in his diary on one occasion. Despite his evident love for the child, he would find an afternoon's childcare, on top of everything else, 'something of a strain'.[5] This was an age after all when most men did not take easily or kindly to childminding: Moorehead and Clifford, it could be argued, showed a rather cavalier attitude to childcare when they 'tried to tow (John's) pram home behind the car'; unsurprisingly 'he was very upset and the pram fell over'.[6]

Above all, there were substantial worries about work. Clifford contemplated following Moorehead to India so that he too might cover the Cripps' mission, but he decided, in the end, that the *Mail* was insufficiently represented in the Middle East and leaving Cairo for an indefinite period would be a mistake. A further frustration was the persistent bitterness about censorship which was shared by the press as a whole. At the conclusion of a briefing by Brigadier Shearer on 3 March, for example, there was 'a terrific blitz against the RAF press hand-outs and censorship. It appears that everyone has been harbouring rancour against them for some time.'[7] The American war correspondent Edward Kennedy was one of them; he found what the censors had done to his dispatches 'disheartening', citing one such example: 'The word "wells"', he wrote, 'a cablese form (of) "as well as" was deleted for violating the rule against mentioning water resources in the desert.'[8]

Even at his lowest, though, Clifford recognised that things could be worse: he was thankful he wasn't a prisoner-of-war, for example. In recognition of that blessing, towards the end of March, he 'sent a parcel of food to Eddie Ward (who) is living in a nice castle somewhere just outside Florence'.[9]

✷   ✷   ✷   ✷

Moorehead's arrival in India on 28 March coincided with Cripps' first press conference where, to an audience of 'two hundred journalists, mostly Indian, in a lofty chamber in New Delhi's magnificent imperial palace,' Cripps lit himself a cigarette and muttered the words, 'Here is the document'.[10] Sir Stafford Cripps was lofty, ascetic and muscular, with a face etched with lines. A Labour politician and a barrister, he was 'a man of warm heart and sympathies but of inexorable logic', according to Matthew Halton.[11] The document he presented to the assembled journalists was just 800 words long, but its purpose was to seek a change in the course of history.

Cripps began work, taking the first prearranged steps in the long diplomatic ritual – the game of quaint practices and protocols which must be followed. Meetings should be conducted according to unwritten rules; invitations to drinks in the city's grand staterooms (where the cocktails were disappointingly thin) must be given only to the appropriate delegates; interviews with those with whom Cripps must reach agreement should conform to the accepted way of doing things. Given the complexity of the task and the evident intransigence of the participants, one wonders whether such reliance on old-fashioned diplomacy could ever have succeeded. In essence, the proposal on the table envisaged the promise in due course of Indian independence, subject to sustained support against Britain's wartime enemies. The complication was the bitter rivalry between the various parties in India.

Under a broiling sun one mid afternoon, Moorehead and Busvine were given an interview with the Nationalist leader Mahatma Gandhi. Moorehead found himself impressed by the aura surrounding Gandhi, but unsettled by what he saw as his evasiveness. They also interviewed the future prime minister of India Jawaharlal Nehru, as well as the Muslim leader Muhammad Ali Jinnah, whom Busvine, with his aggressive questioning, provoked into a full-blown argument. At one point, Busvine suggested that 'there was no essential difference between Hindus and Muslims, which was rather worse than telling a Nazi that there is no difference between an Aryan and a Jew'.[12] The response was furious: 'They worship cow. I eat cow,' Jinnah bellowed. 'We are utterly different.'

Meanwhile, the persistent, earnest Cripps ploughed on with his cycle of talks, beset by exactly the levels of animosity and difference that Busvine's questions had provoked in Muhammad Ali Jinnah. Sometimes there was a hint of progress, a cautious step forward – only for it to be followed by three rapid steps in the opposite direction. For his part, Moorehead was struck by the stark difference between old and new Delhi, the old city's disconcerting smell balanced by the glory of the flowers in the Imperial Hotel's gardens and elsewhere. He had brought with him from Cairo a copy of *War and Peace*, a wise choice given its length and the painfully slow progress of the talks. He read and explored the city. Eventually, with no conclusion in sight, Moorehead drove to Agra and visited the Taj Mahal, the beauty of which took his breath away, despite the scaffolding and distant machine-gun fire. When he got back to Delhi it was clear that the Cripps mission was in deep trouble and, indeed, on 11 April, it was announced that no agreement could be reached. Suddenly the would-be dealmakers, the secretariat, the security men and the rest could identify a dozen places they would rather be than Delhi: it was time to move on. Moorehead received instructions to go to Colombo in Ceylon, since there was a looming threat to the island from the Japanese. He and Busvine left Delhi for Bombay on 16 April aboard the Frontier Mail. To pass the time on the train they played honeymoon bridge, a game of Moorehead's own devising. Vainly, Busvine tried to interest Moorehead in the sights from the train window, but Moorehead's attention was fixed entirely on the playing cards. 'Come on, chum,' he would say, 'it's your deal.'[13]

Moorehead never warmed to big port cities – Bordeaux, Marseilles, Alexandria, Naples, none of them appealed – and Bombay was no different, an antipathy not helped by being unable to leave it. Attempts to fly out were thwarted (sometimes by senior officers pulling rank). Once Busvine thought he had successfully negotiated an escape until a surplus of mailbags on the aircraft was given priority. When he returned crestfallen to the Taj Mahal Hotel, Moorehead just 'guffawed'.[14] Eventually the two of them reached Colombo, where the sight of ships sailing for Australia made Alan homesick. Soon after, he realised that there was nothing to be gained by coming to Ceylon other than finding some decent curry, something which India had signally failed to supply. He visited each of the island's flying fields, flew over the mountains to Trincomali, saw the tea plantations, talked to the forces bigwigs – AOC, GOC, admiral – and wrote. He bathed, ate coconuts and pineapples and played billiards at the club. But he knew that Cairo was where he needed to be and so, when he could, he took a westbound flying boat. Busvine, lucky man, had wangled leave in England and he watched sadly as Moorehead left, before heading back to Bombay and a boat for Liverpool. Moorehead had been a delightful companion, he thought, and he 'was very sorry to see him go'.[15]

✳   ✳   ✳   ✳

Good heavens, 33! He felt 'practically middle-aged'.[16] It was early morning in Cairo on 8 April 1942 and Alex Clifford's birthday. He lay in bed as the sun streamed in through the thin curtains and heard Lucy encouraging John to take a present of some Turkish Delight through to his room. 'Go on! He'll be wide awake!' Indeed he was, his mind running on the passage of time, on growing older and that sad 'feeling of life slipping by without anything achieved'.[17] He shook his head as he reflected on how his birthday seemed invariably to be associated with world disaster – defeat in Greece in 1941 and the debacle in Norway and Denmark the previous year. Before that he had been in Spain and remembered that 8 April had coincided with yet another success for Franco's army.

John Moorehead and his godfather Alexander Clifford. (John Moorehead)

There would be no such catastrophe to mark his 33rd birthday, but he would always associate April 1942 with his growing disillusion with Cairo, its air of decadent ease when so much of the world was in pain, its dancing, al fresco dining, steamy flirtation and shared nights. Six days after his birthday, he noted in his diary that 'there is a Russian Air Force mission in town, apparently unutterably shocked by the luxury and ease of life' in Cairo, while there were 'eighty thousand Poles whom the Russians have suddenly stopped feeding and pushed over the Persian border'.[18]

War reporting had got no easier either; there was a series of bad experiences with the RAF who 'always tend to treat us as though we were half-witted children,' although sometimes compensated for it with a hearty RAF breakfast. There was the time when Clifford visited a squadron based on the road to Alexandria that 'was beautifully equipped with everything but planes'.[19] It wasn't just the RAF who caused problems for the press. One Saturday he caught the 7 a.m. train to Alexandria intending to interview Italian POWs who were to be exchanged – 700 of theirs for sixty of ours – in the Turkish port of Smyrna. Alex arrived late because of an air raid and, when he finally got to the quayside, there was a strange stand-off between the confused prisoners and a group of curious newsmen whose eager questions were met with blank faces and stumbling replies. Initially, the information gleaned was decidedly muddled; soon after, they were denied access, a British orderly blithely explaining that 'they were mental cases – the whole lot were cuckoo'. Alex left mystified.[20]

A week later he returned, intent on a further attempt at interviewing the Italian prisoners. The dockside had been heavily bombed in the intervening days and two ships lay wrecked in the harbour, while much of the quayside had been destroyed. That was all that had changed; the press were still denied access to the POWs, the army insisting that it must interrogate them first, and so Clifford, in company with the estimable Christopher Buckley, returned to Cairo by train. The next day, the interviews finally went ahead, allowing the Italians to embark on a welter of complaints about conditions: 'too little food, too cramped camps, too little washing and sanitary arrangements, too little to do.'[21] For Clifford the most interesting news was about captured war correspondent Eddie Ward whom one of the prisoners knew and who 'had even sent a message to us ... and I got his exact address and everything'. It wasn't all good news: the Italians, it seemed, were not treating imprisoned war correspondents as officers.

That April was brutally hot. Once after dinner, Lucy, unable to sleep in the suffocating heat, persuaded Clifford to drive out of the city to find some cooler, fresher air. They drove – Lucy still in her dressing gown – through some scruffy villages into the countryside, passing coffee shops spilling light and argument into the night shadows. They returned to the flat 'where the insects were appalling'.[22] Heat, disgruntled POWs, substantial RAF breakfasts – it was all too evident to

Clifford that 1942 had yet to see him send a genuinely big story; not about the Middle East, at least. Maybe it was proving different for Moorehead in India? Clifford attended the regular press meetings, including a strange briefing about the imminent visit by the Duke of Gloucester, and went to dinner parties, including one where all the host's books 'down to P.G. Wodehouse and rank pornography are beautifully bound in leather'.[23] He lunched at Geoffrey Keating's, sitting next to the Swedish minister's daughter who lived in Madrid and whose parents were close friends of the Spanish marquesa whom Clifford had known during the Spanish war. It was unsettling to be reminded of those days in Spain, not so long ago, when war reporting had presented one new experience after another. Most of his bright-eyed spirit had gone now, lost in the heat of Cairo and the Western Desert.

In the middle of April a former Reuters colleague of Clifford's, Gordon Young, arrived in Egypt. Young now worked for the *Express* and had travelled out on a troopship with the celebrated photographer Cecil Beaton. Young was a fount of Fleet Street gossip, which piqued Clifford's interest, but also reminded him of how far away from the centre of things he currently was. Moreover, Young was merely passing through en route to India, where the prospect of hard news seemed significantly better than in Egypt. Young's stay in Cairo was brief, but it was long enough for him to have his pocket picked. Clifford was sympathetic but unsurprised; after all, he had returned to his car one night to find thieves in the process of removing his wheels, while on another occasion, he had found an unknown Egyptian curled up asleep in the back seat.

The night before Young left for India on an eastbound flying boat, he and Clifford had attended a fellow correspondent's 60th birthday celebration.[24] The highlight had been the performance by the singer Alice Delysia. 'She must be nearer sixty than fifty,' Clifford wrote, 'but she makes no pretence of being a sweet young thing anymore.'[25] She was dressed in a 'resplendent' blue uniform and was singing in an airless cellar, with soldiers leaning against the walls, khaki against the brick. The song was *Battez les Coeurs*, the anthem of the Free French, unveiled in this smoky basement for the first time. She sang initially in French, then in English, a version which Clifford had written, with stirring lyrics about courage, freedom and the casting off of chains. It had a rousing chorus – '*To Hell With Hitler and his Henchmen!*' – and ended in a thunderous tumult of noise. Alex was 'overwhelmed with emotion', particularly when Delysia 'flung her arms round my neck and kissed me on both cheeks'. For a few fleeting moments, a birthday party in Cairo had foreshadowed victory and the uproarious nightclubs of a liberated Paris.

✳   ✳   ✳   ✳

April drew to a close. There was a garden party at the British Embassy for the visiting Duke of Gloucester: flags flew and the cut flowers wilted in the sun. A brass band played 'God Save the King' and the duke stood to attention at the top of the steps. There was a brief pause, an uncomfortable silence, while everyone stared, waiting for his Royal Highness to move. However 'nothing stirred, except a fly which Lady Lampson whisked away'.[26] Afterwards there was 'second-grade Groppi tea and cakes and ices'[27] while the band neglected to play the Egyptian anthem, an omission which raised eyebrows amongst some and offence in others. An embarrassed Clifford considered writing 'a very cynical little story about it' which would juxtapose the imperial pomp and circumstance, the sunhats and sweat-stained uniforms, the small talk and languid flirtation.

As May approached, it got hotter still. The jacaranda trees were in full bloom. Clifford dined with Christopher Buckley and Clare Hollingworth who 'had some somewhat boring consular people there, great talkers all'.[28] There was a hint of action in the air though: on 1 May, Walter Monckton summoned Clifford to a meeting to discuss a 'very secret project', so secret that Alex was loath to record any details of it in his diary, let alone reveal them to that part of the world that read the *Daily Mail*. Soon after, he decided it was time to return to the desert. It would boost his morale, he thought, ease his conscience and give him a dateline from which he could dispatch with confidence. He felt pleased that he had at last taken the initiative. So it was that he and Lucy went to the cinema on his last evening and saw, with a nice touch of irony, *Foreign Correspondent*. The next morning, the alarm woke him at 5 a.m. and by 6 a.m. he was on board an aircraft, heading once more towards the desert. It was Monday 4 May 1942, three weeks before Rommel went on the offensive intent on the capture of Tobruk.

NOTES

1   *A Year of Battle*, op. cit., p.106.
2   Halton, p.161.
3   *A Year of Battle*, op. cit., p.106.
4   Clifford papers (16727), IWM, file AGC/1/2: diary entry for 3 March 1942.
5   Ibid., diary entry for 1 March 1942.
6   Ibid., diary entry for 10 March 1942.
7   Ibid., diary entry for 3 March 1942.
8   Kennedy Cochran, p.96.
9   Clifford papers (16727), IWM, file AGC/2/1/6; letter of 25 March 1942.
10 Halton, p.162.
11 Ibid., p.165.
12 *A Year of Battle*, op. cit., p.134.

13 Busvine, p.304.

14 Ibid., p.305.

15 Ibid., p.307.

16 Clifford papers (16727), IWM, file AGC/2/1/6. Letter to his mother dated 14 April 1942.

17 Ibid., file AGC/1/2: diary entry for 8 April 1942.

18 Ibid., diary entry for 8 April 1942.

19 Ibid., diary entry for 2 April 1942. The RAF, unsurprisingly, took a contrary view. Air Marshal Tedder, for example, 'was furious to learn in cables from home of more half-baked criticism of the RAF in newspaper leading articles.' See Tedder, *With Prejudice*, p.242.

20 Clifford papers (16727), IWM, file AGC/1/2: diary entry for 4 April 1942.

21 Ibid., diary entry for 12 April 1942.

22 Ibid., diary entry for 18 April 1942.

23 Ibid., diary entry for 9 April 1942.

24 The correspondent was André Glarner of the *Exchange Telegraph*.

25 Clifford papers (16727), IWM, file AGC/1/2: diary entry for 20 April 1942.

26 *Near East* by Cecil Beaton, p.37.

27 Clifford papers (16727), IWM, file AGC/1/2: diary entry for 25 April 1942.

28 Ibid., diary entry for 29 April 1942.

12. The Bonfires of Cairo

Alex Clifford set out for the oasis at Siwa on the morning of 7 May 1942, a year after the military authorities had refused him permission to go there. He was accompanied by Richard McMillan who, having forsworn alcohol, seemed to have improved his potential as a travel companion. Judging by the dilatoriness of the start, though, this was optimistic. He severely tested Clifford's patience with a series of delays: wanting to write a story before they left, then worrying, in turn, about rations and petrol and water. 'And perhaps we might see if we can track down Ron Monson's brother?' Infuriating! Eventually they got going, driving past the abandoned remains of tanks and lorries, their sombre frames already being buried under drifting sand.

They made camp that night on a salt flat in high winds and heavy rain. If this deterioration in the weather wasn't bad enough, the drivers insisted on cooking, something which rang alarm bells for Clifford, although a timely intervention ensured that at least the onions were cooked the way he liked them. Alex was only too aware how fussy he was about what he ate in the desert, despite worrying how that might appear to others. It would have been hard to disguise it, given his loathing for sweet tea (an army staple), cold bully beef or salmon, tinned sausages, cold tinned potatoes, and the army white bread which was invariably stale. He made do with biscuits and cheese, jam, and a few dates.

Next morning, with no obvious distractions in the wilderness for McMillan to seize upon, they managed an early start. The landscape in every direction was disconcertingly the same: empty, barren and unwelcoming. They were at 'the centre of an unvarying disc of flat brown gravel, walled in with mirages and domed by a brassy sky'.[1] Towards midday they began to see strange hills in the distance – abrupt and sheer, fantastically layered and shaped, like cheeses or haystacks. On all sides the sand billowed in vast corrugated waves. Later, they saw a distant green smear of palm trees and, more sobering, a sign on the roadside that warned they were entering a malarial area. Eventually they arrived at Siwa and headed for the camp of the Long Range Desert Group – 'the highwaymen of the desert'[2] – many of whose men sported suitably piratical and ferocious beards. They were welcoming enough but there was no mistaking a degree of cold suspicion towards the press, even on their home ground. The camp included a small airfield and workshops, while the oasis itself was much larger, more fertile and more intriguing than Clifford had expected. He swam in Cleopatra's Pool, explored the ridge above the oasis and, when night fell, moved out into the desert to avoid the clouds of mosquitoes. In the darkness he remembered the stark warning about malaria they had driven past earlier in the day and duly protected himself against the insects 'with a layer of TCP, then a layer of vaseline, and then a layer of my Japanese insect powder'.[3]

Back at RAF Bagush, after the return from Siwa, Clifford sat in the sun typing out a story about the remarkable oasis. The words came easily and quickly, but not fast enough to avoid a blistering suntan. He was already desperate to get back to Cairo, while recognising that he could not hole up there long if he was to retrieve some enthusiasm and purpose. The previous night, after dinner, Cecil Beaton had turned up, enduring his own kind of desert hell, a chronic constipation brought on by the 'excessively public conveniences' in the desert. The 'desert latrines are encased by a transparent flapping sacking,' Beaton wrote later, 'which reaches as high as a man's waist.' It left the enthroned 'sitting like Buddhas oblivious to the world around them' but with precious little privacy.[4] Beaton preferred not to endure such embarrassment, a sensitivity which left him increasingly uncomfortable. For all that, 'the luxury mess of Bagush' appealed to him and he could see 'why certain people would choose to come here for their leave rather than go back to Cairo'.[5] Clifford would have begged to differ: Cairo provided some semblance of civilisation, while the desert was, in all respects, a thing to be endured, and with the potential to break you.

On Clifford's return to Cairo, he was warmed by Lucy's enthusiastic welcome. She had been starved of letters from Moorehead in India and Clifford's arrival helped to dispel her anxiety. That was the sum total of good news. Waiting for Clifford was a telegram from his employers at the *Mail*: they recognised that he would benefit from a change of scene and emphasised that they would love to facilitate such a change but, regrettably, it simply would not be possible for him to leave the Middle East at present, since there was no one else there able to do his job. You'll just have to stick it out, my dear chap.

On 14 May Clifford caught the 7 a.m. train to Alexandria, delighted to find Richard Dimbleby holding pullman seats for Dick Mowrer and him. A hospital ship had been sunk by the Germans and they were on their way to interview the ship's captain. Alexandria had a fresh, clean feel to it, a stark contrast to the gritty dust of Cairo and, moreover, there was the restorative of the city's Union

Bar where he ate a first-class lunch in the company of Christopher Buckley, Kim Mundy and Cecil Beaton. He caught the afternoon train back, his voice nearly gone, 'possibly the result of talking so hard to Dimbleby all day'.[6]

*   *   *   *

Alan Moorehead had been away from Cairo for almost two months. Then, out of the blue, on 17 May 1942, Lucy received a telegram indicating that he would be home the following afternoon. It prompted a momentary panic: 'My hair!' she shrieked. Clifford was amused that 'the whole day revolved round Alan's homecoming' so that lunch was altered 'to suit Alan's palate' and then changed again when it was realised that the BOAC flying boat wouldn't be arriving until 3.30 p.m. When they reached the landing place, baby John Moorehead suddenly wanted to be close to Clifford and 'ran about, tried to fall in the river, wet itself, sat in some mud, and generally kept Lucy on the simmer'.[7] Finally the aircraft arrived and Moorehead emerged, though John failed to recognise him, maybe because of the 'atrocious sun helmet' Moorehead was wearing which 'would baffle anyone' Clifford thought. Later, listening to Moorehead expounding on Indian politics, he regretted even more that he had not travelled there, partly because he was convinced that he would have warmed to the Indian point of view. The Mooreheads and Clifford slipped easily back into the previous *ménage*, although there was no avoiding the fact that Moorehead was deeply tired. On a picnic three days after his return, when they went *en famille* to the barrages outside of Cairo, he immediately fell asleep in the shade of a tree, while Lucy, Alex and John played on the grass nearby.

Both Moorehead and Clifford were bone-tired, longing for some respite. Soon after arriving back in Cairo, Moorehead boycotted a briefing by the Director of Military Information, preferring to enjoy a long siesta. As well as being unprecedentedly tired, he could not rid himself of the longing to see Australia again; if that was not possible, *any* change of scene would do. To complicate matters, his agent in London cabled him on 21 May – the same day that Moorehead had fallen asleep under a tree while Clifford and Lucy played with the baby – indicating that the publishers Hamish Hamilton were interested in a sequel to *Mediterranean Front*. Their enthusiasm was clear: 'length not shorter preferably longer'. A natural and instinctive writer, Moorehead would in normal circumstances have jumped at the invitation, but for once, in his current state of exhaustion, a curt instruction to aim for brevity might have been preferable. At least Hamish Hamilton was prepared to wait for a while, should Moorehead deem it necessary: 'not pressing for book for which willingly wait until spring if you any doubt adequate material.'[8]

Moorehead's return coincided with a renewed surge of interest from London in the war in the Middle East. Clifford sensed the changing mood and wrote a 'deep, well-balanced piece which cancelled itself out neatly and meant absolutely nothing'.[9] It was one of those familiar moments when he was caught between maintaining interest in the present situation and not compromising security. A resumption of meaningful hostilities in the desert – with both sides planning offensives – was clearly imminent, and Clifford's diary was the first victim. A terse entry on Sunday 24 May was to be his last after nearly two years. On that final day he noted his attendance at a briefing from the Polish General Anders, described how he, Lucy and the baby went out of Cairo 'in the cool of the evening' to play in the 'steep, soft sand', and observed the 'formidable' gathering of war correspondents whose steadily increasing numbers were a clear sign that hostilities were about to resume.[10] Sure enough, the balloon went up on 26 May when the Germans attacked the Gazala line and Clifford's diary failed to record it. The diary stayed blank thereafter.

✳   ✳   ✳   ✳

'Of the six *Daily Express* staffers now assigned to the Middle East, only Moorehead had sensed, in that great cliché of 1942, the "turn of the tide".'[11] He was so Cairo-hardened, so desert-burned, that he above all was best placed to recognise that events were on the turn. To the rest, the end of May seemed no different from what had gone before. There was the usual overture to battle – skies thick with aircraft; the mounting rumble of trucks and tanks; the radio traffic – and it prompted the usual exodus of correspondents from Cairo. But the prevailing view was that this was just another short-lived convulsion, not a life or death moment. Clifford, Dimbleby and a number of others set up camp at Gambut, on the coast to the east of Tripoli, in a patch of unremarkable desert between the road and the sea and close to General Ritchie's 8th Army HQ. They chose 'a sheltered cove with some green scrub and palm trees'.[12] As night fell, the Luftwaffe began its 'insomnia raids', calculated to keep the enemy awake through the night, though Clifford slept on, oblivious and undisturbed, curled up in a sandy trench.

Next morning, the prevailing noise was that of lorries moving east, away from the Germans, stirring clouds of dust in their haste to get away. No 'turn of the tide' here, more like more of the same. Later, in the confusion, Clifford found himself perilously close to the enemy: 'I lay on the hot stones, while lizards darted over my bare legs, and peeped over the brow of a little rise at the Nazis.'[13] More worrying still, he feared he was witnessing a full-scale retreat and without doubt the 'soft' transport was in a consummate hurry to get away. The faces of the drivers 'were so caked with dust and sweat that they looked as though they were wearing beauty specialists' mud-packs'.[14] Was the noise getting louder? Undeniably there was an increasing number of vehicles approaching quickly, occasionally shifting direction like a disturbed nest of ants. The camp, too, suddenly became a swirl of activity, with kit being hurled into lorries, and cars speeding to and fro. This was no time to stand and stare – instead, grab your rucksack and bedding and get a bloody move on! By now Clifford could recognise a 'flap', that situation 'when enemy tanks cut loose among soft-skinned, undefended transport',[15] and this was evidently a major flap, a desperate retreat, all discipline and plans discarded, confusion replaced by panic. This was the battle for 'Knightsbridge' and Alex did what he could to follow the battle, skirting cautiously around its edges, squinting into the teeth of another sandstorm.

The fighting here was intense and the dangers considerable. For example, when the sun finally emerged from the whirling sand, its brightness made it very difficult to identify aircraft – Stuka or something more benign? Decisions of this kind were often last minute and instinctive, resulting in a sigh of relief or a desperate dive into a trench. At one point Christopher Buckley, who had now teamed up with Richard McMillan, found himself 'facing the Afrika Korps alone!'[16] The two of them drew to a halt on a slight rise alongside a crashed Hurricane and watched with dismay the 'volcano of smoke and fury' below them as the enemy's guns directed their fire on the fort of Bir Hacheim. Buckley trained his binoculars on the enemy tanks, trying to work out their next move. 'They've started up again,' he said, 'Now they're turning. They're turning – and they're going back the way they came.' It was a day of blistering heat, the midday sun beating down so hard that the metal of the tanks became 'almost too hot to touch'.[17]

Meanwhile Alex Clifford found himself slowly picking his way through minefields in a fog of dust and smoke, almost as thick as a sea fret. He was confident that Rommel's attack would eventually peter out, but it troubled him that the British were showing so little initiative: only once in three weeks, he estimated, had they stirred themselves and tried to make things happen. Information seemed in short supply too and it was discouraging to realise that he 'knew more about what was going on than did Army HQ'.[18] Just as worrying was the fact that the German prisoners that Clifford met seemed 'self-assured and almost pitying in their condescension'.[19]

By now Clifford and Moorehead were reunited, and were sheltering with three American correspondents amongst a nest of rocks at El Adem, south of Tobruk. They ate one of Kim Mundy's hot curries ('curried bully and a special treat, *fried* potatoes'),[20] drank whisky and talked far into the night, before falling asleep in a hole so deep it felt like a tomb. They were woken by an explosion from a cache of ammunition triggered by the storm, specifically, the *khamseen's* 'electrical properties'. Columns of fire lit the sky and they surmised that they were caused by burning lorries from the Indian division which had blundered into their own minefield. Suddenly things turned distinctly nasty and the correspondents were obliged to pack in a hurry – it took just seven minutes – before fleeing the enemy advance. It proved a truly terrible day: they crashed into a derelict tank, then a front-line cemetery, grinding a gravestone beneath their wheels. The American reporter, Frank Gervasi, searched the ground on his hands and knees and realised with horror that he was holding the wooden upright of a cross. More broken wooden crosses lay under their wheels and they could hear the truck behind them splintering other graves. The disturbed human remains did not bear contemplation, but at least they had avoided careering blindly into a minefield and adding to the broken bodies.

It had been a day they would not wish to repeat. They unrolled their bedding and slept fully clothed, each taking one hour's watch. Such caution spoke volumes: it was becoming transparently clear that the Gazala line could not hold, despite the stand made in this 'grimmest battle in desert history'.[21] Tobruk had been bombed without cease and when Moorehead drove around the city for the last time, he was appalled at its ruined state. It finally fell to the Germans on 21 June. It was a moment of despair for those who had followed the ebb and flow of the desert war over the years. Alex Clifford thought the loss was the lowest of many low points, the bitterest moment he had known in the desert. Richard Dimbleby was close to tears, welling up at the thought of so much sacrifice for so little gain.

By 25 June, Clifford had been in the desert for a month, reduced to washing his clothes in the sea. Alan Moorehead had already decided to make his way back to Cairo, thinking that such urgency would give him the best chance of fooling the censors and getting the news of the defeat out to the world. He found a city where the proximity of the Germans was becoming more alarming by the day. The abandoned Gazala line had been all of 400 miles away, but now the city seemed well within Rommel's grasp. It was just three days after the loss of Tobruk that Alaric Jacob, who had replaced Alan at the front, heard the word 'Alamein' mentioned for the first time, by a staff officer who confided that it was 'where we are going to fall back to, if we have to'. Jacob expressed astonishment at Alamein's proximity to Alexandria. 'Sixty miles away, old boy,' agreed the staff officer.[22]

When Tobruk fell, the reaction amongst Cairo's military chiefs was to begin burning files of sensitive documents. Bonfires fed by secretaries and soldiers threw up ashy spirals of official typescript which fluttered over the hitherto tranquil gardens of government buildings, blown on the breeze. Lucy Moorehead was handed a box of matches and instructed to burn Auchinleck's correspondence with the prime minister and the War Cabinet. The first day of July was dubbed 'Ash Wednesday' to mark the time when the city's military and diplomatic quarter was thick with smoke. Cairo's peanut vendors, meanwhile, seized the opportunity to use those half-burnt secrets to wrap their cones of peanuts.

The retreat towards Alexandria began, long trails of dispirited, bitter men kicking up a tunnel of dust as they trudged east. 'Transport was to be seen nose-to-tail crawling along four deep', all chaotically mixed up – tanks, trucks, bulldozers, guns.[23] Clifford was spared having to march at least, but vehicles in the desert had their drawbacks too, brought home when he and Richard McMillan were stranded, miles from anywhere, with a leaking radiator. They tried plugging the hole with candle grease and chewing gum, with no luck, before getting a tow to the coast.

When he finally reached Cairo, Clifford struggled with how best to represent the unfolding disaster to his readers back in Britain. He 'used to sit at (his) typewriter trying desperately to write something that would be neither too pessimistic nor too optimistic, and would at the same time get past the censor'.[24] Across the city, there was widespread, mounting anxiety. Cecil Beaton overheard one of the secretaries at HQ saying, 'Oh, I can't get a thrill out of the desert any longer. It's always a case of someone going backwards or forwards.'[25] In truth, by now the movement was all backwards. On 28 June Beaton noted in his diary that 'German radio announced that their armies would be in Alexandria on the 6th and in Cairo by the 9th'.[26] The following day, the Germans reported they had taken Mersa Matruh. There were plans to shift GHQ to Gaza, and although the ambassador, Sir Miles Lampson, 'in a conspicuous demonstration of *sang froid*',[27] sought to quash the rumours by having the embassy railings painted, as if everything in the garden was forever England, people still worried that all was lost.

On the last day of June 1942 Christopher Buckley and Moorehead left Cairo on the desert road once more, accompanied this time by Russell Hill. They met an ominous tide of traffic going the other way, vast numbers of lorries in a long line, nose to tail. The three correspondents argued about whether continuing against the flow was the wisest course of action; Moorehead was convinced that it would be madness to continue, since they could all too easily get cut off. Buckley staunchly backed him, and Hill accepted the majority view. So they turned off on a side road towards Alexandria. The city had an ominous quiet, the streets deserted because of the 8 p.m. curfew and its defences seemingly unmanned. Obtaining rooms in the Cecil Hotel was disconcertingly easy. That night Moorehead lay awake, troubled about the prospects of imminent heavy air raids on Cairo and whether Lucy and John were safe.

The next morning Buckley, Moorehead and Hill drove back along the delta road, in a landscape of canals, dark, fertile soil and villages of mud-hut dwellings, the three of them 'perched on the roof of the truck like three strange birds on a housetop'.[28] Back at GHQ in Cairo they found that the 'Flap' had worsened and the thoughts of many had progressed from burning papers to getting the hell out of Egypt. Moorehead and Clifford eventually prevailed upon Lucy to leave on the special evacuee train to Palestine, taking baby John with her. This despite the fact that the Mooreheads had sworn never to do such a thing, heeding the wise counsel given them years before by a member of the Dutch government: 'Never, never be a refugee,' he had said. 'It's always better to stay where you are.'[29]

Having now seen what bombing could do to a city, Moorehead had changed his mind about staying put and phlegmatically seeing the thing through. In all probability the British hold on the city would soon be over – why, the city's taxi drivers had a new and pointed joke, 'Today I drive you to Groppi's – tomorrow you drive me!'[30]

So, after some hurried packing, the Mooreheads and Alex Clifford rushed to the station where the flap seemed greater than ever – bribes being offered, 'take no prisoner' scrambles for any vacant compartments and seats, people tripping headlong over each other and their luggage, oaths, arguments and tears. Lucy busied herself with the clutter of chamber-pots, nappies and food, her heart in turmoil, but determined to maintain a quiet dignity. The three-day journey to Jerusalem was an ordeal. An air raid forced them to abandon the train temporarily, exchanging the carriage for a vigil in the sand, the passengers standing directly in unforgiving sunlight, with nothing to see but the train and the desert stretching away to a shimmering horizon. Later, at a Customs post, there was an attempted suicide by a Czech Jew who was standing next to Lucy. Told that his passport was invalid, he reacted by slashing his wrists, spilling blood over baby John.

Moorehead, back at Cairo Central and oblivious to the unpleasantness that lay ahead for his family, simply felt relieved that they were on their way to safety. He turned to Clifford standing beside him on the platform, smiled as the train pulled out of the station, and suggested dinner. Both men, as they strolled down the station platform, could be forgiven for harking nostalgically back to the days before the Durban flying boat had brought Lucy to Cairo; but in truth they knew that circumstances were much changed, and so, in their hearts, were they.

*   *   *   *

Early in July 1942, Christopher Buckley wrote a piece in the *Telegraph*[31] which explained the significance of the forthcoming battle in the Middle East. Under the headline 'Main Battle Joined in Egypt Bottleneck', he described the 'grim, desperate race against time with tired men on either side struggling to get the last ounce of effort and endurance out of themselves and their machines'. The battle which would decide the fate of the Middle East began at 6 a.m. at El Alamein, 60 miles from Alexandria. Buckley hammered the dispatch out, crouched over his typewriter during a brief stop amongst sand dunes and roadside scrub, with bombers prowling overhead, a constant stream of aircraft attacking the German supply lines.

Moorehead and Clifford would soon join Buckley back at the front, travelling by train, a journey which brought back memories for Moorehead of trips he had taken to Lérida during the Spanish Civil War. It seemed that the critical moment had come at last and strangely Clifford, the natural pessimist, was one of

Digging Slit Trenches: El Dab'a, Western Desert, Ivor Beddoes. (IWM, LD 1698)

Afternoon at the Gezira Club, Cairo, Edward Ardizzone. (IWM, LD 2592)

Entering Tobruk, 1942, Edward Bainbridge Copnall. (IWM, LD 5738)

Aid to Russia: Trucks on the Road to Teheran Crossing the Paitak Pass, Edward Bawden. (IWM, LD 4397)

Opposite top: *The Retreat of the British Armoured Brigade in Greece, 1941*, H. Johns. (IWM, LD 3353)

Opposite bottom: *Halfaya Pass*, Jack Craddock. (IWM, LD 3403)

Troops and Civilians Looting in the Town of Reggio, Italy: on the day of its occupation, 3rd September 1943, Edward Ardizzone. (IWM, LD 3453)

Opposite top: *Alice Delysia Gives a Concert Aboard a Fighting-French Warship*, Anthony Gross. (IWM, LD 2331)

Opposite bottom: *The Black Watch Landing in Sicily at Red Beach*, Ian Eadie. (IWM, LD 3807)

British Infantry Greeted by the Populace of Torre Annunziata, Bay of Naples, Italy, 1943, Tom White. (IWM, LD 3763)

Once Proud City – Cologne 1945, William Warden. (IWM, LD 5972)

Human Laundry – Belsen 1945, Doris Zinkeisen. (IWM, LD 5468)

the few who could see a successful outcome. Certainly, for the time being at least, the Germans were being held at Alamein, gratifying the correspondents since Alexandria was now close to the front and it proved possible to drive out there in the morning and return to Alexandria at the day's end. It made the Alamein line the answer to a reporter's prayer. The drawback was that the morning jaunt to the front could be dangerous, not least when they were subjected to sudden Stuka attacks from a clear blue sky. These would provoke Kim Mundy to bellow 'Scram!' and the three of them would simultaneously dive for cover into a roadside ditch. At other times, they would stand on the truck to get a grandstand view of how the offensive was progressing. Their campsite by the sea was an idyllic spot, some 15 miles east of the line and near the 86km sign on the road to Alexandria. They swam naked, soothed by the beauty of white sand and soft waves reflecting the sun's glare; then they would eat supper, yet another stew in all probability, while the sand dunes loomed white, lit by a ghostly moon. Finally they would talk into the night, cloaked by the pitch-black desert night. It would be light at 6 a.m., but it was the arrival of the flies which prompted them to get up. The morning light would be golden, the birds would be stirring, and each of the camp beds lined up by the truck would be drenched in a heavy dew. Moorehead would shave, using the reflection in the lorry's rear-view mirror. The daily routine would rarely change: eggs for breakfast, then the first argument of the day about plans for the hours ahead, Kim Mundy pleading with them to make up their minds. The mail would usually arrive around 7.30 a.m., always an anxious moment when some correspondents might well open 'their cables to announce that they had to go to Peru or Moscow'.[32] Half an hour afterwards they would have departed, spirited away by some editorial desk or other, and their presence forgotten within the hour.

Early on the morning of 5 August, the prime minister visited the Alamein front. He endured an unpleasant breakfast in oppressive heat, sitting in 'what looked like a wire cage full of flies'.[33] Subsequently, he and General Auchinleck conferred in a caravan whose lack of air was made worse by Churchill's glowering, disapproving presence and the thick clouds of cigar smoke he generated. The RAF and Shepheards Hotel collaborated to produce a sumptuous lunch which improved the prime minister's mood, and he ate on the beach at Bourg el Arab off a crisp white tablecloth and with silver cutlery reflecting the sun. Soon after, Auchinleck was replaced by General Alexander, while Montgomery took command in the field.

The battle halted the seemingly irresistible German advance and Moorehead thought the situation had become secure enough for Lucy and the baby to return from Palestine. Both he and Clifford were now desperate for some rest and relief from the treadmill of desert conflict. To Clifford, it was like 'a sort of hangover'[34] in which he suffered exhaustion and felt both run down and utterly dispirited. It

Winston Churchill at Alamein in the Western Desert, 1942. (IWM, E15299)

also left him unsure of what made a news story work. Moorehead was similarly troubled, finding it all too depressingly familiar to the extent that he felt he knew each grain of desert sand. By midsummer 1942 they had both reached the point where continuing as they were was not an option. Moorehead cabled Arthur Christiansen at the *Express* and successfully negotiated a break. The Mooreheads would leave for the United States in August, while Alex Clifford would be flying home in mid-August by flying boat, the route a circuitous one via Khartoum, Lagos and Lisbon. Ah, Europe! In the neutral Portuguese capital he was amused to find himself having lunch next to a young German he had known not so long ago in Berlin. How different they were, Atlantic Portugal and Mediterranean Egypt! Lisbon was delightfully refreshing: the soft light, its benign temperatures, the fresh clarity of the air, the sense of lazy neutrality. There were memories too of Spain: he took in a bullfight and drank glasses of dry, chilled sherry, the first taste of which transported him back to a hotel bar in Saragossa years ago and the married marquesa pressed tight against his side.

Eventually, the flying boat arrived in Ireland, its blinds drawn down on the promenade deck to prevent passengers from observing anything which might be deemed secret or sensitive. He was undeniably in a different kind of Europe from sleepy Lisbon. Once out of the plane, England looked grey, gloomy and wet, and soon Clifford began to miss the glare and warmth of Cairo.

* * * *

Only Christopher Buckley of the Trio was in Egypt at the critical moment. On 19 August 1942, *The Daily Telegraph* reported a series of significant changes in the Middle East: General Alexander was to replace General Auchinleck ('whose future post is not named'), with Lt General Montgomery taking charge of 8th Army. The paper reported that 'Strafer' Gott would have been named as commander had he not been killed in an air crash. With the 'turn of the tide' came a different hand at the helm. Buckley watched developments with a wary eye, observing the abrasive energy of the new commander whose first act was to ditch all Auchinleck's plans for an orderly withdrawal – 'Trenches? You won't be needing those I can tell you!' There were those who found the action distasteful and disrespectful to his predecessors: 'It was petty, insensitive and grossly insulting,'[35] but, without doubt, it made clear that things would be done differently from now on.

NOTES

1   Clifford, p.239.

2   Beaton, p.74.

3   Clifford papers (16727), IWM, file AGC/1/2, diary entry for 9 May 1942.

4   Beaton, p.75.

5   Ibid., p.80.

6   Clifford papers (16727), IWM, file AGC/1/2, diary entry for 14 May 1942.

7   Ibid., diary entry for 18 May 1942.

8   Moorehead papers, NLA, MS 5654. By January 1942 Hamilton had sold upwards of 7,000 copies of *Mediterranean Front* and were printing a further 3,000. Two consignments of the book sent to Cairo were presumed sunk, according to a letter of 17 June 1942 to Moorehead from his agent.

9   Clifford papers (16727), IWM, AGC/1/2, diary entry for 20 May 1942.

10   Ibid., diary entry for 24 May 1942.

11   Collier, p.131.

12   (Richard) Dimbleby, p.267.

13   Clifford, p.248.

14   Ibid., p.249.

15   Ibid., p.258.

16   *Rendezvous with Rommel* by Richard McMillan, p.58.

17   (Richard) Dimbleby, p.269.

18   Clifford, p.255.

19   Ibid., p.250.

20   Gervasi, p.391.

21   (Richard) Dimbleby, p.272.

22   Jacob, p.192.

23   *Operation Victory* by Major-General Sir Francis de Guingand, pp.123–4.

24   Clifford, p.284.

25   Beaton, p.89.

26   *The Years Between: Diaries 1939–1944* by Cecil Beaton, p.183.

27   *Cairo in the War* by Artemis Cooper, p.196.

28   *A Year of Battle*, op. cit., p.216.

29   Ibid., p.217.

30   Cooper, p.196.

31   *The Daily Telegraph*, 2 July 1942.

32   *A Year of Battle*, op. cit., p.227.

33   Cooper, p.199.

34   Clifford papers (16727), IWM, file AGC/2/1/7, letter of 30 June 1942 to his mother.

35   Cooper, p.213.

13. From Suez to Syracuse

The liner *Zola* lies in the port of Suez. It is August 1942 and Alan Moorehead is standing at the ship's rail looking down on the lines of German prisoners on the quayside below. It is another hot North African day and, although on deck there is a gentle breeze off the sea, on the dockside the air feels stifling, as if it has been breathed many times before. The desert-hardened Germans, caked in dust and in shabby green-grey uniforms, show little sign of being discomforted by captivity; they do not even look defeated. Their marching sets the gangplank swinging and they are whistling and singing as if they own the ship and do not anticipate being POWs for long. The *Zola*'s sweat-stained British crew are watchful, acutely conscious that the Germans outnumber them. Moorehead watches the third mate spit into the oil-streaked sea, then turn towards him. 'More trouble,' the mate says. 'I expect we'll be having more trouble with these bastards.'[1]

The 'trouble' had been a prisoners' mutiny on *Zola*'s previous trip. It had been quelled eventually, but it had been disturbing enough to make the ship's crew wary, on a constant lookout for a further riot. The pitiless heat of the Red Sea put paid to that possibility. It was hot enough to provoke 'red spots in front of your eyes in the daytime'.[2] Under a ferocious sun, no one wanted to move, let alone mutiny. Initially, when the Germans had been confined below decks, many had succumbed to heatstroke and it soon became clear that there was no alternative but to allow them up on deck at night. Even there, or in the upper deck cabin which the Mooreheads occupied, the heat made sleeping very difficult.

As *Zola* trended south, Moorehead increasingly felt that he had embarked on 'a voyage of personal discovery'.[3] For almost three years his focus each day had been the constantly changing battle plans of a string of here-today, gone-tomorrow generals, the present strength and intentions of the enemy, the state of military hardware and morale, and politics – largely in London or GHQ Cairo. Now his mind was free to think on other things, not least the direction and purpose of his

'The novelty of holding baby John in his arms.' (John Moorehead)

own life. What is to become of me and mine? What made that harder was that his memories of England were indubitably hazy; after all, it had been some five years since he had last thought of London as his home. So, with the ship sailing away from Egypt, Alan savoured the novelty of holding baby John in his arms as the deck moved beneath his feet and he watched the flying fish chasing the waves, or lying idly back in a deckchair watching the sun unhurriedly crossing the sky, or *Zola* carving a path through the sea, while he allowed himself to contemplate a future quite different from the immediate past.

There was a fresher feel to the weather once *Zola* entered the Indian Ocean and, by the time they reached Durban, a cold winter had arrived, with soft rain falling. From South Africa, they sailed across the Atlantic, arriving in Halifax, Nova Scotia in a dense, unwelcoming fog. Momentarily, just before they docked, the fog had lifted, revealing a thin sun and a convoy bound for England. Then the fog closed in again, as quickly as it had arrived. Once *Zola* had tied up, the Mooreheads took the train to New York, arriving there towards the end of September 1942.

* * * *

On the morning of 23 October 1942 Montgomery briefed the correspondents about the desert battle to come, but not before an officer had alerted Christopher Buckley and the rest: 'The General does not smoke; please put out pipes and cigarettes.'[4] Monty was characteristically bullish – 'We will proceed to hit Rommel for six out of North Africa' – while the press exchanged significant glances. Buckley, like the rest of the reporters in the room, wondered quite what the War Office had unleashed on them, on 8th Army, and, of course, on Rommel. Was it plain arrogance or was this spiky egoist capable of breathing life back into the North African campaign? Heads were shaken, cautious words scribbled down in notebooks, shoulders were shrugged. But there was no mistaking this diminutive general's self-confidence and poise. As the press left the marquee, he had a parting shot: 'You can go anywhere you want in the battle. When I have something more to tell you, I'll call you again.'

Montgomery's briefing triggered a flurry of hasty arrangements amongst the press, including the teaming-up of Christopher Buckley with Richard McMillan and the Australian reporter, Jack Hetherington.[5] They were to follow the 51st Division into action. The fighting around Alamein in the coming days would be chaotic and confusing to the extent that the correspondents had little sense of the bigger picture. Indeed, even the highly respected Buckley, 'versed in every campaign from Stonewall Jackson to the Dardanelles', could be heard complaining at the daily press conferences, 'Can *anyone* give me the tactical answer?'[6] Nevertheless, by 4 November, Buckley's front-line report described

Christopher Buckley, with Richard McMillan (centre) and Doon Campbell (left), in Italy, January 1944. (Anthony Grey)

infantry, with their bayonets fixed, moving steadfastly through fields of mines and booby traps towards the German lines.[7] A pale moon glimmered on a rocky, desolate landscape which was lit more brightly by the occasional flashes of aircraft flares and gunfire. Three days later, he was able to report that, according to Montgomery, 'the Boche is completely finished'.[8] In Cairo, the cathedral bells heralded the victory and, for the first time since the war had begun, bells were rung in churches across England too.

Christopher Buckley mulled over the long desert road he had travelled – the Stuka attack at 'Knightsbridge', Christmas at Benghazi, the yo-yo campaign along the Libyan coast, the tasteless food, the biting cold, the violent desert storms;

the mines buried in the sand – and wondered if everything really was about to change. How long would it be before he set foot on European soil again, with victory finally in sight? One thing was certain: only he of the Trio would be there at Montgomery's desert headquarters, in early November, to hear the General Officer Commanding 8th Army address a group of war correspondents in that reedy voice with those quirky rolling 'r's', claiming a victory that was both complete and absolute.

*   *   *   *

At the critical moment, when the tide finally turned, Moorehead was still in New York, while Alex Clifford was at sea, en route from Glasgow to the west coast of Africa. Before he left, Clifford had broadcast for the BBC in German, Swedish, English, Spanish and French, and he would happily have offered Italian and Dutch too, had they been required. In many ways, Cairo and the desert were little changed when Clifford finally returned, although perhaps the city was even more frantic, wild and expensive. Nearer to the battlefield, the dangers remained much the same: the minefields were still there and so too the tattered corpses rigged up as booby traps. Occasionally there were sights which were different enough for Clifford to log them in his notebook: for example, when he saw some enemy graffiti on a white wall: 'Englishmen, may your stay here be short and unhappy.'[9] For the most part, though, what lay ahead was familiar: '… there was the long pursuit – the countless miles through a desert that froze you, and drenched you, and blinded you with sandstorms, and parched you, and bogged you and sometimes gave you a miraculous carpet of wild flowers to walk on'.[10]

*   *   *   *

On 22 December 1942, Arthur Christiansen wrote to Alan Moorehead, informing him that, since the Australian had been appointed chief correspondent in Africa, he would expect him to make 'on-the-spot decisions when it is not easy to consult Foley or myself'. His letter went on to list the eight reporters at Moorehead's disposal.[11] 'I know,' Christiansen wrote, 'that you can count on the co-operation of all these men in any emergency.' The American interlude was demonstrably over. Moorehead's journey back to the UK involved taking a train from New York's Grand Central Station to Montreal, then flying by Liberator to Scotland, a trip which took ten hours and involved a hazardous take-off from an ice-strewn runway. Scotland seemed so gentle, green and soft to a man with desert grit in his mind's eye. He took an all night train down to London, enjoying the luxury of having his own cabin, with hot water, and morning tea brought to him. Home at last! It struck him powerfully that nowhere else had anything like his adopted country's 'efficiency ... courtesy and precision'.[12] Its weather had its drawbacks, though: a fog blanketed the capital, giving it a spectral feel; buses and taxis emerged from the grey and disappeared as if they had been swallowed. It was so bad that night that Moorehead felt obliged to walk ahead with a torch to help the taxi driver keep his cab on the road.

Moorehead spent Christmas in Ireland, contemplating a winter voyage to North Africa in the corvette *Exe*, due to sail from Londonderry. *Exe* did not impress, being 'the ugliest and most uncomfortable ship I ever expect to sail in'.[13] For all that, he was to become a staunch defender of the ship, valuing 'her skill, her manners, (and) her company'. She sailed on Christmas Day, but reports of U-boat activity resulted in an emergency recall to port. Moorehead avoided a return by crossing from *Exe* to the destroyer *Loyal* by means of a complex system of ropes, over a quarter of a mile of murky ocean. There was a high sea running too, while the ropes burned his fingers ('removing most of the fingerprints' as he put it), and the crew members were pessimistic – the manoeuvre transporting him from ship to ship was 'bloody well impossible' was a typical judgement.[14] To Moorehead's untrained eye the waves seemed enormous and he feared the worst. He might actually succeed against the odds and get across, he thought, but in the process he might lose all his precious war correspondent's gear, acquired from lessons learned over many months. There was the 'flat metal typewriter bought in Macy's in New York that winter, a soft cowhide kitbag made in the native quarter in Cairo and stuffed with such things as shirts and a large silver whisky-flask, a featherweight metal stretcher bed and fleece-lined canvas sleeping bag just bought in Fortnum and Mason's'.[15] Clinging on desperately to the rope and with spray lashing his face, he slowly inched his way across, conscious that the gap between the two vessels seemed to be growing wider, rather than diminishing. Above the wind's roar, he heard a voice bellowing through a megaphone: it was the captain of the *Loyal*, evidently relishing the newspaperman's lubberly discomfort. 'I don't see you taking any notes!' he yelled from the bridge.[16] Moorehead was unamused by the skipper's frivolity, but he smiled with relief when he finally reached the opposite deck, his kit thoroughly soaked and the cowhide bag from Cairo almost lost forever below the waves. A stiff whisky was enough to restore his good humour.

Loyal sailed fast, reaching Algiers in the first week of 1943. Dry land it wasn't; nor did it feel like Africa. Instead, the city was wet and cold, suffering from a spell of wild weather, including torrential rain. Moorehead's hotel was gloomy and down-at-heel, while the prevailing atmosphere in the city was one of deep suspicion. It did not take him long to develop a hatred of the place. Philip Jordan of the *News Chronicle* felt the same way, describing Algiers as 'the sewer of the world'.[17] The weather remained grim throughout January, an unforgiving wind flinging rain against dreary windows. The smell of drains was nauseating and permanent. The city's politics stank too: Philip Jordan was convinced that it was the Vichy, pro-German French who held power, while A.B. Austin of the *Daily Herald* was of the same opinion: 'I wondered what would happen if I told some of my friends at the front that things they were supposed to be fighting to abolish were still flourishing in Algiers.'[18]

Press conferences in Algiers were somehow in keeping with the pervading gloom. They were held in a long narrow room with two rows of desks – 'like a grown-up schoolroom' Austin thought – and to a format which scarcely wavered. On the wall at one end of the room was a drawing-pinned map of the front. In front of it, an officer would slowly read out an official communiqué, while a second then added detail which was both predictable and dull, mundane footnotes explaining perhaps that such-and-such a place was a mountain, or a village; or that the fighting had been 'hard'; or the weather 'a hindrance'.[19] Scarcely the stuff of headlines or human stories. Meanwhile the uniformed correspondents would type busily, only too aware that the news was being managed for them, but seeing no alternative. A.B. Austin thought, 'It was like standing far back and watching the battle reflected in a distorting mirror'.[20] The intention was to render the position reassuring, the news palatable. Thus the press was told that 'one can do nothing in these narrow waters without (the) RAF', or that the British and Americans were 'welded together into one happy family', and that there was 'no difference between the US or Britain'.[21]

The unsatisfactory nature of press briefings made expeditions to the front both attractive and necessary, although such trips had their associated problems. A.B. Austin summed up the war correspondent's dilemma thus: 'whether to place himself as far forward as possible with the front line troops where the news is freshest but transmitting it a problem; or to maintain constant contact with his communications head'.[22] Imagine, though, the sheer pleasure of exchanging the oppressive briefing room for the open road! An hour's drive on a mid-January late afternoon took Moorehead through a sunlit green valley to the hills above Tunis. There were peasants ploughing in the fields, preparing the ground before sowing the winter crop, while cattle browsed beneath eucalyptus trees. Alan stood on the car's front seat, his head emerging through the roof, on the lookout for enemy aircraft. There were none, and instead he found himself soothed by the tranquil, green farmland.

There were other welcome escapes from Algiers: on 22 January Moorehead flew to Casablanca to cover 'the unconditional surrender conference' between Churchill and Roosevelt.[23] Soon afterwards, he and Philip Jordan drove the 250 miles east to Constantine. Away from the coast, spring seemed close and, on the roadside, the almond blossom was 'like smoke on a windless day'.[24] It was a relief to be on the move again, even though Jordan was quiet, his mind racing with alternative titles for the book he was working on, based on his diary. A reporter for the *News Chronicle*, Philip Jordan was someone else with experience of the Spanish Civil War. He talked more the following day as they motored further east, into Tunisia. The drive was a beautiful one, over spectacular mountains at one point, and for once it was warm and the earth smelled of a change in the seasons. At one point, they saw three storks, one nesting high on a chimney pot, and more the next day, as well as some Luftwaffe Ju88s. The storks 'were beautiful and their wings as steady as those of aeroplanes'.[25]

As they drove, Moorehead and Jordan talked enthusiastically about their ideal newspaper where advertising would be banned, salaries small and all the editorial staff would be shareholders. Talent and principles would be the determining factor in recruitment. 'We want a technical editor with no policy, and a proprietor with no policy. We want whoever owns the paper to say that all news is to be treated according to its real value in terms of a belief in justice, and all the other "rights of man".'[26] Both men were painfully aware that neither of their present employers fitted such a model. There was a certain irony too in the fact that the following day Moorehead received a cable from Arthur Christiansen offering him a salary rise.

They were intent on reaching Tripoli, but initially they headed south in the direction of Tebessa. The desert seemed ever closer, the air colder and drier, and the landscape increasingly barren. Tebessa though proved to be glorious, with its city walls, Roman ruins, pinewoods and golden stone. The road to the American army headquarters outside the town took them through a deep gorge of rocks which had the feel of bandit country.

They left at nine the next morning, 4 February, in two jeeps, having checked out how safe the road ahead was likely to be. They knew all too well the dangers of the open road – minefields, enemy patrols, Luftwaffe sweeps – recognising that 'there would be far less correspondents in German camps if more had taken this precaution'.[27] At first they travelled through dull tree-strewn country whose combination of deserted road and low hills left them vulnerable to patrols of enemy fighter aircraft. Soon the hills were replaced by a barrier of high mountains which they laboriously climbed, hairpin by hairpin. At one point, they drove past a sign that warned them to 'watch out for enemy aircraft'. Jordan's American driver was unimpressed, yelling, 'Are you serious, darling?' as they roared past in a flurry of dust. They approached the desert, 'not true desert yet, for it was covered with camel thorn, and very lovely in the benign sun of midday,' and then got lost in a maze of cactus. They drove past sheep and goats grazing, through a sparse and barren landscape, into more mountains of contorted and chaotic stone. It took all day to reach the idyllic oasis of Tozeur, travelling without maps and relying on instinct to find the way, and when they arrived at dusk the place struck them as both biblical and romantic, huddled beneath a huge minaret, with a mist hanging over the low roofs, and clouds of white smoke from numerous cooking fires drifting into the stillness of the evening. Tozeur was not just romantic, but a strategic milestone: 'the virtual junction of the 1st and 8th Armies', the point where the eastbound and westbound Allied armies met. 'Tonight,' wrote Jordan, 'I dined with a man who has come overland from Cairo.'[28]

All too soon, on 6 February, winter returned, with rain and a cutting wind. The cold was ferocious as they set out on the return to Tebessa – Jordan, cocooned in a balaclava and face mask, thought it colder than Moscow – and both men were frozen stiff. An apologetic, limp sun finally appeared as they entered the mountains, but by the time they reached journey's end, they were numb with cold and exhaustion. The following day, the two of them went their separate ways – Moorehead turning for Algiers in response to another cable from Arthur Christiansen, while Philip Jordan set off alone for Constantine, driving 859km in just two days. It took Moorehead five days to reach Algiers where, instead of the freedom of the open road, he was obliged to resume a life of interviews and cocktail parties – at the Agricole, for example, where correspondents and top brass mingled in a ritual dance of champagne flutes and canapés, uniforms and medals, questions and obfuscation, and the frustrated muttering of the press.

Anywhere but Algiers! If such a confined existence was not enough there was the city's persistently evil weather, more driving rain, coupled with gales and a bone-aching cold. What a relief then when Moorehead was summoned back to London. He flew home on 24 February, via Gibraltar, returning to a grey and gloomy capital still in the grip of winter. Nonetheless, there were heart-warming compensations: lunch or dinner at the Ivy, perhaps, or the Savoy or Waldorf, with David Woodward or Charles Foley, or the minister for information Brendan Bracken, perhaps, or Philip Jordan, Osbert Lancaster and John Strachey. It was a world away from scratch lunches in the roadside dust of Libya. Back now in the centre of things, Moorehead found himself thinking hard about what his future might hold. He no longer felt the carefree bravado which characterised the early part of his war. Indeed he now thought that being a war correspondent was a 'fickle irresponsible job' – so much so that he was contemplating joining up. He wrote to Lucy who was still in the United States: 'If I joined the Army I would have at least four months' training in England when I could see you and John fairly constantly … I want the quality of inevitability in my life.'[29] Three days after his arrival in London, he was summoned to meet Lord Beaverbrook at the *Express* owner's house, Cherkley Court, near Leatherhead. They argued throughout the weekend, but it was clear that Beaverbrook held him in the highest regard: 'He would, I think, really like to see me in a place of some power after the war,' Alan noted, observing that the two of them might be politically in opposite camps – 'He's Right. I am Left. I will not sell out and he cannot.' Beaverbrook, however, knew that Moorehead was too precious a commodity to be allowed to leave easily, and made clear to his star reporter that he 'would be a damn fool' if he joined the army.[30]

Moorehead's leave in England was all too short – less than two weeks – and he flew back, via Lisbon and Gibraltar, in the company of Philip Jordan. In Gibraltar, they dined with the governor, and the left-sympathising Jordan was particularly affronted to find that one of the other guests was Sir Samuel Hoare (a former appeaser who had been bundled off to Madrid as British Ambassador). It quite spoiled Philip Jordan's dinner. Later, he and Moorehead were shown around the Rock's defence system, miles of complex tunnels bored deep into the limestone. In Algiers, the weather was unchanged, but at least the military situation showed signs of improvement, with the Americans slowly advancing, and by the beginning of April, Moorehead was in Thibar, closing in on the city of Tunis, warmed at last by the tangible signs of spring through the northern valleys, as well as the prospect of an enemy in retreat.

*   *   *   *

All three members of the Trio were now in North Africa. While Moorehead was in the north-west of the continent and heading east, both Alex Clifford and Chris Buckley were with the 8th Army, following Montgomery's advance west on Tripoli through the Libyan Desert. By Christmas Eve 1942 Clifford was in Nufilia, Tripoli, contemplating the prospect of yet another uncertain, strange Christmas: 'possibly we shall have a roof, but most likely not'.[31] On Christmas Day that year Clifford stood with others 'in rows on a barren hillside singing carols'.[32] Into the new year, he found that the desert had not lost its capacity to surprise: camping in the fields beyond Sirte, halfway between Benghazi and Tripoli, Clifford saw swathes of beautiful flowers so colourful, scented and rich, that he frequently gathered enough in the evening to put in empty cans to give the dinner table just a hint of old-fashioned elegance.

Through the spring of 1943 the advancing correspondents became increasingly short of basic supplies of all kinds, including paper. Perhaps the one thing that had yet to run out was Clifford's luck: one hot afternoon, he had stripped naked to wash off the caked desert dust, and sat down in the sun to dry off and write. Suitable subject matter for the *Daily Mail* reader? Perhaps the poor quality of British bacon compared to the Americans'? Or the urgent need for a tasty substitute for bully beef? Or the perpetual curse of these pesky desert flies? He slid a precious sheet of paper into his typewriter and, as the first sentence began to emerge, so did the Messerschmitts roaring in fast and low over the sand. Without the camouflage effect of his khaki uniform, Clifford was as visible as a fly on a white wall, and in an instant it dawned on him that 'the pilots must see me clearly as a conspicuous pink figure bounding across the countryside'.[33] The gunfire missed, ploughing up channels of sand instead of pink war reporter, and the aircraft thundered away, leaving Clifford to still his thumping heart and write the next sentence. On reflection, it seemed wiser to wait until he had dressed, glad of his uniform's sand-coloured anonymity, before hitting the next key on the battered typewriter.

The advance towards Tripoli became a headlong pursuit, but Clifford could not dispel his unease at the contrast between the rural location, with its 'fair grassy slopes and little pockets of olive trees and here and there an almond tree just bursting into miraculous blossom' and the dismembered corpses scattered amongst the trees. At one point, he 'nearly trod on a German who was stretched on his back with a stomach wound, looking round with staring eyes and calling deliriously for water'. Despite the sight of Tripoli in the near distance, Clifford was deeply troubled, so much so that he would remember that he had never 'hated war so much as I did that afternoon'. Tripoli eventually fell on 26 January 1943 and Christopher Buckley, following close behind the armoured cars of the 11th Hussars, was one of the first to enter the city, shortly after sunrise. British military police were already directing traffic and patrolling the roads while the Union Jack flew from the town hall in the Piazza Italia, Tripoli's main square. When Clifford entered the city he was wearing 'a special pair of whipcord trousers I had been saving and my last clean pair of socks' and he sat in the heat of the sun-drenched square to write a dispatch.[34]

The sense of triumph was short-lived, however, overwhelmed by the usual wartime irritations: the hotels with no running water, restaurants with no food, 'laundries but no soap, cinemas but no films, shops but nothing to buy'.[35] Clifford moved into a seafront hotel, the misnamed Grand, which was a grim building painted a shabby grey, where the sheets were clean, but the wine was ghastly. He wandered through the palm trees and white buildings reflecting on what had been and what still lay ahead.

Through February and March, Montgomery's 8th Army continued its advance, driving through 'Tunisia like a plunger being pushed into a tube'.[36] The next objective was Tunis itself, some 500 miles to the north-west along the coast from Tripoli. An even more significant objective was witnessing the much-anticipated rendezvous between the Americans and the British 8th Army, the latter scarred by its long journey from Egypt, 'reddened with the sun and dusty with the sand, already dressed in dirty shirts and ragged shorts'. The Americans, by contrast, 'had mackintosh wind jackets and baggy trousers and gaiters and boots and iron-grey vehicles' on their journey west.[37]

By mid-April, Clifford was still some 100 miles south of Tunis, in the coastal town of Sousse, which the fighting had reduced to a confusion of charred and twisted metalwork, lumps of stone and masonry, piles of shattered furniture and sunken ships. Despite the devastation, the town provided two heart-warming moments. First, on 13 April, Clifford met a Frenchman on his bicycle who, when asked if he could direct Clifford to a restaurant, was both generous and insistent. 'No, there is nothing,' he said, 'But if you care to lunch at my house I shall be honoured.'[38] Later, Clifford was sitting in a car, parked in the main street, writing a dispatch, still aglow with the generosity of the bicyclist's French family whose womenfolk had all worn small paste crosses of Lorraine, proud emblems of France which had been hidden of necessity for months. He glanced out of the car window to see three war correspondents walking down the road: surely that's Ward Price of the *Daily Mail*? And yes! – that's Buckley and Moorehead with him![39] It was a moment to be cherished: the Trio had not met since the previous summer when Moorehead had left for America, and there was so much to talk about.

Like Clifford, Christopher Buckley was to remember Sousse fondly: there had been a high wind blowing as he entered the town and, in order to write his dispatch, he had to find some shelter from the gusts. He holed up in an abandoned woodshed, typing seated on 'a pile of faggots', and watched by a number of children. After a while, they disappeared, and then 'returned carrying bouquets of flowers'.[40] Later that day, he saw first Alan Moorehead, then Alexander Clifford and, soon after, Geoffrey Keating rolled up, followed by Russell Hill. Suddenly, in the middle of this battle-scarred town, so far from home, was the wherewithal to establish the unofficial Sousse Bridge School. They stopped for the night in a villa by the sea, a building entirely untouched by bombing or artillery fire and whose rooms were in a good clean state. Before getting the bridge cards out, they fell easily into their comradely routine, with Clifford cooking as always – Moorehead 'would no more have dreamed of interfering with Clifford's cooking than he would have thought of instructing me on the lighting of the stoves or the unpacking of the trucks'.[41] Keating, ever the smooth operator, took responsibility for petrol and rations as usual, no one better at wangling both necessities and unlikely luxuries. It turned out to be an occasion Clifford would never forget for the rest of his life, as enjoyable an evening as he had ever spent, the war set aside for a while, and the focus instead on cooking, cards and conversation, the shared pleasure in the lives of others.

It proved to be a brief interlude. The Trio could rarely resist for long the compulsion to set out on the road to the front, a Michelin map open on the passenger's knees, the driver squinting into the sun, a firm grip on the jeep's steering wheel while the vehicle bounced and rolled, trailing yellow dust and grit in its wake. So it was this time. Faced with the classic war correspondents' dilemma – stick with the troops as they moved on, or sit tight and write up the story even though it was already in danger of being upstaged by the next – the urge to keep close to the front usually won. The urgency stemmed partly from each correspondent's innate restlessness, but editors back in London expected the very latest news, and they were not easy men to ignore. For example, soon after the Sousse reunion with Buckley, Moorehead, and the rest, Clifford was working with Chester Morrison of the *Chicago Sun* and Ned Russell who was employed by United Press. Morrison's instructions from Chicago brooked no argument: find some heroes, preferably from your employer's city. For his part Ned Russell was told: 'Keep it coarse – hell, this is war.' Clifford was no stranger to the seamier sides of newspapers: take the time that London instructed him to 'probe into the secrets of Montgomery's boudoir'.[42]

By the beginning of May, the fall of Tunis was imminent and the mood in the city was volatile, even wild. The streets were crowded with the liberated, as well as trigger-happy soldiers, exhausted after months of unrelenting foot-slogging. There were still Germans there too, penned in and increasingly desperate, and eruptions of street-fighting were liable to occur at any time. Accompanying Alan Moorehead was the intrepid Christopher Buckley and A.B. Austin, who 'seemed to derive a strange satisfaction from being fired at', together with Sidney Bernstein, a filmmaker with the Ministry of Information. Bernstein was discomfited by much of what he saw – the broken bodies of dead Germans, as well as those seeking to surrender to him, and by the civilians trying to thank him. One dead German he saw was 'lying on his stomach … his face turned sideways and his eyes wide open. His map case still hanging from his shoulder lay beside him.'[43] Elsewhere a tank crew had been trapped in a burning tank, the smell of cooked meat testifying to their failure to get out in time.

Entering the village of La Mornaghia in the early afternoon of 7 May, Moorehead passed a sign in German warning that there was typhus in the village. Then, by a signpost which pointed the way to Tunis, 14km away, he met up with Alexander Clifford once again, steadfastly hitchhiking there. Moorehead 'drove up and offered me a lift,' Clifford wrote later. 'He had penetrated still further into the town and he had come from lying in a ditch with the bullets chipping away the plaster of the wall above his head.'[44] The sheer speed of the Allied advance caught many Germans by surprise, so that instead of being dug in behind walls or lurking in cellars, they were being shaved or having their hair cut by the local barbers, or sitting in the pavement cafés or on the terrace of the Majestic Hotel enjoying a drink. One officer from the 11th Hussars likened it to 'three German armoured cars (having) driven up to Shepheards Hotel in Cairo'.[45] It had begun to rain but it failed to dampen the enthusiasm as they drove into the captured city, Alex Clifford viewing it all from the truck's roof. It was 2.45 p.m. on 7 May 1943. Much later that day, at dusk, Moorehead and Clifford drove back together to Thibar, through the rain, numb with an exhaustion so deep that they scarcely flinched when a Spitfire crash-landed close to the road and burst into flames.

A few days later, they spent the night with Randolph Churchill at a villa he had
secured at Sidi Bou Said, about 10 miles from Tunis. It was another of those evenings
when the war seemed to exist somewhere else, in a parallel world. The village had
wonderful views of the Mediterranean and perhaps for both correspondents its
location hinted at the kind of life that might be theirs when the war finally ended.
A villa on the coast. They talked, the two of them, of what constituted happiness,
'the best things in life – reading and writing and good conversation, good food and
wine, sitting in the sun, swimming in the sea, making love. Especially making love
– the setting was perfect.' For a brief moment they were both deeply at peace. But
the next day the recurring fear that they might miss the crucial moment became all
too strong; there was news out there somewhere, happening as they daydreamed.
There was another motive too: 'Clifford and I were keen to do a little looting, a
sport at which we had become adept in the desert'.[46]

They enjoyed an exhilarating drive back to Algiers, stopping every so often
for a swim in the Mediterranean. In particular, 'the last 600 miles were superb,'
Clifford wrote to his mother, 'the most wonderful road I have seen anywhere',[47]
this after he had been 'madly busy conquering Tunis'. By the time he arrived
in Algiers, he had driven all the way from Alexandria, a distance of over 1,500
miles. It had been a sapping experience, invariably uncomfortable and sometimes
dangerous. He had not had a hot bath for three months, sleeping arrangements
were often primitive, perhaps on the roof of the truck, or in some slit trench
scratched in the dirt; rations were often in short supply and frequently nauseating;
the bugs continued to bite and sting, and the Luftwaffe still had the power to send
them scurrying for the shelter of a roadside ditch.

May 1943 marked the end in Africa for the Duo. They had arrived in Algiers
in a 'liberated' Volkswagen, a replacement for a similarly looted Fiat which had
blown up soon after its requisition. Clifford's colleague on the *Mail*, Ward Price,
saw Alex greatly enjoying 'driving his captured German car about' the city,
and wrote to Alex's mother to tell her so, adding that he looked 'in the very
best of health'. Generously he told her that her son was 'by far the most able
correspondent produced by this war'.[48] The Volkswagen was soon stolen, the
result of carelessness by an airman to whom Clifford had lent the car: he had left it
unlocked and with the key in the ignition. The theft could have happened in any
wartime city of course, but it reinforced Clifford's antipathy towards Algiers. And
wasn't it just typical that the army's public relations unit had lost the draft of *Three
Against Rommel*, his recently completed book about the North African campaign?
The Algerian blight even struck Clifford's pleasure in swimming. For the past
three years he had swum naked, without a moment's thought for modesty, from
dozens of beaches along the Mediterranean littoral, but now in Algiers a more
decorous world intruded. Without a moment's hesitation, Clifford had dived into
the sea not wearing a stitch, with no thought for women on the beach. He soon

realised his mistake and had to 'scream to someone on shore to bring me in a pair of pants'.[49] Algiers! The end in Africa could not come soon enough.

*   *   *   *

Alan Moorehead had already left Africa and was back in London, absorbed once again into the unreal world of luncheon engagements and dinner appointments with the likes of Michael Foot, Arthur Christiansen, Sydney Bernstein, the war correspondent Noel Monks, the socialite Lady Colefax, and the *Express* cartoonist Osbert Lancaster. On 13 June – Whit Sunday – he travelled the 40 or so miles to Clifford's parents' house at Lindfield in Sussex, bringing them news of their long-exiled son. It was a typically generous act of friendship by the Australian, the more so as his mind was preoccupied with plans for the future. A scheme had been devised in which Moorehead would exchange roles with Charles Foley, the foreign editor at the *Express*. This would allow Moorehead to become resident in London once again. There was, however, a major flaw in the proposal: it would not be permanent. That revelation appalled Lucy – how could her husband have agreed 'to return to the work he had claimed to hate'?[50] It was an arrangement which Moorehead was also unhappy with, realising the unwanted consequences of his ambitious streak, and he manifested it during his stay in London by being both defensive and abrupt. He believed himself to be in the wrong at the time, and later, after he had gone back to the war, he would admit it, writing Lucy an apologetic letter conceding that he had behaved very badly when he had been with her in London. By then he was on his way back to the war which, in the months he had been away from the Middle East, had rapidly moved on. In July 1943, Allied troops had landed on the European mainland. As he looked down from the aircraft window at the island of Sicily where the invasion had taken place, Moorehead's prevailing mood was relief that he would soon be back at work, much as he regretted the way he had said goodbye to England. At least the struggle now was closer to home, in Europe rather than North Africa, a thought that went some way to consoling him as he set foot on the runway at Syracuse. It was 9 August 1943, a month to the day since the invasion of Sicily had begun.

NOTES

1   *The End in Africa*, op. cit., p.11.
2   Ibid., p.13.
3   Ibid., p.18.
4   *Rendezvous with Rommel*, op. cit., p.89.
5   Like Moorehead, Jack Hetherington was born in Melbourne.
6   Collier, p.136.

7   *The Daily Telegraph*, 4 November 1942. The dispatch was attributed to both
     Buckley and Ronald Legge.

8   *The Daily Telegraph*, 7 November 1942.

9   Clifford, p.325.

10   Alexander Clifford in the *Daily Mail*, 6 June 1946.

11   Moorehead papers, NLA, file MS 5654.

12   *The End in Africa*, op. cit., p.30.

13   Ibid., p.39.

14   Ibid., p.50.

15   Ibid., p.49.

16   Ibid., p.50.

17   *Jordan's Tunis Diary* by Philip Jordan, p.124. He and Moorehead were the first
     two pressmen identified for the Algerian campaign – see Jordan, p.20.

18   *Birth of an Army* by A. B. Austin, p.66.

19   Ibid., p.67.

20   Ibid., p.68.

21   Moorehead papers, NLA, file MS 5654. All these notes were handwritten in
     Moorehead's 1943 diary.

22   *IWM Review, no. 6*, p.23. A. B. Austin was to die later in the year near Naples.
     Christopher Buckley thought him 'the one who really preferred the battlefield
     to the camp. He was both brave and dogged.'

23   Austin, p.72.

24   Jordan, p.168.

25   Ibid., p.173.

26   Ibid., p.171.

27   Ibid., p.175.

28   Ibid.

29   Letter to Lucy Moorehead in New York, dated 10 March 1943 (and written
     when Alan was flying from Gibraltar to Algiers); see Pocock, p.142.

30   Moorehead papers, NLA, file MS 5654; letter of 10 March 1943.

31   Clifford papers (16727), IWM, file AGC/2/1/6.

32   Clifford, p.325.

33   Ibid., p.330.

34   Ibid., pp.343–4.

35   Ibid., p.349.

36   Ibid., p.382.

37   Ibid., p.383.

38   Ibid., p.384.

39   There is a discrepancy over dates as to when this meeting took place: Clifford
     has 13 April, while Moorehead's diary has the 12th.

40   Buckley, p.122.

41   *The End in Africa*, op. cit., p.156.
42   Clifford, p.386.
43   *Sidney Bernstein* by Caroline Moorehead, p.154.
44   Clifford, p.401.
45   *Desert Conquest* by Russell Hill, p.153.
46   *The End in Africa*, op. cit., p.207.
47   Clifford papers (16727), IWM, file AGC/2/1/7.
48   Ibid., file AGC/5/4.
49   Ibid., file AGC/2/1/7; letter of 18 June 1943.
50   Pocock, p.150.

PART 2

The Trio: Sicily to Lüneburg

14. The Villa in Sicily

Some weeks earlier, on 29 June 1943, Christopher Buckley had sailed from Suez on board the luxury liner *Strathnaver*. When he had left Cairo four days before, it had been under cover of darkness, reflecting concerns about enemy espionage and the need to keep the forthcoming invasion of Europe a secret. There were those in Cairo only too ready to note 'the conspicuous departure of even a single War Correspondent' and realise the implications.[1] An army truck took him and his 65lb kitbag to the port, arriving as the dawn light slowly spread from the east and the cool of early morning began to fade. Once settled on *Strathnaver*, Buckley passed the time reading, playing chess and finally, 'as is the fate of all war correspondents', giving lectures to the troops on board. Eventually, on the morning of 5 July, the fleet set sail from Port Said, its steel-grey ships in ordered ranks under a cloudless sky, each vessel making its ponderous way through placid water. It had the feel of a holiday cruise, if you turned a blind eye to the ubiquitous khaki. Breakfast was splendidly old-fashioned, while four-course dinners were served by discreet Indian waiters in crisp white jackets; the food was comfortingly traditional: 'clear soup, vol-au-vent, lamb cutlets, macedoine of fruit'. It was all very reassuring.

That sense of gentle cruising was not to last. The weather began to deteriorate on the afternoon of 9 July and the sea became rougher, threatening a delay in the invasion hour, a last resort since any postponement could increase the likelihood of the enemy being alerted to the armada of ships in the darkness. As it was, at around 11 p.m. that night Buckley began to prepare himself: clothes (bush-shirt, khaki trousers, pullover), lifebelt, water bottle, binoculars and steel helmet, gas mask; rations for two days, washing and shaving gear, portable typewriter and 'enough copy paper to have written *War and Peace* and *Gone With the Wind*', and a copy of Fanny Burney's *Evelina* 'lest there should be *longeurs* in the process of conquering Europe'.[2] Soon after, Buckley and the troops of 231 Brigade were given mugs of tea and tots of rum before settling into the landing crafts. The stars were visible and 'a reddish half-moon was tilting downwards towards the sea'.[3] The waves, which had seemed benign from the liner's deck, looked huge seen from the open boat. Buckley and the rest soon became uncomfortably cold and wet and, in many cases, seasick. It was dark and the air smelled of the nearby land, its vegetation parched by the summer heat. Buckley worried about whether he would be able to keep his typewriter and paper dry. Every so often waves would break over the boat's bows, the faint moonlight catching the surf. Then he felt the boat touch the beach and he jumped out, holding his kit high above his head. 'I felt one foot splash in shallow water and then the other struck soft sand, three thousand years of history rushed towards me, and I stood again in Europe.'[4]

It was 5.30 a.m. In the grey half-light, passwords were exchanged: a cautious 'Desert Rat!' eliciting the response 'Kill the Italians!' Stumbling in some haste away from the beach as the light began to spread, Buckley gave no thought to the possibility of mines, stepping quickly across a ditch, past a farm and cottages fronting a white and dusty lane, next to a stubbly field, and pools of water. This was not the invasion he had created in his imagination; to begin with the landscape was strangely peaceful, seeming 'nostalgically English' in the early morning light before the sun had risen high enough 'to give it the hard Mediterranean glitter'.[5] That first night ashore he spent in an abandoned cottage in a meadow looking down on the sea.

The Sicilian summer was unforgivingly hot and the island was cursed with mosquitoes which, so the joke went, were more unpleasant than the Italians, though not their German military counterparts. Both the dry heat and rugged landscape were reminiscent of Spain, while the kind of warfare was in marked contrast to that fought in the desert, the broad acres of tank country replaced by narrow country lanes. Buckley often found himself sleeping under the stars, perhaps in a clump of olive trees when the night might be as warm as high noon in an English midsummer. Sometimes there was a malevolent atmosphere abroad on the island: when Buckley went to Syracuse, for example, he was unsettled by the resentful, sullen faces of those queuing for food, of whom there were many. The question everywhere was, 'Are you bringing food?'

By comparison, the correspondents' problems were neither life-threatening nor painful, just frustrating. As well as the heat, mosquitoes, mountainous terrain and the fierce German resistance, there were the usual transport problems. With insufficient vehicles available, it meant reporting the war from a static situation too far from the front, something which Buckley reckoned reduced his effectiveness by half. For all that, Sicily had its compensations. There was, for example, the time Buckley picnicked with an elderly Sicilian shepherd, the two of them companionably sharing a tin of grapefruit which the Englishman had been carrying all the way from Cairo. Then, near Lentini, Buckley happened upon some twenty of his colleagues, camped in a recently cut hayfield – a well-chosen spot with some patches of shade, a stream with drinkable water, low stone walls and ripening blackberry bushes, as well as trees from which to rig up mosquito nets. He thought again of Spain, remembering the 'miserable fortnight in August 1938 when I was detained at Alicante on some technical formality and had to sleep in a hotel which had no mosquito nets in a town totally unprovided with other remedies against the creatures'.[6] His escape from malaria he put down to a benign providence.

The days in Lentini had a set rhythm: they would wake, perhaps, to the sound of Spitfires heading for Messina; then after breakfast there would be a briefing, an opportunity to ask questions, after which the correspondents would sit on packing crates in the shade for 'an hour of vigorous typewriter-pounding', each of them writing as if in 'the final half hour of any public examination'.[7] Soon after 11 a.m. the whole pack of them, in small groups, would set out in search of the next day's story: there would be a visit to an army unit here, an offer of a mug of tea there, a recce for a suitable vantage point, perhaps, then a stop in the shade for a picnic of sardines, biscuits, the inevitable 'corpse-like' bully beef, and a drink of fiery Sicilian red wine. Buckley would sometimes entertain his colleagues by reciting pastoral poetry, or they would pass the time by inventing ideal meals – salmon mayonnaise perhaps, with strawberries to follow, washed down with cider cup. As the daylight began to fade, they would drift back to camp to write up the day's notes under flickering candlelight before eating dinner under the stars. Buckley would smile at how it all resembled the outlaws' banquet in the Forest of Arden in Shakespeare's *As You Like It* and how, given the chance, he would cast Clifford as Jaques perhaps, and the absent Moorehead as Orlando.

That was the Lentini routine: waking before the day's heat had built up, in a dawn light, and glad of the reviving mug of tea beside the typewriter. Such routine might have been mildly comforting, but there was no denying that the fighting each day had now acquired an even greater brutality. On one occasion, Buckley saw a lorry explode some 300 yards further up the road and watched with horror as the bodies continued to burn long after they had died. That was a fact of war that he had not previously known. He had learned much in North Africa about survival in a battle zone – the importance, for example, of keeping tucked in to the side of the roads, since ditches, hedges and walls all provided varying degrees of cover, and anti-personnel mines were more likely to have been placed in the middle of the road, rather than at its fringes. That was the theory anyway...

By the beginning of August 1943, Christopher Buckley and Alex Clifford were in Catania. Buckley would long remember squatting down contentedly on the steps of the cathedral in the sun to type a story, and being accosted by a pretty girl who capriciously draped a scarf around his neck. He and Clifford had driven into Catania together, remembering as they did so the other conquered towns they had entered side by side: Tripoli, Tunis and now this down-at-heel port in

Sicily. The third member of the Trio was in their thoughts too as they strolled through Catania's narrow streets, seeking shade. For his part, Alan Moorehead was only a matter of days away from joining them. The Trio was about to reconvene.

✳   ✳   ✳   ✳

By midsummer 1943 Moorehead's star was in the ascendant, and he was recognised widely as one of Britain's greatest war correspondents. That June *A Year of Battle* had been praised during a debate in the House of Lords – it was judged a 'very remarkable (and) inspiring' book,[8] while a month later, a letter from his father Richard in Australia commended the same book for its maturity and style. Moorehead had progressed from journalist to writer: 'You've got your public now,' his father wrote with evident pride, 'your book public as distinct from your newspaper public'.[9] For all that, when the younger Moorehead looked to the future, there was uncertainty; he sensed that the war was far from won and he knew the road to Rome could prove long.

Moorehead arrived in Sicily just four days after Buckley and Clifford had been exploring Catania together. He found Alex Clifford one late afternoon 'on a dusty plain outside Lentini. He had pitched his bed under one of those formal orange trees which one sees so often in Italian frescoes and medieval woodcuts.' He was fast asleep beneath a mosquito net suspended from the tree, its 'ripe fruit hanging from the branches like yellow lanterns on a Christmas tree'.[10] It didn't take Moorehead long to see that his friend had changed – he had lost weight and looked pale and exhausted. Initially Alex had enthused about Sicily – it provided 'the most wonderful free tourism' he told his mother.[11] It was the changed nature of the fighting which troubled him, its proximity to the civilian population. No longer was the war 'a soldiers' tournament in empty space'.[12] Like Moorehead, Alexander Clifford had become a household name, with a reputation as 8th Army's most celebrated correspondent. Eating away at him, however, was the intense suffering the war caused, and his fear of what was still to come. His letters home reflected his growing doubts and disillusion. On 31 July 1943, for example, he told his mother that he was determined not to write another book: 'Everyone seems to be writing books,' he wrote, adding a self-deprecating, 'I shall write no more unless this one is extremely successful which I don't think it could be.'[13]

There was, however, some comfort in the reconvening of the Trio. It was in Sicily that Christopher Buckley fully recognised 'the beginning of the triumvirate which lasted for many months'.[14] They had become increasingly close over three long years: initially in Athens, then journeying 'around together on a dozen battlefields in North Africa and Tunisia'. They had teamed up 'by mutual consent', sharing in a friendship which went far beyond rivalry and was characterised by trust and respect and mutual admiration.

And so, in mid-August 1943, the Trio came to Taormina. Apart from Messina, it was the last major town in Sicily to be captured. It had been the German HQ and yet it had been surrendered without a shot, so desperate was the Nazi withdrawal. As for the Italian troops, rather than fight to the end, they seemed more enamoured with the idea of pragmatic surrender. Just a few hours before, the war artist Edward Ardizzone and Major Geoffrey Keating of the Army Film Unit, had '(captured) the town of Taormina plus a Colonel and four hundred Italian troops'.[15] Soon after, at an enemy radio and signalling station, Christopher Buckley found a note written in English by an Italian naval captain asking the invading British and Americans if they could see their way 'every morning at eight (to) give some food to the pigeons in the Greek Theatre'. *Tenente* Carlo Zuccaro, who signed the note, was also keen to point out that he was married to an American and that 'the armchair here belongs to Miss Dora Bell, an Englishwoman'. Buckley shook his head in astonishment, unable to 'take a nation seriously whose soldiers go to war and leave notes for their enemies asking them to feed the pigeons'.[16]

Perhaps the town's magic had reminded the Italians of how fine a peacetime life could be; certainly for the British war correspondents, Taormina proved to be a kind of oasis, with idyllic days 'in the sun, drinking wine, swimming from the beach, meeting the women'.[17] The Trio stared in wonder at its beauty – the intense blue of the Mediterranean at the foot of the towering cliffs, and the looming shadow of Mount Etna. Alan Moorehead would later describe the time spent in the town as the 'Taormina Summer School', with its full programme of wine, swimming, bridge and nocturnal conversations in the garden about art and books as the night insects whirred in the darkness. He and Alex Clifford shared a room in a picturesque villa precariously situated high above the town's hotels, with a steepling view down to the Mediterranean, while General Montgomery, having decided that Taormina was too exotic for the troops – 'It smells of love. It would take their minds off the war'[18] – set up his HQ in one of the hotels below the villa. Freddie de Guingand, Monty's chief of staff, was one of many visitors who drifted in and out of the 'Summer School' villa, for bridge, or company, or food and wine, or reminders of home.

The days merged into one another: the sun shone; the sky was never anything but blue; wine and conversation flowed; Ardizzone painted; Buckley read *Barchester Towers* and browsed amongst the villa's library where he found a copy of his favourite cricket story *Spedegue's Dropper*; music drifted through the gardens; heated arguments about art or literature lasted deep into the night. When tiredness finally prevailed, they would fall asleep on the terrace. Moorehead and Ted Ardizzone introduced the American war correspondent Frank Gervasi to the poetry of John Donne, the war artist later confiding to his diary that Moorehead's 'unaffected erudition' impressed and surprised him.[19] Monty was proved right about the town's erotic charge: Alan Moorehead, for one, was much struck by the glories of local girl Mariella who 'in her bathing suit was a girl of bursting vitality. She was frankly and consciously sexual. She made an aggressive innocence of her body that had become too early ripe in the Sicilian sun.'[20]

*   *   *   *

It could not last, Taormina's interlude of peace. Across the strait, the Italian mainland was clearly visible and preparations for the invasion were well advanced. On 2 September Montgomery sent a 'Personal Message' to be read to all troops: 'To the Eighth Army has been given the great honour of being the first troops of the Allied Armies to land on the mainland of the continent of Europe. We will prove ourselves worthy of this honour … Good luck. And God Bless you all.' That night, before the momentous crossing of the Straits of Messina, Buckley slept in a wood on a bed of wet pine needles, waking early on a glorious morning to witness the Allied artillery bombardment. He found himself contemplating where he had been on the equivalent day in previous Septembers: wondering whether he would get out alive from Warsaw (3 September 1939) or from Athens (1940), reflecting on the pleasures of Cairo (1941), and the turning of the tide at El Alamein (1942). After a breakfast of a mug of tea and some sausage rolls, Buckley duly crossed the narrow strait between Sicily and the mainland, leaving at 9 a.m. under a cloudless sky. Once he had crossed, he secured a lift into Reggio. Clifford and Moorehead, meanwhile, together with the American Frank Gervasi, crossed with Montgomery himself, glad of a sea that was placid, stirred only slightly by the occasional white ripple. Halfway across, after Montgomery had spent time at the ship's bow staring at the smoke-cloaked enemy coast, they went below for fortifying biscuits and coffee.

The town of Reggio proved to be wretched and dispiriting, 'a desolation of twisted shutters and broken wire',[21] while the looting which had seemed somehow more acceptable in the desert was shocking to many. The war artist Edward Ardizzone, for example, was disturbed by the sight of a 'soldier with two dozen coat hangers and two alarm clocks' tucked under his arms. Reggio was the kind of place that you longed to leave, its buildings and roads broken and scarred by fire and largely deserted except for the legions of scavengers. The summer school in Sicily was conclusively over and what lay ahead was the long, painful slog up through Italy. Ominously, the skyline to the north and east of Reggio was dominated by high mountains; the more thoughtful of those soldiers and correspondents moving north that autumn would readily have imagined the trouble to come.

The more optimistic amongst the invaders held high hopes, however, of wintering as far north as Florence, but as autumn turned towards winter, such

Montgomery scanning the Italian mainland from the Straits of Messina, September 1943.
(IWM, NA 6211)

thoughts soon faded. The plans for Florence in February were soon replaced by
those for the 'winter school' in Naples. To make life worse, some old complaints
resurfaced: there were severe reporting restrictions laid upon them; transport
was impounded and, at one point, Moorehead was sufficiently incensed by the
censorship that he 'suggested that we had better go up into the hills and write
Nature Notes'. His letter prompted a long explanatory response from Allied
Forces HQ (Public Relations Office) in Algiers, and then a facetious paragraph
taking its tone from Moorehead's letter of 22 September. 'In the meantime if you
are serious about writing a book on nature, I hope you will present me with a
copy. I am particularly interested in the ways of lizards, scorpions, flies, fleas and

war correspondents in winter time.'[22] Moorehead was at least informed officially that he was 'free to move in 5th Army area providing you don't expect them to transport you or transmit your messages at the expense of those correspondents already within 5th Army'. The principle to which Public Relations adhered was that 'the number of correspondents in the Theatre of Operations must be governed by the amount of transmission available'. In other words, the press were thrown back on their own resources, something which the Trio had perfected over the years. Moorehead and Clifford borrowed a truck from the Army Film Unit, while Buckley, Monson and others secured the services of a 'pre-historical Humber'. They were mobile now at least and could head north into the mountains and the Italian winter. Not every correspondent was so lucky. In Cairo, for example, a reporter with the Melbourne *Argus*, Richard Hughes, described for his readers how 'frustrated war correspondents here are chanting their new song "What's it all about?"' Most lines were too rude to print, he wrote, but two of the more acceptable were: 'We never write a line, we never get a beat / We only keep our weight off our big flat feet.'[23]

That autumn Moorehead listed in his diary the names of those war correspondents who had been killed in the war or been taken prisoner. Instead of his normal busy scrawl, the names were neatly written, as if by doing so he might keep himself safe, and their memory not forgotten. The first eight were those who had died: Massey Anderson, lost when he was torpedoed in the Mediterranean in December 1941, Ralph Barnes who was the first reporter to die – on an RAF night flight which crashed into mountains in Yugoslavia in November 1940, Harry Crockett, drowned after being torpedoed in the Mediterranean in February 1943, the Paramount cameraman, Freddie Bayliss – he of the six-egg-per-person omelette in Libya – burned to death when his transport plane crashed in the summer of 1943, and A.B. Austin, Bill Munday and Stewart Sale, all killed in Italy in September 1943. The remaining four names – Eddie Ward, Ronald Noble, Larry Allen and Godfrey Anderson – were all prisoners-of-war. Death or imprisonment must have been an increasingly threatening spectre as the Allied armies edged north, fighting the winter weather, the high mountains and the dour, resilient Germans.

NOTES

1   Buckley, p.15.
2   Ibid., p.27.
3   Ibid., pp.28–9.
4   Ibid., p.32.
5   Ibid., p.34.

6   Ibid., p.80.

7   Ibid., p.82.

8   *Parliamentary Debates: House of Lords, vol. 127, No. 67, for Thursday, 3 June 1943.*
     The debate was on 'military despatches and publicity'.

9   Moorehead papers, NLA, MS 5654. Letter dated 19 July 1943.

10   *A Late Education*, op. cit., p.136.

11   Clifford papers (16727), IWM, file AGC/2/1/7; letter to his mother, 31 July
     1943.

12   *A Late Education*, op. cit., p.137.

13   Clifford papers (16727), IWM, file AGC/2/1/7.

14   Buckley, p.131.

15   *Diary of a War Artist* by Edward Ardizzone, p.44.

16   Buckley, p.138.

17   *Eclipse* by Alan Moorehead, p.5.

18   Pocock, p.156.

19   Ardizzone, p.50; diary entry for 2 September 1943.

20   *Eclipse*, op. cit., p.7.

21   Ardizzone, p.52.

22   Moorehead papers, NLA, MS 5654; letter of 29 September 1943.

23   *The Argus*, 11 August 1943.

15. 'My Treasure. I am Coming Home.'

At first, all the signs were good in that fifth autumn of the war as the Trio motored north, spinning contentedly along idyllic country roads with the Mediterranean a startling blue to one side and the mountains standing tall to the east. They were often welcomed as liberators by the Italians: once an elderly man kissed the gritty, undemonstrative Australian war correspondent, Ronald Monson, who blanched at the indignity. The days were disconcertingly similar: troops would trudge up the coastal road, then stop at the first blown-up river crossing, thwarted until the sappers arrived to repair the damage. This was a Herculean task; after all, 'a thousand bridges were said to have been destroyed between Rome and Taormina',[1] some by the Americans. Of the Germans, there would be no sign. For the correspondents such routine meant much wracking of brains as to how best to report the same story in a dozen different ways. Although the Italians had surrendered, it soon became clear that the Germans intended to fight for every inch of ground. As well as the broken bridges, the advance was held up by mines buried in the roads by both sides, in a seemingly haphazard way: Christopher Buckley shivered when he was told that he had just driven over a British-laid mine.

On the morning of 9 September the Allies landed on the beaches at Salerno, to the south of Naples. Four days later Christopher Buckley found himself on the flat roof of a villa near Nicastro, idly eating grapes and reading *War and Peace* in the autumn sun. Salerno was 200 miles away to the north and it dawned on him that, with the Italian surrender, the land between Nicastro and Salerno had become a tempting no-man's-land, fit for journalistic buccaneering. The prospect was enticing enough to prompt a two-car expedition of impatient correspondents, including Ron Monson and Christopher Buckley. Close behind were Moorehead and Clifford in their borrowed Army Film Unit truck, having decided to find their way to the US 5th Army in the north, this despite having 'no

driver, no spare wheel, no tools, no rations, no petrol, no oil, and no maps'.[2] They
kept to side-roads in a ruse to avoid mines and, every so often, they would draw
to a halt alongside curious Italians standing by the roadside and ask whether there
were any German troops in the area. Reassured, they would then cautiously press
ahead, never entirely confident about what lay behind the next corner. Once, just
after passing through the village of Bulgheria, Buckley's driver suddenly slammed
on the brakes and brought the car to a shuddering halt. It prompted oaths, yelled
questions and, in the back seat, arms flung up to the leather seat backs to cushion
the impact. The emergency was not the sighting of some well-armed Nazi patrol,
but rather having 'just caught sight of the most beautiful girl I had ever seen in my
life'.[3] So stunning was she that they had all got out of the car to stand and stare.

Clifford and Moorehead finally caught up with the advance party in mid-
afternoon on a wooded ridge having a picnic amongst the oak trees. The group
included Captain John Soboleff (from Public Relations), a larger than life figure
who had the enviable knack of acquiring supplies of all kinds. In Sicily, for example,
he and Ron Monson had liberated 'all the French champagne that remained in
Syracuse'.[4] On another occasion, he produced forty hard-boiled eggs to grace a
war correspondents' picnic. When the other two members of the Trio turned up,
Buckley was once more pondering on the Forest of Arden, those outcasts 'feasting
alfresco' amongst the shadowy trees; then who should emerge through the woods
but 'Orlando, in the persons of Clifford and Moorehead, who appeared in their vast
truck, hungrily demanding food and drink'.[5] After a trying journey during which
a tyre had burst, followed by crashing into a concrete road-trap in the darkness,
they needed food and rest, and so they ate and considered the next move. Monson
left the shelter of the trees to drive ahead and reconnoitre, returning soon after to
report the sighting of a German armoured car driving towards them. It reinforced
the importance of proceeding with great caution and they decided that the wisest
thing would be to hole up in a château in Castelnuovo suggested by Soboleff. This
was typical of the man, both knowing of the house's existence and able to call in
a friendship, there in that remote countryside deep in the Italian south. That night
they all dined at a long polished table, Buckley sitting beside Clifford, the two of
them chatting like dinner guests at some suburban house in Surrey, oblivious to
the dangerous world beyond the subdued lights and elegant hospitality.

The next morning, 15 September, they left the château at dawn, travelling in
three cars. They soon discovered that they had been close to the Americans, rather
than any German patrols, although a series of blown bridges presented them
with a logistical problem. Eventually, after an abortive search for some bicycles
to complete their journey, they came face-to-face with the Americans. It was
a fraught encounter: 'We came round a bend of the road to find an American
half-tracked vehicle proceeding slowly up the road in front of us'[6] and, more
worrying still, a tommy gun being trained on them, until someone waved his

British army cap in the air. Unarmed, the group of war correspondents were some 40 miles ahead of Montgomery's advance guard. It had been a daring and determined initiative, but it 'brought them a stinging rebuke from Montgomery's press department'.[7] Such official disapproval lay ahead. For now, after driving some 120 miles through no-man's-land, Buckley was too exhausted to sleep, and so he talked late into the night with two young GIs from Texas.

✳ ✳ ✳ ✳

With the autumn, the Allied advance began to slow. Despite the loss of summer, there were some lingering, delightfully blue days which tempted Clifford into dreams of buying an Italian vineyard when the war was over. On 12 October, a day of glorious autumn light and blue sky, the Trio travelled to Capri carrying with them 'a letter from Gracie Fields to the tenant of her villa on the island'. Buckley wasn't sure 'how the note had succeeded in reaching us, but we felt that for once in our lives we were touching the fringe of real greatness'.[8] The Trio's three days in Capri were a delightful interlude, though not comparable to that in Taormina, and Clifford was discomforted by the island's 'sinful' atmosphere. As the autumn continued, though, Capri was revealed as an isolated pleasure. All too often the campaign had a sour taste to it, typified by the time they were turned away from the Imperiale Hotel in Bari because, without Italian civilian ration cards, they were 'not entitled' to lunch there. There was a bad-tempered row in the same town with an American lieutenant (from the Psychological Warfare Division) who bellowed at Alex and Alan: 'Get out of the hotel!' Clifford, showing an unexpectedly belligerent temper, slowly took off his glasses and said quietly, 'Just try and do it!'

The first days of the Allied offensive aimed at the German's winter line coincided with two days of fine weather. The sky was an egg-shell blue; there was snow on the distant mountain crests, blue-grey mists which drifted over red-tiled roofs in the valleys, and above the mist, puffs of smoke like flowers which proved to be shell bursts.

The offensive might have begun amidst such optimism, but it wasn't to last. The swollen rivers and the sequences of ridges over which the roads climbed and fell made the advance tortuous and slow. It was also unquestionably bloody and Buckley, for one, was disturbed by the Allied armies' tactics, what he termed their 'excessive rigidity'. Clifford, for his part, was worried about the quality of military information, believing that General Alexander's HQ at San Spirito near Bari 'was rather a side-alley', somewhat out of touch with events and working on the basis of 'curiously belated' information.[9] More generally, there was no escaping the pervading gloom, the heavy rain and bitter cold which turned the mountains into a series of grim obstacles. Rome still seemed so far away. The correspondents held a sweepstake as to when the Allied armies might capture the city, the consensus being that it wouldn't be until January 1944. Ever the realist, Buckley thought it would be as late as 26 February. It became increasingly difficult to get to the front and back in a day, and the Trio began to struggle with low spirits, with Alex in particular suffering from occasional depression, triggered in part by too much travelling. 'I somehow got my laundry strung out in villages all through Italy', he wrote to his mother, even claiming to have seen people wearing his clothes.[10] He had had enough.

The Trio often thought back to the days when they had dreamed of being in Florence by the time winter closed in; in fact, they spent Christmas in Naples, nearly 300 miles to the south. Geoffrey Keating acquired a twelve-room flat (complete with its own hungry fleas) on the waterfront, with a view across the bay to the Sorrento Peninsula, and the Trio moved in, together with Edward Ardizzone. They found Naples squalid and with a disturbingly violent undercurrent. Clifford had his car stolen again, while the BBC's Frank Gillard had left £3,000 worth of recording truck in a Naples street only for somebody to drive off with it. There was a flourishing black market and most Neapolitans were desperately hungry and, to Ardizzone's eye, suffering from 'the final humiliation of begging from the people they had tried to kill'. By contrast, life for the victors, despite the occasional theft, was apparently a heady diet of 'opera, sun, restaurants, movies'. But, beneath the surface, all was not well: drinks at the flat could end in 'gloomy conclusions', with Alan 'being Tolstoyan', while Naples itself could be unpleasant, its streets dirty and its 'people completely lacking in pride'.[11]

A few days before Christmas, Moorehead and Clifford had turned up at the flat, armed with a live turkey, having been away with 8th Army for a couple of days. Christmas Day itself was beautifully sunny, the ghost of long-lost summer, with drinks on the terrace, a head-clearing climb up Vesuvius to follow and then a heroic rescue of the festive dinner by Clifford who assumed responsibility from the drunken cook who was lying in a stupor on the kitchen floor. The correspondents' flat hosted some 200 guests over the next three days and the celebrations drifted on into the new year.

Christopher Buckley's Christmas was considerably bleaker. He and Richard McMillan had been with 8th Army whose fighting at Ortona was to continue unabated through Christmas Day. Their billet was a damp coastguard cottage – 'a bleak square toiletless house on the edge of the Adriatic'. The correspondents called it 'Dysentery Hall'.[12] As many as thirty correspondents and others lived there. It was a grim location: at one point Buckley discovered an old woman in a cottage surrounded by four dead children. He spent New Year's Eve wrapped in blankets against the cold. A fierce gale was blowing, gusting through the windows where the glass panes should have been. 'The screaming blast tore at shutters, soughed through the rooms, whistled around the eaves, sent the brown-grey waves lashing over the derelict Italian strongpoints on the edge of the beach.'[13] Buckley occupied the time by reading *Persuasion*, a choice of book which could not have been more at odds with the state of the world. It left him distinctly underwhelmed.

In mid-January he made a brief visit to Cairo, but once there, typically, he was worried about 'being caught out of position' – in the wrong place at the right time and missing the big story. He soon returned to the siege of Monte Cassino, 'the fortified mountain crowned by the vast Benedictine monastery which barred the road to Rome'.[14] He would remain there, covering a gratifyingly big story for three months, staring at the mountain's towering presence and driving each day to an observation point near Cervaro. From there, 'on a cold blue February morning' he watched several hundred Flying Fortresses bombing the abbey. 'They flew in perfect formation with something of that arrogant dignity which distinguishes bomber aircraft as they set out on a sortie.'[15]

By the spring of 1944, the Trio had split up for a while, Buckley choosing to stay at Monte Cassino without his two stalwart friends. In fact, he was soon unique: 'Of all the pressmen who had been in Sicily, I alone was left.'[16] In early January Alan Moorehead paid a brief visit to Cassino and it was from there that he sent his last report from Italy before leaving the country. At much the same time, Alexander Clifford took a flight over the snow-capped cordillera of central Italy. From above, under bright sun, he was given a privileged view of that cold, confined and mountainous land, his eye following the bends of an occasional white road snaking through a green valley, or the chill-blue of a river in spate. He was glad to be leaving.

*   *   *   *

In the last months of 1943 Moorehead had grown increasingly anxious to be home in time for the opening of the second front in France. Moreover, he had a new project in mind and wrote to Lucy on New Year's Day 1944 about it: 'I have an idea for the next book so fragile and reeking that I scarcely dare to write about it. It's a book about our summer school in Taormina and our winter school in Naples.'[17] His writing continued to be highly regarded and he was cheered by the success of *The End in Africa*, the first edition of which was soon sold out. His publisher wrote telling him that his 'stock has never stood higher with the British public',[18] and the reviews were extremely positive too: *The Listener* described him as 'easily the best of all the group (of war correspondents)' while his work was 'shrewd, realistic, compelling' (*Evening Standard*) and 'most brilliant, the most imaginative' (*New Statesman*).

His New Year letter also revealed some good news: 'My treasure. I am coming home. Christiansen cabled today.' Shortly before Christmas, Arthur Christiansen had written to Moorehead's father, Richard, in Australia, describing Alan as 'this war's greatest correspondent'. It was a generous letter, praising the correspondent's dynamism, observational gifts, his gift of words, and his loyalty. Christiansen concluded by apologising ('I am sorry that he has not been able to get home'), since he recognised that Alan had been very anxious 'when Australia was in danger of invasion'. He signed off with 'cordial greetings for much happiness in 1944'. It was a letter to make a father very proud, and Moorehead too when he saw it years later.[19] With the new year in sight, the *Express* editor had relented and decided to bring his star correspondent home.

Moorehead and Clifford flew initially to Algiers before, in the third week in January, continuing on to the UK, enjoying a flight in General Eisenhower's personal Flying Fortress, before going in different directions. This parting of the ways coincided with a certain coolness between the two old friends which had been apparent, truth be told, for some time. Moorehead's perception was that 'Alex had never really liked the desert', but was more at ease now he was back in Europe, deploying his gift for languages and settling readily into the Italian way of life. Clifford preferred, Moorehead thought, living on a diet of 'roast chicken and Chianti instead of bully beef and tea, baroque churches instead of tents and Bedouin huts'.[20] Alan's perception of the desert was very different, not least because a physical life in the open air – its simplicity – appealed to him. The campaign in Italy had certainly seen a change in their relationship. Moorehead was often 'irritable and mentally breathless', while Clifford just 'continued calmly on his way'.[21] In addition, Moorehead could not help comparing the stage he had reached in his own life with where Clifford was in his, asking whether Alex might 'end up at that point where I had found him in Athens so long ago'. After all, Clifford was 'still alone, still a dilettante of many different things and a dedicated professional in none'. Hanging over both men, and Buckley too, was the murky uncertainty of the future, not least when exactly the invasion of France would happen. The issue of the second front 'hung over us', Moorehead wrote, 'like the prospect of a major surgical operation that one keeps putting off from month to month, even from year to year. And yet we knew we had to face it in the end.'[22]

* * * *

Once he was back in London, Moorehead was absorbed by a new and hectic life: he wrote a regular column for the *Express*, broadcast on the radio ('congratulations broadcast wonderful'), and embarked on a busy social round which scarcely slowed. In his 1944 diary he logged a relentless tour of classy lunch and dinner establishments – the Dorchester, the Ivy, Claridges, the Grosvenor, the Athenaeum, the Savoy – as well as convivial meetings with establishment people – the writer J.B. Priestley (on 18 February), Ernest Bevin (a week or so before), John Betjeman, Harold Nicholson, Michael Foot, John Soboleff and fellow correspondents (George Millar and Richard Busvine). He lunched with the hero of Alamein, General Montgomery, and at the end of February spent some days following him around as he visited army camps, giving pre-invasion pep talks to the troops. There was something reminiscent of Gandhi about Montgomery, Moorehead thought, while Montgomery evidently respected the Australian correspondent. In January he had written thanking Moorehead for the 'very kind letter' which he and others had sent before Christmas. Monty vowed to 'keep it always' and was at pains to record his gratitude for the way 'you and your comrades played the game' and for not taking 'advantage of me when you might well have done so'.[23]

That spring of 1944 was filled with a sense of waiting, a pause before the downward rush to the war's ending. It was a symbolically appropriate time for both Moorehead and Clifford to be 'mentioned in dispatches' for a second time, 'having rendered signal service' and been 'held in the highest estimation by the Armies to which (they were) attached'.[24] During those spring months, Moorehead spent some nights fire-watching in the capital when there was a renewed threat from the German V1s which began to fall randomly across London. It prompted the Mooreheads in April 1944 to rent a cottage in Jevington, a village close to Eastbourne in Sussex. Years later his son John would wonder about the wisdom of choosing a village in an area vulnerable to misfiring V1s.[25] Perhaps it was the very Englishness of the Sussex Downs which prompted the move, since during that spring and summer before D-Day, Moorehead found himself reflecting on what it was about England that moved him so and what he would miss if he left the country: the English spring, books, girls and draught beer, he thought, as well as the country's timeless quality, its evident desire to cherish a way of life.

By midsummer the lanes of southern England were full of army vehicles, while 'the bright plumage of military uniforms in London dimmed as the capital thinned out'. Restaurant tables and taxi cabs in London became much easier to obtain.[26] Christopher Buckley was using the time to write, telling the military theorist and historian Basil Liddell Hart towards the end of May that he was completing a book about the campaign in Sicily and Italy and just passing the time until the invasion began. There was little doubt that it would be sooner rather than later: 'As the last week of May arrived, there could be little doubt that D-Day was near. The blood – in large, clearly marked canisters – had landed.'[27] Blood was a battlefield necessity and it had a life of two weeks at most.

Finally, on 30 May, Moorehead and the other war correspondents were summoned to the Public Relations Office of Supreme Headquarters Allied Expeditionary Force (SHAEF) at Egerton Gardens, Knightsbridge; they duly collected their field equipment from the Duke of York's Headquarters in Chelsea, and the next day Moorehead left London for Virginia Water. This was for the final pre-D-Day briefing which took place at Wentworth Golf Club, the golf course's trees casting pools of shadow across the grass. The turreted clubhouse and the sprawl of fairways and greens were a reminder of a certain kind of English heaven, in abeyance for the duration. Now its car park was full of dull green army vehicles. Alex Clifford wasn't there – he was to miss D-Day with a bout of jaundice – but, after the briefing, when the pressmen were all given their tasks, Moorehead wandered through the gardens clutching a mug of tea, in company with David Woodward, Richard McMillan, Noel Monks, Chester Wilmot, Ed Kennedy and other old reporter-friends.

Later he set off for camp in the suburbs of Southampton, now fully aware that they were indeed heading for France (an official issuing of francs had scotched any hope of withholding the secret any longer for those due to sail).

It was 1 June when Moorehead went on board his invasion ship and on the day itself he wrote a terse 'Sailed for France' in his diary. Back in London that first night of D-Day, 6 June 1944, Lucy and Alex were both convinced that Alan was already dead.

NOTES

1   *A House in Sicily* by Daphne Phelps, p.9.

2   *Eclipse*, op. cit., p.27.

3   Buckley, p.177.

4   Ibid., p.178.

5   Ibid.

6   *Cossack At Large* by I.S.K. Soboleff, p.174.

7   *Eyewitness* by Noel Monks, pp.207–8.

8   Buckley, p.217.

9   Liddell Hart papers, LH 11/1944/11.

10   Clifford papers (16727), IWM, file AGC/2/1/7; letter from Calabria, dated 22 September 1943.

11   Ardizzone, p.85.

12   Campbell, p.38.

13   *Twenty Angels Over Rome* by Richard McMillan, p.121.

14   Pocock, p.174.

15   *The Daily Telegraph*, 16 February 1944.

16   Buckley, p.302.

17   Pocock, p.173.

18   Moorehead papers, NLA, MS 5654; letter of 17 November 1943.

19   Moorehead papers, NLA, MS 5654; letter dated 23 December 1943.

20   *A Late Education*, op. cit., p.138.

21   Ibid., p.139.

22   Ibid., p.140.

23   Moorehead papers, NLA, MS 5654, letter of 14 January 1944.

24   The National Archives, WO 373/94. The awards were in March 1944.

25   Interview with the author, 13 November 2013.

26   *The Guns at Last Light* by Rick Atkinson, p.25.

27   Ibid.

16. The Lion D'Or, the Ritz and the Canterbury

From the deck, Moorehead looked over the Channel swell towards the invasion beaches, noting the bodies, the wreckage, the churned sand, the craters and shell-holes, crippled tanks, fires and coiled wire. Despite such scarring of the landscape and his enforced lengthy absence from the country, he could still sense the apparently unchanging nature of France. There was the beach, the grey sea, red-roofed houses on yellow cliffs, a windmill high on a hill. It was, Moorehead thought, 'incredibly and inexplicably the same'.[1] Behind him, spread over the water for miles about, was the invasion armada grappling with a heavy sea, the legacy of the bad weather which had threatened the success of the operation. Instead of going ashore that day, Moorehead was forced to wait until the following morning before he landed in France, glad to be away from the ship's rolling movement and the endless, infuriating swing music aboard the American ship. He was carried ashore by a strapping US soldier who hoisted him on to his shoulders and then deposited him, and his mercifully dry typewriter, safely on the sand. He was in France again after five long years.

So, Moorehead was emphatically still alive, despite Lucy and Clifford's fears. He soon teamed up with Christopher Buckley and the two of them wandered around the beachhead observing the seashore's devastation and, in the hinterland to the east and south, the still pristine green fields of France. Moving away from the landing beaches, they set out for the town of Bayeux, some 7 miles inland, through countryside reminiscent of England, with its 'high hedges, leafy lanes, meadows, many tall trees and grey stone villages'.[2] Bayeux had an air of Gallic permanence: the cathedral spire soared upwards, there was Camembert cheese in the shop windows, wine carts slowly creaked and jolted along the streets, and flags fluttered in the breeze. They stopped at the Lion D'Or Hotel hoping for some lunch and expecting the company of other correspondents. The hotel was quaintly provincial, ramshackle and 'set back from the road round a courtyard, coloured canvas awnings over the windows'.[3] The menu had echoes of peacetime: 'soup, omelettes, steak, vegetables, cheese', with some gritty bread, *café nationale* and a dry white Sauternes. As they ate in relative peace, however, collaborators were being beaten not far away in the town's square, blood spilling on the stones and young men with tommy-guns running through the streets.

✳   ✳   ✳   ✳

Alex Clifford was still in England with 21 Army Group, sleeping on the floor of 'a somewhat derelict stately home' and thoroughly dissatisfied with being at HQ, a role which he had 'always steadily avoided doing'.[4] He was acutely aware that 'Alan and the others (were) getting wonderful stuff' in France, and he found the thought depressing. Soon though he crossed the Channel and the Trio reconvened; what the left-wing journalist Tom Driberg called that 'close and formidable caravan'.[5] This late in the war, the three of them were set apart from the rest. Other reporters would look askance when they arrived at HQ to see them already leaving, presumably separately briefed. 'They made an interesting jeep-load,' one correspondent noted. 'Moorehead short, neat, compact like a coiled spring; Clifford, square-shouldered, shy, detached, peering uncompromisingly through his glasses; Buckley, tall, rangy, never looking too comfortable in battledress, unstuffily schoolmasterish with a twinkle or chuckle.'[6] One thing that each member of the press faced was the overriding suspicion of the military, both during the invasion and afterwards, the forty war correspondents being seen as 'an annoying and mysterious band of roving gypsies'.[7] By the time they reached Bayeux, the number of British, American and French war correspondents had increased to sixty.

By 13 June, Clifford reported, the beachhead was 'solid for 60 miles' and Montgomery, in his tank corps beret, cord trousers and grey sweater, confirmed this when he met the correspondents to brief them on progress. 'The beaches,' he said, 'are now behind us'. For a while Clifford lingered in Bayeux which he liked, not least the comforting routine of a regular dinner table at the Lion D'Or, with its excellent food and dreadful service. He would drive back the short distance from the front, 'drinking the rough Norman cider and listening to the guns and watching the flicker of them in the summer night sky'.[8] There were difficulties though: the battlefront remained close enough for the town to be subject to fierce enemy shelling, and Clifford fell foul of the authorities 'about the right to censor our own letters'.[9] He was unwell too with suspected malaria which he had first contracted earlier in the war. He noticed that the mosquito-borne disease afflicted a number of other correspondents who had been in Sicily.

By 3 July Clifford was reporting from Caen, some 15 miles south-east of Bayeux, on the Germans' 'precarious lines of communication' which were subject to constant heavy shellfire and bombing.[10] Caen itself had been reduced to such a state of desolation that it resembled the craters of the moon, the air thick with swirling, choking brick dust. All three members of the Trio felt a mounting despair at the sickening destruction they saw everywhere and the one-time frisson of excitement in the vicinity of danger had now become something of which to be wary. Such caution was heightened by the constant fear over enemy snipers. While the younger and less experienced reporters were readily stirred by events they judged newsworthy, the Trio's default response was a strict adherence to the professional, coupled with an impassive war-weariness. Moorehead saw it as being 'the end of the world, end of the war, the final expression of man's desire to destroy. There was nothing more to see except dust.'[11] When one enthusiastic correspondent, faced with yet more shattered buildings, excitedly pointed out that it was four o'clock and that they just had time to catch the final edition, Alan was unmoved. To him, now, there was little to be gained by describing yet more piles of rubble.

*　*　*　*

Clifford finally moved on from Bayeux in late August with the bout of malaria no longer troubling him. The bosses at the *Daily Mail*, however, were not so easily brushed off. Clifford was disturbed to learn that he would now be required to write for the *Sunday Dispatch* as well. He was also worrying about the quality of his writing – 'worse than ever' he felt, and yet 'the Mail never makes any comment at all'. By the end of August he was contemplating joining the staff of the *Manchester Guardian* after receiving an invitation to write for that paper as well as *The Observer*. 'I don't believe,' he wrote to his mother on 29 August, 'that the *Mail* is going to be any good.'[12]

Moorehead was even more uncertain about the future. In June he had written to Arthur Christiansen indicating that, in September, he wanted to take an extended leave in England, partly to coincide with the new Moorehead baby's arrival, and partly to work on a book. On the last day of July he wrote again, a long letter explaining the reasons. He thanked Christiansen for his generous and fair response, before going on to say that he 'would not dream of asking for leave in September if we were at the gates of Paris or in the midst of a decisive battle'.[13] It came down to wanting to write in a different way, Moorehead wrote, not 'quick, straight and clear', but with greater complexity and tightness, and with less reliance on cliché. He no longer wanted to be seeking the 'quick angle': he recognised that most correspondents 'succumb to the angle that we think the subs will like'. Writing the way he wanted was not possible, Moorehead wrote, 'from the back seat of a jeep bumping around the bridgehead every day'. In a book, the whole story could be told. Moorehead recognised that the *Express* had paid him well and published his prose 'in a very big way', but he now wanted a changed relationship with the newspaper, an arrangement that would keep him clear of journalism until 1947.

*　*　*　*

Towards the end of August, the Trio, together with David Woodward, set off for Paris in a liberated Volkswagen. Woodward had by then recovered from the wounds he sustained during a D-Day glider accident, but other war correspondents continued to prove how dangerous their profession remained. The *Daily Mirror*'s Ian Fyfe had been killed on D-Day itself; Philip Jordan and Evelyn Waugh were both hurt in July when their aircraft crashed; while Russell Hill was wounded when his jeep hit a mine near Aachen. His driver and the *New Yorker*'s David Lardner were both killed, but Hill was lucky enough to escape with bruises and a 'possible fractured arm'.[14] Driving towards Paris, Woodward and the Trio were pleased with the VW's performance – 'it had covered only five hundred kilometres when its owner, a German captain, had been shot dead'[15] – but they were also worried that driving the 'German people's car' – Clifford's words – they might be shot at by the *maquis*.

On the outskirts of Paris, they were halted by a truculent Free French checkpoint and were disconcerted that a pass from Eisenhower's HQ cut no ice at all; only a direct order from General le Clerc would do, and that they didn't have. Eventually they talked their way through and, after some adroit navigation, they were soon on familiar ground, driving through Paris, with the sun shining and recent rain rapidly drying on the pavements. It was as if they had never been away: the cafés, boulevards, *les flics*; 'the racing, changing colours of the city, the uplift of a Paris street.'[16]

The correspondents, censors and the rest were instructed to gather at the Hôtel Scribe where harassed reception staff shook heads and shrugged: 'We have no more rooms'. Clifford would remember the *impasse* the day he returned to the hotel in March 1946 when he was eventually turned away in odd circumstances. At the Ritz, where the roomless war correspondents proceeded, the reception was more accommodating, although the sight of Ernest Hemingway loudly presiding over the dining room while quaffing a bottle of Perrier-Jouët champagne was disconcerting. The American writer had evidently 'completely forgotten he was a war correspondent' and instead had installed himself as the head of a group of *maquis*, 'having lent his portable typewriter to another correspondent'.[17] On his arrival at the Ritz, Hemingway had been promptly given rooms for his 'Private Army' and then proceeded to order a large round of drinks. 'The bartender could not be found and the cocktails were mediocre. But Ernest was finally in nominal possession of the Ritz.'[18] Unperturbed, the occupants of the liberated German people's car settled back for a good lunch and champagne of their own.

Later, the Trio, with Moorehead at the wheel, drove the VW slowly down the Champs Élysées in a nose-to-tail convoy in the wake of the regal General de Gaulle as he marched ahead. On all sides vast crowds sang 'La Marseillaise', the noise increasing as de Gaulle slowly and stiffly bent to lay a wreath. When Alan glanced round at the other occupants of the car he saw that they were all in tears. Alexander Clifford wept all the way from the Arc de Triomphe to Notre Dame where gunfire from snipers changed the mood. It was, he thought, an unsurpassably emotional moment, triggered for him by seeing a list of Spanish Civil War defeats daubed on the sides of armoured cars driven by members of the Free French. Ironically, the *Mail* had not wanted him in Paris, but rather to stay at the front, an instruction which he resented and ignored. Indeed there was enough of a *contretemps* with the paper to prompt him to request a recall to England. 'Nothing on earth', he wrote, 'was going to stop me.'[19] The solution was to be there but not to file a single word. 'I don't know what the *Mail* will say when they find I was there'. Nor did he care much. It was enough to be there and witness what the city's liberation meant. That meaning was brought home to Moorehead in an interview with one French citizen: 'I'll tell you what liberation is. It's hearing a knock on my door at six o'clock in the morning and knowing it's the milkman.'[20]

There was another kind of liberation on Moorehead's mind, infinitely less newsworthy, but even more personal. While he was in Paris, he was also still corresponding with Christiansen about the future. On 3 September 1944 he wrote to the *Express* editor declaring that he did not wish to be the paper's Paris correspondent in the longer term, although, 'since Paris is becoming the centre of everything in Europe I should become the nominal head of the bureau here for the next few months'.[21] Working in the French capital was chaotic, with a series of difficulties caused by the need to find suitable offices, the creaking telephone system, and the city's transport. He went on to say that he was leaving for the front and the anticipated liberation of Brussels.

On 6 September Christopher Buckley reported, 'We chased the Germans back into Brussels this evening and we chased them out the other side. It was the climax of an advance in which the British armoured forces advanced 73 miles between sunrise and sunset.'[22] The Germans had almost gone, but their stocks of wine remained behind – about 80,000 bottles of a 'remarkable' claret – and it fuelled a glorious celebratory binge which continued for ten exhausting days. If the liberation of Paris had been stirring and memorable, the taking of Brussels was wild, chaotic to the point of being crazed. 'Paris', Moorehead thought, 'was a pallid thing compared to this extravaganza.'[23] It was Alex Clifford's intuitive sense of timing which had brought him to Brussels at the very moment when the city was about to fall, with the result that the *Daily Mail* correspondent accompanied the first five tanks as they burst into the city on 3 September.[24] The tank-led charge was fraught with risk, but irresistibly exciting. There was also something neatly rounded about re-entering the city where he had been on the very day war was declared. A tank battle was raging in the Boulevards, but Clifford used his knowledge of the backstreets to skirt trouble and soon 'captured the best hotel which the Germans had just that minute moved out of'.[25] The reward was 'floods of champagne' and the hotel's Royal suite where, despite 'frightening bills', he stayed two weeks. When Alan Moorehead arrived in the city the day after its fall, the Trio was reunited and in a position to savour the pleasures of Brussels.

The Belgian capital exceeded all other liberated cities in its celebrations of freedom. It was 'a glitzy sin-city, with countless bars, night clubs and cabarets for most known and unknown forms of entertainment'.[26] At the Canterbury Hotel where the press foregathered, a pliant officer kept tabs on which correspondents had 'company' with a carefully updated list in the mess. There were parties too, for one of which Lucy Moorehead provided from London a record of the Broadway hit *Oklahoma*. David Woodward and Michael Moynihan of the *News Chronicle* stayed at the Palace Hotel in Brussels but 'fed at the Canterbury, and treated ourselves to a well-earned whoopee'.[27] Moynihan's view of the Trio – the 'Big Three' as he called them – was typical of some reporters. Since Normandy, he claimed, they had 'waxed fat on luxurious, expense-paid living, rarely bothering to visit front-line troops'; moreover, he resented their 'supercilious air of having seen it all before'.[28] This ignored the simple fact that they *had* seen it all before. They also shared a brittle weariness which came from long years of war and led to a profound 'bleakness of the soul'. Clifford spoke for each member of the Trio when he wrote in November, 'Oh God I wish it would all end'.[29] Moorehead, for one, sensed that they had changed, having become 'more cheerful and yet more selfish, more materialistic than we were before'.[30] Certainly these survivors of a long war had grown more cautious, reluctant to risk taking a stray bullet as the end approached. Soft living in Brussels – the oysters, champagne, the long lunches – was infinitely preferable to a painful spell in a field hospital. In Clifford's case, the temptations of Brussels even included the attentions of 'the brewer's wife' who had fallen in love with him (and whose clutches he was keen to evade).[31] Escape he did, but only to fall in love elsewhere.

In the summer of 1944 an honorary associate of the Trio emerged, in a way its unofficial fourth member …

NOTES

1   *Eclipse*, op. cit., p.100.
2   Ardizzone, p.128.
3   *Eclipse*, op. cit., p.103.
4   Clifford papers (16727), IWM, file AGC/2/1/8; letter dated 10 June 1944.
5   Driberg was a former *Daily Express* journalist.
6   Pocock, p.187. The correspondent was Doon Campbell of Reuters.
7   Atkinson, p.30. He is quoting the reporter Don Whitehead.
8   *Daily Mail*, 6 June 1946.
9   Clifford papers (16727), IWM, file AGC/2/1/8; letter dated 2 July 1944.
10 *Daily Mail*, 3 July 1944.
11 *Eclipse*, op. cit., p.133.
12 Clifford papers (16727), IWM, file AGC/2/1/8; letters dated 13 and 29 August 1944.
13 Moorehead papers, NLA, MS 5654; letter of 31 July 1944.
14 The National Archives, WO 229/21.
15 *Eclipse*, op. cit., p.148.
16 Ibid., p.151.
17 *Papa Goes to War* by Charles Whiting, p.93.
18 *Ernest Hemingway* by Carlos Baker, p.495.
19 Clifford papers (16727), IWM, file AGC/2/1/8; letter dated 29 August 1944.
20 *Eclipse*, op. cit., p.168.
21 Moorehead papers, NLA, MS 5654.
22 *The Daily Telegraph*, 6 September 1944.
23 *Eclipse*, op. cit., p.182.
24 Clifford was proud of his sense of timing which he thought had been remarkably good from the very start of the war.
25 Clifford papers (16727), IWM, file AGC/2/1/8; letter dated 17 September 1944.
26 Campbell, p.88.
27 Moynihan, p.130.
28 Ibid., p.131.
29 Clifford papers (16727), IWM, file AGC/2/4; letter dated 1 November 1944.
30 *A Late Education*, op. cit., p.141.
31 Clifford papers (16727), IWM, file AGC/2/4; letter dated 19 October 1944.

17. 'Some News For You'

Jenny Nicholson is sitting alongside Alan Moorehead as he drives an open jeep through the tumultuous, liberated streets of Brussels. To the observer, she and Moorehead look as if they are the comfortably devoted couple, with Alex Clifford in the background. Indeed both he and Buckley are rather uncomfortably perched on the jeep's back seat. A photographer snapped the group on that liberation cavalcade: Jenny looks small – she can even look up to the diminutive Moorehead. Pudgy-cheeked and toothy, she looks homely rather than flirtatious. Clifford, in beret and sunglasses, has an earnest look, his hands clasped, as if nursing some unknown anxiety, while Christopher Buckley contrives to look as if his uniform and officer's cap were made for a different, bigger man. Moorehead's grin is broad, as if he is enjoying the moment for itself, the riotous liberation and, perhaps, the evidence that love is in the air! He has the air of a man who leads others as if by right – and after all, in the Trio, he is presently the only married man.

Jenny Nicholson was the daughter of the poet and writer Robert Graves – it was by dint of her mother Nancy Nicholson's insistence that her daughter took her name. Jenny had been in the Women's Auxiliary Air Force (WAAF) since 1941 and had followed the invasion forces from the early days in Normandy. At one time, early that summer, she had flirted with Moorehead, but she soon realised that he was spoken for, clearly in love with his absent wife, and so she and Clifford were increasingly drawn to each other. From a camp in Belgium she wrote to Basil Liddell Hart reporting that her neighbour in the next-door tent was his friend, Alexander Clifford. Jenny, at 25, was ten years younger than Clifford, born on 6 January 1919. She was attractive rather than beautiful, tactile, bursting with confidence and invariably talked loudly and often. Moorehead watched the affair burgeoning, regarding it as 'the least predictable of attachments and the most inevitable'.[1] Jenny had the very qualities which Clifford lacked – vivacity, a certainty about her social position (her godparents, for example, were

Siegfried Sassoon and Max Beerbohm, while she was related to the painters Sir William and Ben Nicholson). She was energetic, eager, willing to take risks. 'Alex rose from the depths like a leaping trout,' Moorehead wrote later, reflecting on how Clifford had been neatly hooked and landed, breathless in Brussels. Alex was inordinately proud of her and her sudden appearance in his life seemed the perfect antidote to the impending grim foray into defeated Germany, with its ruined cities and desperate people. When she wasn't there, he missed her terribly – 'there is something cheerless about going to bed alone which I have never felt before'.[2]

* * * *

Towards the end of October, Alan went back to England for the birth of his second child. Clifford reported to his mother that Lucy had 'apparently produced it in about ten minutes when no one was looking – even the nurse was not properly there'.[3] He, Buckley and David Woodward entertained each other by making up a list of potential names for the little girl, born on 28 October 1944. The navy-obsessed Woodward 'wanted to call her Formidable'; Christopher Buckley, who was to be the baby's godfather, proposed 'Alamein' and 'Old Man's Beard', while Clifford 'plumped for the good old Spanish name of "Contracepcion". We all thought Fatima was good.'[4] In the event, the Mooreheads, despite Buckley and Clifford's whimsical suggestions, called their daughter Caroline.

The weather in the autumn of 1944 was often bad – cold and wet, leaving the roads slick with mud. Not every night was spent carousing in the fleshpots of Brussels; more typical was the night, not far from Arnhem, when they wandered for hours through the town's darkened streets looking for somewhere to stay. They were a sorry sight: muddy and 'desperate looking', some of their kit lost and with one of them showing signs of coming down with malaria. Throwing open a welcoming door to such a motley crew on a black night of rain and wind would have meant a considerable act of faith.

Beyond the gloom of autumnal Northern Europe there was the murk of the future to worry about too. Alex Clifford, for example, was asked to write a biography of Rommel, but turned the idea down since it would mean 'an awful lot of work' and perhaps require the energy and drive that he was presently lacking. At one point, he was approached by the *News of the World* to see if he would consider moving over to them; meanwhile the *Mail* offered him 'a substantial increase in salary', evidently worried about losing their special correspondent.

* * * *

'Liberating two capitals like Paris and Brussels in ten days – it's – it's more than humans can stand!'[5] That was how Richard McMillan explained away his and

Ronald Monson's weary response to yet another sustained bout of vigorous kissing, this time by a 'slender young girl', evidently overflowing with liberated gratitude. 'Let's get into an hotel and shut ourselves in,' yelled Monson, and the two correspondents took flight. There was only so much celebrating that a liberator could endure after all. Those correspondents who had been there from the beginning were exhausted. It was clear to everyone, bar the most stubborn Nazi, that the war was all but over, but when would it actually stop? That sense of an ending subtly changed attitudes. Moorehead caught the mood when he asked, 'What was the sense of being killed at the eleventh hour?'[6] In Britain, the talk largely centred on what kind of new world would replace the old one, once the fighting had stopped. The fighting itself was of secondary interest and in London, newspaper editors had taken to spiking stories, in response to what they saw as the changed context. The *News Chronicle*'s Michael Moynihan discovered later that only seven of his pieces were used out of twenty-four written over a thirty-two-day period. In mid-October, Montgomery's chief of staff, Major General 'Freddie' de Guingand felt the need to intervene: 'I gave one of my periodical [sic] talks to the war correspondents on October 18th and tried to help them'.[7] But everyone recognised that only a renewed sense of progress towards the German border would really help.

For weeks there was little respite from the drudgery of briefings, eating and drinking, reading and sleeping, but at last, on 16 November, the long-awaited Allied offensive began. Michael Moynihan for one was relieved: 'Thank God the waiting is over and there is something to do and write about.'[8] The advance proved hard going, however, so much so that 'the seven armies, straining forward together side by side, were measuring their gains only in thousands of yards',[9] something which raised the prospect of trench warfare. But there was progress of a kind: the lines of sullen German prisoners in their grubby green uniforms testified to that, as did the confidence exuding from their US guards, gum-chewing and alert, their guns raised, waiting to crush the first sign of trouble.

By December the advance had reached the borders of Germany itself, in grim winter weather. The snow fell from sombre skies, seemingly without end, and the front was a mix of churned mud and frozen ruts. Petrol froze; even the anti-freeze succumbed to the cold, while 'men froze to death in their fox-holes in the night'.[10] The front itself had become 'as fluid as Niagara',[11] making the reporting of developments uncertain and confused. Then, on Saturday 16 December, the Germans under Field Marshal von Rundstedt launched a surprise counter-attack in the wooded hills of the Ardennes, its speed such that their troops appeared in rapid succession in village after village from which the Allies had been obliged to retreat. The following day things were clearly out of control, a situation made worse by a thick fog which had descended on the battlefield, cloaking everything in confusion. Around Brussels and Liège the fog had a milky quality, while in the heights of the Ardennes, above the blanket of fog, there were 'mile upon mile of untrodden snowfields under the clear and frosty lamp of the winter sun'.[12] The sky was ice blue, the trees crusted with white frost, and high above, the Flying Fortresses spun vapour trails across the sky. The Australian correspondent Noel Monks, after driving around the frozen hills for ten hours, 'had to be hauled bodily from jeep to hotel' so benumbed was he by the cold.[13]

Many of the correspondents spent Christmas at the Canterbury Hotel in Brussels, including David Walker and Michael Moynihan who looked askance at some of his fellow reporters: 'The Big Three … Monty's blue-eyed boys from the desert war days, were much in evidence'.[14] Moynihan disapproved too of Jenny Nicholson, thinking her 'status as a WAAF appeared merely academic'.

Meanwhile, back in the UK, the overriding concern was the weather: 'A group of Southwark housewives … besieged their town hall demanding help',[15] so desperate were they about the spate of burst pipes in what was the coldest winter for fifty-four years, and the shortage of plumbers. The Channel was tinged with ice, while Big Ben froze. So too did milk bottles on the doorsteps of London, fingers of solid milk bursting the frost-bound glass. In Berlin, von Rundstedt's offensive was seen to be 'the most beautiful Christmas present for Germans one could wish'[16] – but it wasn't destined to last into the New Year.

✳   ✳   ✳   ✳

Clifford stared out of the window at the wintry streets of Brussels and contemplated the Christmas he hadn't had in England. As if that wasn't bad enough, he was preoccupied with how best to tell his mother the most startling news of 1944. It could not, he thought, be postponed any longer. He had nursed hopes of telling the family when he was home for the festivities, but the last-ditch German offensive had put paid to that, so it must be done by letter.

The Trio had become adept at making a wartime Christmas acceptably festive, whether it was celebrated in Benghazi, Naples or some miserable desert sand-trap. It usually involved last-minute searches for suitable yuletide poultry, confused cooking arrangements and stellar Boxing Day hangovers. This time, in Brussels, Jenny had organised Christmas stockings for Clifford and the others; there had been breakfast in bed, a concert by the Hallé Orchestra and goose for dinner, enjoyed with ample supplies of champagne from Rheims. Wondering what Christmas in Lindfield had been like, Clifford began to write.

'I have some news for you, though I am sure I don't know if you're going to like it.' He hesitated, then after a moment of uncertainty, got to the point: 'The fact is, I am proposing to get married. I don't know when, but it could easily be quite soon since the young person concerned is over here and we must take the best opportunity'.[17] Having got that off his chest, he turned to 'the girl in question', explaining the apparent anomaly of her name – 'an odd idea. But she is quite legitimate', and reassuring his mother that she shouldn't worry about the age gap. He could all too easily imagine 'mama' remarking 'but she's so much younger than you!' so he stretched her age to 26 which is what she soon would be. He touched on her 'bizarre and curiously unsuitable' career, reporting that 'she has in fact been one of Mr Cochran's young ladies, a ballet dancer, a chorus girl, an actress; a radio writer for the BBC'. He described her book *Kiss the Girls Goodbye*, an account of life in the WAAF, as 'more or less a best seller' and explained that she was working while in Belgium, writing articles for American and British papers as well as developing the script of an official film about the invasion. 'She doesn't drink, or smoke and she is definitely plain,' he wrote. He smiled, imagining the cat unsettling the Sussex pigeons.

* * * *

The drab autumn preceded a ferociously bleak winter and it became increasingly clear that there was still much hardship to endure. Early 1945 was a time of floods, freezing temperatures, bone-hard ground and famine, all rendered more intolerable by the Germans' desperate resistance. It made for bleak reporting. If there was a glimmer of light it was the evident change in Alexander Clifford. That early spring, Moorehead could see that his old friend had changed greatly, being more confident, more at ease with those around him, more tolerant of minor officials, and more generous. He looked different too, perhaps the result of those long years in Africa and the legacy of the French summer: he was deeply sunburnt, tall and handsome. It wasn't hard to find a reason for the overall transformation – 'plain' Jenny Nicholson.

NOTES

1 *A Late Education*, op. cit., p.142.
2 Clifford papers (16727), IWM, file AGC/2/3; letter to Jenny Nicholson, 12 October 1944.
3 Ibid., letter of 8 November 1944.
4 Ibid., letter dated 3 November 1944.
5 *Miracle Before Berlin* by Richard McMillan, p.88.
6 *Eclipse*, op. cit., p.210.
7 De Guingand, p.424.
8 Moynihan, p.112.
9 *Eclipse*, op. cit., p.208.
10 Ibid., p.217.

11   Moynihan, p.123.

12   *Eclipse*, op. cit., p.217.

13   Moynihan, pp.127–8. Monk's wife, Mary, had left him for Ernest Hemingway.

14   Ibid., p.131.

15   *London 1945* by Maureen Waller, p.155.

16   *The Daily Telegraph*, 31 December 1944.

17   Clifford papers (16727), IWM, file AGC/2/1/8; letter dated 28 December 1944.

18. 'That's What You're Here For'

On 14 January 1945 Jenny was summoned back to England by the Air Ministry and immediately posted to RAF Northwood, while Alex Clifford remained in Brussels, missing her, and worrying about how his family in Sussex would view the proposed marriage. 'She isn't the sort of person you probably expected me to get for a wife,' he wrote, admitting too that the Ministry's recall of his wife-to-be appeared to be because she was in some sort of trouble, something which 'she often seems to be' he admitted in a letter home written the day she left.[1] He needn't have worried about his mother's reaction: 'Papa and I are *delighted* … your Jenny will fit herself into the family, and she will be *very welcome*.' A relieved Alex reported the good news back to Jenny soon after, adding, in an uncharacteristically ill-chosen phrase, 'It only remains for you to make a good impression'. He encouraged her to visit her prospective in-laws, giving the most detailed instructions: 'the telephone number is Lindfield 96 (a toll call). That is really the telephone number of Pages, the local bakery, and we have an extension, so you must insist on Mrs Clifford.' She must take the train to Haywards Heath; turn sharp right out of the station; make herself known to the 'lady with spectacles' who would arrange for a taxi to Walstead, 'a village of about twelve houses beyond Lindfield, and my house is the very first house you get to'.[2]

Clifford had more on his mind than his mother's reaction to his wedding plans, or even the bitter winter war that was being waged close to the German border. His health had become a matter of growing concern. He had 'an outbreak of leprosy or some other skin disease',[3] the visible signs of which were a running sore on his face. The cause was unknown and the medics seemed nonplussed – was it frostbite perhaps? – and they had tried to hospitalise him, something which Clifford initially managed to prevent, but rapidly had to accept. He was admitted to a hospital situated some distance from Brussels, suffering from an 'obscure and anonymous malady', as he put it, but hopeful that he was getting better and would be out fairly soon. His visitors included Christopher Buckley whose visits were never less than entertaining. For example, 'The day the Russians broke through', Alex wrote, 'he was so full of champagne he could scarcely speak. In addition somebody had sent him a book of 700 pages about the battles of Monte Cassino in 1757 or something, so he was blissfully happy.' On another occasion he brought champagne and a map with him, proceeding then to brief everyone on the ward about the latest military situation. Once, he arrived in the middle of a concert party and blithely walked in front of the stage to where Alex was sitting in the front row, carrying a 'war game, a PR bag, half a dozen maps, some assorted books, a tin of coffee and some clean underclothes'.[4] Buckley (or 'Xopher' as Clifford usually wrote) was struggling to write an alternative ending to *Road to Rome* which his publisher Heinemann thought too gloomy. 'Now he is closeted in the Canterbury, pecking at his typewriter by candlelight, trying to come up with a happy ending to replace the bloodbath of Monte Cassino.'[5]

A week passed and Clifford remained hopeful of being discharged, although he was not convinced that he was much better, and, in the event, the following day he suffered a relapse. He suspected that it might be because he was allergic to penicillin. Jenny too was in hospital in England and in a long typewritten letter, he tried to look beyond the here and now into a better, more certain future. He touched on the importance of their having a baby, and about buying a house together in Dorset, or perhaps the two of them taking off for a skiing holiday in Chamonix. He was keen that the Mooreheads should be told of their wedding plans 'because they will feel hurt if they hear it definitely from another source', and worried that Jenny's melancholy might return in his absence.

While he was incarcerated in hospital there were further signs that, amongst the younger war correspondents, the Trio was not universally popular: 'the lower orders of Warcos revolted and claimed that the old gang was forming a close oligarchy'.[6] There was considerable comfort in the fact that, when it came to an election, despite the rumblings of discontent, the old War Correspondents' Committee was duly returned, since the Trio were all active members and Moorehead was the committee chairman. Ironically, when a meeting was proposed between the new committee and the chief of staff of 2nd Army 'it turned out Alan was in England, I was in hospital, McMillan and Monson were hopelessly drunk and Illingworth and the American were in the front line'. So the malcontent young warcos went instead.

Beyond the hospital, the Belgian winter was profoundly depressing – the cold was unrelenting and brutal: there was a shortage of coal, electric light was banned during the day, there was no heating day or night, and there were no trams running after 7 p.m. Alex spent his time censoring the letters of 'other ranks' and, in occupational therapy, using Perspex to make a shoe horn, a holder for his shaving stick and some candlesticks. He toyed with starting a book, but

'The wedding cake was cut with an SS officer's knife' – the wedding of Alex Clifford and Jenny Nicholson. (IWM, Clifford Papers)

the atmosphere in the hospital felt completely wrong. His sense of isolation was heightened by the fact that letters from Jenny would often arrive in bulk, but would then often be followed by days of dispiriting silence. It seemed that he would never get out of hospital.

It was early February before he was released and the wedding of Alex Clifford and Jenny Nicholson took place soon after, on 22 February, in the Royal Chapel of the Savoy Hotel in London. Only the immediate family were there, although there was a celebratory party in the Savoy's River Room that evening. Jenny's father, Robert Graves, who had written a poem to mark the occasion, arrived for the ceremony without a tie, a crisis resolved when Jenny cut and fashioned him one from the room's velvet curtains. The wedding cake was cut with an SS officer's knife which Alex had looted from a train in Holland.

* * * *

Once the Cliffords had honeymooned in North Wales, the Trio was reunited, entering Germany together through 'lush green countryside', the fields full of cattle, with farms that seemed rich and fertile. It was the Germans themselves who revealed the true level of suffering, 'reduced to the state of herded animals'. Each guesthouse or shop had 'a discoloured patch on the wallpaper' where Hitler's picture had been removed.[7] The Trio progressed from one farmhouse or small hotel to the next, invariably enjoying comfortable billets and obsequious service from Germans who cleaned the rooms, washed clothes and acted out the required rites of defeat. The villages through which they passed were crowded with refugees from bombed-out towns and cities. When they reached Cologne they were stunned by its ruins, the only recognisable landmark still standing being the twin spires of the city's cathedral. Most of the other buildings had simply collapsed into dust and rubble. With the dark twin towers of the cathedral behind them, they sat on the steps eating a cold chicken, looking at the city's ruins and contemplating both the crossing of the Rhine and the sheer scale of the destruction. As ever, when faced with the detritus of battle, they took the opportunity to indulge in a little gentle looting. Earlier, in Wesel, it had been deeply disturbing to see Pathfinder flares tumbling from the sky, knowing that the town 'had just about ten minutes to live' before the bombs rained down on the glowing target.[8] In the middle of March Christopher Buckley had seen some 3,000 foreign workers – Russians, Poles, French, Dutch, Belgians, Italians, Spaniards, Czechs, Serbians and Armenians – sitting patiently inside unlocked prison cells, or wandering in confusion through the prison's tiled corridors, or stoically standing in long, unmoving queues in the forlorn expectation of food. Germany, it seemed, was on the verge of collapse.

It was a time of poignant contrasts. At night the Trio slept under down and feather-filled white German bolsters; the lanes through which they drove were green with new leaf and in the evening they wrote dispatches by candlelight, fuelled by rare old French wine, rescued 'from a mob of Russians and Poles who were looting and smashing them' and yelling for beer.[9] Once they stayed 'in a quiet old-world rectory with a harmonium in the parlour'. When they eventually decided to move closer to the front, the unprepared Buckley was thrown into a panic: his bed disappeared under mountains of packing and, in the confusion, he lost his bedroll, but compensated for that by finding some rations which had been missing since the early days of the invasion in Normandy many months before.

German resistance was much in evidence as they moved east, both its intensity and its forlorn nature best symbolised perhaps by the trainloads of V-weapons stranded in bombed-out sidings, the rail tracks twisted and bent beyond immediate repair. The Trio lived in fear of lone snipers potentially lurking around each corner, and they argued amongst themselves about the most fitting way to treat the Germans. The war artist Edward Ardizzone was moved by their plight: 'so English-looking and frightened-looking too that one can't help feeling sorry, though one shouldn't'.[10] He was obliged to carry a revolver at all times; it was, he wrote, 'the bane of my life'. David Woodward and Clifford were judged by colleagues to be 'too kind' to the enemy; Alex noted that 'the worst thing is repressing the brutality of Alan (who) gets annoyed because I am so soft'.[11] On 9 April 1945 the Trio arrived at Diepholz where the press had set up camp in an inn, and that evening they enjoyed a grand reunion with Ardizzone, Geoffrey Keating, Ted Gilling and Ron Monson, before moving off next morning towards Bremen, bowling along the sleek German autobahn smiled upon by a bright sun and blue sky. They did not suspect the darkness to come.

On 13 April, towards nine o'clock, two German colonels drove up to the British lines, accompanied by half a dozen Hungarians. They carried a white flag and requested a truce, since there had been an outbreak of typhus among the 60,000 or so prisoners in a nearby concentration camp. They were near the village of Belsen, to the north of Hanover. The approach to the Belsen concentration camp gave no hint of what lay beyond the wire. It was wooded and beautiful. Then they saw the signs warning of typhus and the dark truth began to be revealed. They were sprayed with anti-louse powder on arrival and then conducted along a path strewn on both sides with emaciated bodies. 'The living men, women and children looked like walking skeletons'.[12] But there were corpses too, thousands of them, many of them naked, 'stacked one on top of another, limbs awry and twisted, carelessly flung in like so much garbage'. The stunned correspondents walked around the camp, each revelation adding to the horror of it all, stumbling around with handkerchiefs pressed to their noses because of the smell. It was 'a stench that you feel will never get out of your nostrils', Clifford wrote later. What they were witnesses to was incomprehensible and left Alex 'groping for some ingredient of human mentality which could explain it all'.[13] At one point they were shown a doctor who had injected 'creosote and petrol into the prisoners' veins' and who would occasionally inspect their huts, complain of the excess numbers, and then shoot at them randomly with his revolver. It was truly a nightmare – 'a journey down some Dantesque pit, unreal, leprous and frightening' – and Moorehead, for one, found he could not look for more than a second before turning his head away. It was impossible to 'distinguish men from women, or indeed to determine whether they were human at all'. Finally he said, 'I've had enough of this,' but the British officer conducting them round was insistent that they continue on into the men's huts. 'That's what you're here for,' he said.[14] Alan Moorehead would never forget what he saw in the Belsen camp and, while he could write about it, he did not talk about it afterwards. His daughter Caroline never knew about what he had seen that day until she read her father's account in *Eclipse*. 'It was too awful for him to talk about,' she said.[15]

Later, towards the end of the month, Alex Clifford reported that 'six white-faced German mayors, with handkerchiefs clamped to their noses, walked through the hell of Belsen concentration camp today. They had been brought to see it on behalf of their villages, and what they saw was still hell.'[16]

Entering the concentration camp at Belsen. (IWM, BU 3927)

Three weeks or so after the war ended, Moorehead received a letter from a government official in Whitehall asking him to 'consider again how desirable it is to say what you have done about looting by troops and the beating up of SS men at Belsen'.[17] There was already concern that such descriptions might 'provide material for the propagandist of the future'.

*   *   *   *

Faced with painful memories of the Belsen camp, the Trio tried hard to cling to some kind of normality with Clifford inevitably continuing to act as 'shopper and cook and housekeeper and interpreter for our whole party'.[18] He even gave Buckley a driving lesson, a task 'that really is dangerous'. Christopher Buckley's sole job, it seems, was 'to put fresh flowers in the flower vase in our limousine' and he was prone to forget even that 'cushy number'.[19] Over convivial dinners with Ardizzone and others, the Trio consumed bottles of wine from 'a better collection of French wines than we shall ever drink in our lives again'.[20] But they could not avoid witnessing the stark reality of what Germany had become as they travelled across the country, passing through dozens of towns and cities where three years of heavy bombing had wreaked havoc and the ruins still breathed smoke. 'Many of them had no electric light or power or gas or running water, and no coherent system of government.'[21] The destruction eventually became unbearable and each member of the Trio decided not to go to Berlin to witness the final rites. 'We are all at the stage', Clifford wrote, 'when we are telling one another that we are old and broken and written out and need a holiday.'[22] Instead of wandering disconsolately through the ruins of Berlin, aghast at how little remained, they abruptly stopped their trek eastwards and opted instead to stay for a while 'in the most delicious little house – the sitting room all window and light and the most enchanting meandering river'.[23]

*   *   *   *

At 6 p.m., on an early May evening, on roads slick with rain, the Seventh Armoured Division, the Desert Rats, drove into the city of Hamburg. At their head was 'the German garrison commander, General Wolz, riding a captive car'. It was, Moorehead wrote, 'the climax of England's war'[24] – and, of course, the nadir of Germany's. Soon after 5 p.m. on 4 May 1945, on an afternoon of gusting winds and scudding showers, the war correspondents gathered in a tent at Montgomery's headquarters. The guns were silenced at last, presumably not to be heard again. Uncharacteristically, Montgomery's press briefing was 'a masterpiece of simplification and condensation';[25] then, more in keeping with his reputation, he made the Germans wait an additional thirty minutes, before leading the way back to his caravans on the hill above the heath. The Trio was together as the surrender was signed: Clifford described watching 'a group of glum – though gaudily dressed – German Wehrmacht chiefs sign';[26] Moorehead observed that Montgomery 'conducted the proceedings rather like a schoolmaster taking an oral examination';[27] Christopher Buckley, in a *Daily Telegraph* piece, wrote: 'At 6.25 this evening, in a tent on a windswept heath under grey, lowering clouds, five German plenipotentiaries, in the presence of Field Marshal Montgomery, put their signatures to the surrender of the German armies of the north. This is the end.'[28]

Two days later they were all in Copenhagen – Buckley, Clifford and Moorehead, Geoffrey Keating, Ted Ardizzone – the extended Trio – with the war artist driving them around the city to see the Danish celebrations, after which they settled down to a long lunch at the Tivoli. Later they flew through ominous cloud to the Norwegian capital, Oslo, and were greeted with a flamboyant Nazi salute from a

Surrender at Lüneburg Heath, May 1945. (IWM, BU 5208)

German colonel (who was 'festooned with medals') and by two air commodores. The colonel extended a hand which no one would shake and this was followed by a fleeting moment of uncertainty before the multilingual Clifford – exhorted to 'Keep him talking Alex!' by the press cameramen – successfully deployed his German to negotiate surrender. The anticipated aircraft from Scotland, with key officials aboard, had yet to arrive, but the polyglot Clifford's German was fluent enough for the enemy commanders to accept the fact of defeat and surrender without further delay. Had they been Russians, he was told, then there would have been resistance, an idle threat which made Moorehead smile, 'since our force totalled a dozen men against at least a hundred thousand Germans in Norway.'[29]

Flying out of Norway, the Trio, still together, reflected on the past five years' journey, from those early days in Cairo, on through the length and breadth of Libya (and back again), south into the heart of Africa, then Syria, Iraq, Iran, Algeria, Italy, France and Belgium. In particular, Moorehead contemplated 'the three of us who had made that long march up to Taormina in Sicily so long ago'.[30] Eventually he settled back into his seat and looked down on a cloud-draped Europe before beginning to doze. Both Buckley and Clifford were already fast asleep.

With the war in Europe over, what lay ahead? The easy part was deciding to drive back to London together. With Alan at the wheel they set out on the familiar Lüneburg-Hanover road. They drove past prison camps where the inmates were still staring blankly out from behind the wire, the peace so far having by-passed them. There was a chill moment when they drove past Belsen, each man silent and wrapped in his own memories of the horrors they had seen. They argued, as they often did, about the conduct of the war, sometimes even agreeing. Germany in that early summer often looked green and pleasant – until they drove through yet another town where there was nothing left to bomb. Moorehead drove them past the twisted wreckage of the Ruhr; over the Ernie Pyle bridge in Dusseldorf (named for a celebrated American war correspondent who had died just weeks before); and on towards the west. In Liège there was nowhere to sleep, so they bedded down, in a poignant reminder of other ad hoc billets, in a barn over a garage.

Eventually they reached London. The relief now that it was all over was immense: 'Five years of watching war,' Moorehead wrote, 'have made me personally hate and loathe war, especially the childish waste of it.'[31] He, Clifford and Buckley – together with other survivors of the conflict – had now to make their uncertain ways into a very different world. They were each scarred by what they had seen, tired beyond belief, and would now embark on a future where their paths diverged. Like the war, the Trio's time had passed.

NOTES

1   Ibid., file AGC/2/1/9; letter dated 14 January 1945.

2   Ibid., undated letter from Clifford to Jenny.

3   Ibid., letter of 14 January 1945.

4   Ibid., letter of 20 January 1945.

5   Ibid., letter dated 3 February 1945.

6   Ibid., letter dated 26 January 1945.

7   *Eclipse*, op. cit., p.220.

8   Ibid., p.230.

9   Clifford papers (16727), IWM, file AGC/2/1/9; letter of 23 April 1945.

10 Ardizzone, p.192.

11 Clifford papers (16727), IWM, file AGC/2/1/9; letter of 3 April 1945 to Jenny Nicholson.

12 Soboleff, p.180.

13 Clifford and Nicholson, p.221.

14 *Eclipse*, op. cit., pp.254–5.

15 Interview with the author, 13 March 2013.

16 *Daily Mail*, 25 April 1945.

17 Moorehead papers, NLA, file MS 5654.

18 Clifford papers (16727), IWM, file AGC/2/1/9; letter of 23 April 1945.

19 Ibid., letter of 14 April 1945.

20 Clifford papers (16727), IWM, file AGC/2/1/9; letter of 30 April 1945. Edward Ardizzone thought the wine 'exceptionally fine', consisting as it did of Mouton Rothschild, Lafitte, Haut Brion 1895 etc., much of it in jeroboams. See Ardizzone, p.204.

21 *Eclipse*, op. cit., p.260.

22 Clifford papers (16727), IWM, file AGC/2/1/9; letter of 26 April 1945.

23 Ibid., file AGC/2/3; letter dated 1 May 1945 from Alexander Clifford to Jenny Nicholson.

24 *Daily Express*, 4 May 1945.

25 *Eclipse*, op. cit., p.269.

26 *Enter Citizens* by Alexander Clifford, p.245.

27 *Eclipse*, op. cit., p.270.

28 *The Daily Telegraph*, 5 May 1945.

28 *Eclipse*, op. cit., p.281.

30 Ibid., p.285.

31 Ibid., p.289.

PART 3

The Trio is Broken: 'No One Can See Very Clearly'

19. And Now the War is Over

In the summer of 1945, the Trio met up for a reunion at the Savoy, the swish hotel in London's Strand which they had always regarded as their London club, regretting no doubt that they could no longer charge it to expenses. They already inhabited different worlds now and they each had plans to take themselves further apart, the need for comradely support having faded with the peace. The Mooreheads were living in a flat in Belgravia and the Cliffords had plans to move abroad, while Christopher Buckley was hoping to marry, once his wife-to-be had secured her divorce. By mid-July, the separation had gone further: Alan and Lucy were touring Europe for a month, Buckley was in the Far East, while Clifford was in Italy. None of them had lost the urge to travel, some internal demon driving them on. Moorehead's 1945 diary, for example, records over twenty foreign trips between June and November 1945: Rome, Naples, Malta, Cairo, Catania, Athens, Cairo again, Baghdad, Teheran and Jerusalem in July alone, and on he went, month after month. When he flew from Croydon to Le Bourget airport near Paris on 5 October 1945, he was observed to sink into sleep as soon as he took his seat in the back of the Dakota.[1]

Married life evidently appealed to Alex and life for the Cliffords seemed rich with promise. 'It is extraordinary,' he wrote to his mother, 'how much nicer it is being a foreign correspondent when one is married.'[2] He professed himself 'enchanted with Rome' and the couple duly moved into a flat there on 14 July 1945. Their finances were greatly helped by the *Daily Mail* offering Jenny a £1,000 a year contract: it made them, Clifford claimed, in that tone he often used to his mother but to no one else, 'simply stinking rich now'. Like Moorehead, Clifford could often be seen slumped in the back of some aircraft or other, criss-crossing the Mediterranean, having 'breakfast in Rome, lunch in Athens, dinner in Cairo, breakfast next morning in Baghdad and lunch in Teheran'.[3] At one point he returned to where he had stayed in Athens and 'found a number of things left there in 1941' – tents, shoes, a brand new suitcase – clear signs, he thought, that he 'had intended to take to the mountains when the Germans came'.[4] When he flew to Cairo to collect sheets, knives and forks and spoons from the Gezira flat, an outbreak of bubonic plague on Malta kept him confined to the airfield, denied the tempting lights of Valetta. In Cairo, all was well enough, although the moths had begun to eat the khaki uniforms hanging in his wardrobe. Jenny missed him terribly, she told his mother, adding that she and Clifford regarded starting a family as one of the things in life that mattered most to them.

There were signs, however, that not all was well. In June 1945, Clifford travelled to Naples airport to pick Jenny up, waited impatiently for a couple of hours, and was then told that 'her plane had fallen to pieces over France and had to make a forced landing'. Eventually she arrived, unharmed, but it was a disconcerting reminder that life can suddenly turn sour. Moreover, Clifford's health was beginning to give cause for concern. In August, when he was in Athens, he needed medical advice about problems with his eyes, and later, in Salonika, he succumbed to the familiar irritation of sand-fly fever. Nor was the marriage without its tensions. Jenny was a forceful woman, a 'go-getter' of considerable vitality. She could be discomforting: for example, many years later, in a trattoria in Italy, she unsettled the 15-year-old John Moorehead, insisting that he should, 'Come and sit here'. Some thought that Jenny was 'almost scornful' of her husband whose manner was the very opposite of hers, his diffidence and shyness seemingly rendering him vulnerable.[5] Just two months into the marriage, in April 1945, Clifford was writing angrily from 21 Army Group Main HQ, asking her to 'drop the nonsense and start writing nice letters again'. She had the habit of reading 'unpleasant meanings into harmless statements', he complained, and he was deeply troubled by 'the very unkind things you have written to me'.[6] At one point Jenny accused him of discouraging her from seeking a job. It all left him 'struggling with a deep melancholy'. Ironically, in November 1945, he arranged for Jenny to work for the *Sunday Dispatch*. The money was less good, but at least it meant they could travel together. 'It isn't a frightfully good paper as papers go,' Clifford wrote, 'but none of them are much good anyway'.[7]

*   *   *   *

In October 1945 the Cliffords revisited Paris, Brussels and Arnhem, driving back to Rome via Avignon, Vichy, Cannes and Monte Carlo. 'We turned off to a place called Porto Fino,' he wrote, 'which was absolutely enchanting.'[8] It was a place to which they would return. In December 1945, Clifford travelled to Albania (where he came down with jaundice), then moved on to Nuremberg to cover the Nazi trials, before returning to Spain early in February 1946, nearly ten years after the outbreak of the Civil War. He and Jenny had agreed to reconnoitre the state of Robert Graves's house on Mallorca which the poet had been forced to abandon in August 1936 when the fascist rebellion obliged him to leave the island. He had left with a single suitcase and at just a few hours' notice.

On Sunday 3 February 1946 Jenny and Clifford took the overnight ferry from Barcelona to Palma de Mallorca, sleeping in a cabin luxurious enough to encourage them to 'sink back into the comforts of peace'.[9] For years Clifford had usually travelled by air, uncomfortable trips on military aircraft, while sea travel had been confined to assault landings, apart from one sailing in 1942, from the Clyde to Lagos 'in a small and squalid Free French steamer, with an apparently demented crew'. This ship could not have been more different with its bright lights, music and laughter replacing the ever-present fear of torpedoes. When they woke on Monday morning, the ship had docked in Palma harbour, the town beyond the water a brilliant white in the early sun. Suddenly, in February, it was springtime.

Both Cliffords keenly anticipated seeing the poet's house in Deya, set high in the mountains on the island's west coast. Jenny had never visited it before and, to help them find it, Graves had given them 'an intricate and untidy letter' – like a palimpsest, Clifford thought – with a set of detailed instructions. Reassuringly, despite the ten-year gap, some things remained the same: the place where the Deya bus stopped and the identity of its driver, Juan Gelat, were both unchanged. They were all ready to go, it seemed, but it soon emerged that the couple's priorities were very different, with Jenny insisting that she needed to buy some silk stockings. They argued, Clifford feeling that his wife lacked 'typical tact in choosing this moment for a shopping expedition'. Three pairs of stockings later, and after she had dramatically burst into floods of tears in the street, they were reconciled with a drink in the early spring sunshine while Clifford had his shoes cleaned. Then it was time for lunch which was served by a disgruntled 'red' waiter who, in between dispensing plates and glasses, food and wine, complained unceasingly about shortages and bad conditions. Over a table of breadcrumbs and wine stains, the Cliffords resumed their argument, triggered by Jenny's insistence that she needed to have her hair done before they could set out. Clifford waited, sitting in a pew in the city's cathedral, listening to the choir at rehearsal and watching the late evening sunlight fill the stained glass windows with a warm glow.

Next morning, once the sun had woken them, they lay in bed listening to the sea breaking against the rocks below while, across the bay, they could hear the dull rumble of 'trams and bugles and street cries and motor horns' from the city. They breakfasted on the balcony. Later Juan Gelat drove them into the hills beyond Palma, through clusters of almond trees in blossom, the road curving up through sweet-smelling pine trees, before it reached the gaunt and rocky country high above the sea. Deya itself was 'balanced on a pinnacle hill at the bottom of a huge cup of mountains'. Finally they reached Graves's house, a cottage with white-washed walls and a fire burning in the grate. It dawned on Clifford what the poet's rapid exit must have been like on that bitter day so long before, the pain of it, but he was also struck by the way the house had retained its lived-in quality. Robert Graves 'had walked out of it at five hours' notice ten years ago, and he could walk back into it at five minutes' notice now. Everything was in its place – or rather where it had been left.' It felt as if time had stood still, that the clocks had stopped at the very moment when the poet left, his possessions preserved forever, as if in a photograph. There were no layers of dust, no smell from a decade of neglect. Instead there were jars of homemade chutney on the larder shelf, a discarded straw hat still lying on the sofa and oranges ripening in bowls in the sun. Clifford and Jenny wandered through the house, their attention occasionally caught by sheets of annotated paper, shelved books, fragments of stone, cairns of old coins, and a small printing press. As Graves had requested, they watched out for some specific items – a medallion in bronze of the Emperor Claudius and 'a certain photo of Jenny' – but neither was anywhere to be seen.

The spirit of Graves's house in that glorious setting made the Cliffords think hard about finding their own patch of the island. Leaving the cottage, they explored a steeply terraced piece of land, considering the potential for building there for themselves and wondering what the consequences would be, in terms of afternoon sun in the garden, if the front door faced the sea, and whether there was a path down to the fishermen's cove at the foot of the cliff. The prospect was decidedly tempting, to 'live here simply with the sunshine, and the wine and fresh fish and the brown village bread, reading and writing and bathing and talking. Much as, I suppose, Robert did when he was here.' Could the Cliffords manage to live in this island paradise by their writing alone?

Later that day they were invited to eat in the village. The 'enormous feast' began with a paella, a dish which reminded Clifford of Spain in 1938 when 'we were only allowed one dish per meal on Thursdays, as an austerity measure, and it was usually paella'. This time there was no such restraint, with course following course – stuffed chicken and roast veal, salad and new potatoes, squid 'stuffed with pine kernels', omelettes, then oranges picked in Graves's garden and finally an *ensaïmada*. They were also fed ten years of gossip for onward transmission to the absent poet: no one they knew had been shot, or joined the Falange, but Gelat had been incarcerated for four months in a concentration camp 'because he was accused of helping Robert in espionage'. By the time lunch was over, both Cliffords had become enraptured by this 'life of golden simplicity' and were willing to consider leaving the world they knew for a life as Spanish peasants, at least until the warm glow of a heavy lunch faded with the afternoon.

There was another side to Mallorca too. With the meal over, a young man approached the Cliffords. He looked like a village schoolmaster, earnest and serious, but in fact he worked for a group of fascist publications and he wanted to interview Clifford and Jenny about their impressions of his country, its 'social, economic and political' situation. Clifford declined politely, a wise response which nevertheless failed to stop the young man from departing 'in rather a huff'. Clifford's true feelings about the new Spain he kept to himself, the fact that 'the rich are too rich and the poor are too poor, the country's economy is inefficient and corrupt, and I don't like dictatorships anyway'. Other than that, 'it is all much better than when I was here last'. So he described it in writing after he had left the country. But in Spain, at that time, it was wiser to keep such thoughts to oneself, not least because the earnest young fascist would not have smiled amiably and agreed politely to disagree. It did not take much imagination to envisage a bureaucratic net ensnaring the Cliffords, preventing them from their planned departure from Mallorca. In the event, the next day, 6 February, Alex and Jenny left Palma for Barcelona without difficulty on the evening ferry. Leaning on the ship's rail, the Cliffords watched the sketchy hills and flickering lights along the shore disappearing astern and, as night fell, they imagined the kind of life they might lead there and the books they might write.

* * * *

By the early summer of 1945, Moorehead and Clifford were both too disillusioned with the war to contemplate extending their tours of duty. Christopher Buckley, on the other hand, was on leave in London before departing for the Pacific, about which he claimed to know nothing. When the first atomic bomb exploded he was in Cairo on his way to the Far East, and he was in the Iraqi port of Basra when news of the Japanese surrender broke, circumstances which meant that 'the *raison d'etre* of my journey out here was rather lost'. He hoped to go on to China, but in fact, by September 1945, he was in Saigon.[10] Arguably, of the Trio, Buckley had the most certain view about the direction of his working life, seeing himself producing informed political commentary for the serious newspapers, as well as writing both weighty military history and a series of Christiesque detective stories, all leading towards a quiet, academic niche at Oxford. He had marriage in mind too. He had introduced Cecilia Brown to the Cliffords and Mooreheads at his London flat that summer of 1945 and, soon after, proposed to her, an offer she was in a position to accept once the divorce from her American husband, Lincoln Brown, came through. Cecilia was tall, 'dazzling, amazing, vibrant – a bright young thing',[11] with a romantic past and enough of a courageous, independent streak to run away to Canada at the tender age of 18. Like Clifford and Jenny Nicholson, the future Mr and Mrs Buckley were very different from one another.

At that first meeting with the Trio and their spouses, Cecilia, dressed 'in a home-made frock, probably (of) curtain material', was overawed by Lucy – so elegantly dressed, her outfit completed with a fetching hat – while Jenny Clifford seemed 'frightfully gushing'.[12] The members of the Trio, with the war now thankfully over, gave Cecilia the impression that the years of battle had been positive ones, more 'like the end of their last term at a school where they had been happy' than the increasingly corroding experience that, for the most part, it had actually been. She liked Alexander Clifford immediately, warming to his shy charm, while Moorehead flirted with her, despite the fact that she towered over him, something she found amusing since it 'makes a chap look a bit of an ass'.

Cecilia Streeten, the future Mrs Christopher Buckley. (Genista Toland)

Moorehead may have colluded with Clifford and Buckley in sustaining the myth that their wars had been entirely good ones, but he knew in his heart that his life had to change from what it had become, even if at the outset, in those Cairo days for example, there had been excitement and pleasure. 'I simply do not have the heart to go on in the old way rushing from one news event to another'.[13] He had finished writing *Eclipse*, his account of the last three years of the war, the long trek from Taormina to Norway, and had already begun work on a biography of Montgomery. He was also making plans to go to Australia, for the first time in ten years. There he planned to complete *Montgomery* in the peace and isolation of Queensland. Lucy would follow two months later.

Peacetime had not changed his attitude to flying – he loathed it, 'believing it to be the most dangerous, uncomfortable, expensive, and often the slowest method of travel yet invented', and the flight to Australia was desperately long.[14] Anxiously he noted the blood draining from the face of an off-duty pilot sitting near him as they took off from the Ceylon jungle, the heavily laden aircraft only just clearing the canopy of trees. Australia was eighteen hours' flying time away, the lumbering aircraft droning over mile after mile of open ocean. After the first four hours Moorehead's taste for reading had largely disappeared and so he just sat there, slumped in his seat, looking out at the endlessly rolling sea and trying to ignore the occasional stutter from the aircraft engines. At last, he saw the first signs of land, the rhythmic beams of a lighthouse cutting the darkness, but he felt no sense of relief, simply an overwhelming tiredness. The journey wasn't over, of course, since the aircraft had yet to cross Australia, flying all day over another unchanging monotone, this time of red desert sand.

After ten years it was inevitable that Moorehead's view of his homeland would involve 'a curious mixture of nostalgia and personal emotion', the result of 'looking on half-forgotten scenes with different eyes'. Used to the grey monotone of post-war British austerity, he was disconcerted by the fact that the shops were well-stocked (in Sydney, the 'forty dressed chickens and turkeys in a window'), that there were no drab lines of would-be customers, and that ration coupons were non-existent. He was uncomfortable with manifestations of Australian city life: the thin offering of good theatre, the preponderance of American movies, the draconian licensing laws – even the accent bothered him, his own Aussie accent supplanted by an elegant, well-heeled English one, more Surrey than Sydney. Worst of all was the 'mental attitude of the Australian city dweller', and what he saw as their determined pursuit of the average, the insistence on regarding 'all men as your equals' avoiding 'any show of eccentricity' or difference.[15] He did not warm to the 'ugly townships, the advertisement hoardings, the newspapers, and the football and racing crowds'.

All that changed, however, when he left the city for the countryside. 'I sat in the sunshine on a broad verandah and there spread out before me (were) mile after mile of wooded valleys and mountains.' He was staying at his father's house, stirred by the landscape and the proximity of the wild: 'the white trunk of the gum tree on the left ... kookaburras, bell birds and the clear squawk of the magpies ... and a kind of peace here washed down by cups of tea.'[16] There was a hint of Spain in the colouring of the land. The weather was an ever-present, elemental force subject to sudden, powerful change: 'within a few seconds a tearing wind would come up and sink away'. There were forest fires glowing 'with a thousand red eyes' at night; days of blazing sun, clouds of mosquitoes, the persistent cries of jackasses and cockatoos. The rain when it came was on a biblical scale, producing 'smells of indescribable sweetness' from the earth. Opossums nested in the roof and crept into his bedroom to eat the flowers. As he wrote, lizards skittered under his writing table. In this rural paradise, with no telephone or newspapers, and surrounded by this unending display of the natural world, it was no surprise that *Montgomery* was completed a month ahead of schedule. His overriding impression of Australia by then was of the quality of life there, the fact that food, sun, money and leisure were all more plentiful than in England. Someone of 20 'could do far worse than go to Australia at once'; at 30, one might need a trade; at 40, Moorehead's advice was to hesitate, while 'at fifty he should stay at home'.[17] When he wrote this, Moorehead was 36. On the long sea voyage home, sailing from Melbourne with Lucy, he had plenty of time to reflect on where best to live and what his future trade should be.

NOTES

1 My father-in-law, Arthur Spencer, was the Dakota's navigator on that flight. His logbook records twenty passengers, including Moorehead and Princess Alexandra of Greece. The fact that he made a point of noting just those two names gives some indication of Moorehead's celebrity at the time.

2 Clifford papers (16727), IWM, file AGC/2/1/9; letter of 19 June 1945.

3 Ibid., letter of 27 July 1945.

4 Ibid., letter of 3 September 1945.

5 Author's interviews with John Moorehead (13 November 2013) and Caroline Moorehead (13 March 2013).

6 Clifford papers (16727), IWM, file AGC/2/1/9; letter of 23 April 1945.

7 Ibid., letter of 5 November 1945.

8 Ibid., letter of 7 October 1945.

9 Ibid., file AGC/5/1, document entitled 'Finding Robert's House'.

10 Letter from Christopher Buckley to Basil Liddell Hart, 23 September 1945. Liddell Hart Archives, LH 1/125/9.

11   Author interview with Genista Toland, 18 December 2013. Cecilia's maiden
     name was Streeten.
12   Pocock, pp.203–4.
13   Ibid., p.206.
14   *Where Shall John Go?* by Alan Moorehead, *Horizon*, February 1947, p.135.
15   Ibid., pp.135–7.
16   Moyal, p.37, quoting a letter to Lucy Moorehead.
17   *Where Shall John Go?* op. cit., pp.138 and 144.

20. Towards Journey's End

Arriving at the Gare du Nord in Paris on a bleak day in March 1946 was a shock after the warmth of the Mallorcan spring. The French capital was grey and gloomy, with the result that the Cliffords 'peered in silent depression at this dingy, sluttish city where we had come to make a home'.[1] Uncertainly, they headed for the familiarity of the Hotel Scribe, still requisitioned for the use of war correspondents some ten months after the war had ended, but at reception they were told that the Cliffords had already arrived. Clifford smiled wanly and with exaggerated patience said, 'They can't have, *we* are the Cliffords.' Eventually they were allocated room 207 – until Clifford started to fill in the necessary forms. 'I'm sorry, monsieur, wives are not permitted in this hotel.'

'But my wife is a correspondent,' Clifford said.

'She is still not permitted, *monsieur*.'

'Would it be possible if she were my girlfriend?'

'*Mais oui, monsieur*. A girlfriend is quite acceptable, of course!'

Thus finally approved it seemed, husband and wife unpacked and went to bed, only to be disturbed half an hour after falling asleep by an insistent phone call from reception: 'You must give up your room at once!' The other Cliffords presumably had returned. Reluctantly Clifford and Jenny left the Scribe for another hotel which proved to be an unprepossessing building tucked into a side-street. It was 'seedy and lascivious-looking' with windows painted closed, dirt secreted in the shadowy corners of rooms, and 'a pervading smell of never-mended lavatories'. This was not the Paris they had imagined. Next morning they took the Metro to look at the house in Rue de Cambray which Spanish friends had offered to let to them. Variously described as not 'very modern', but 'simpatico' and 'charming', there was always the risk that it might prove just plain ramshackle and down-at-heel. It was a three-storey building with grubby white walls and grey shutters, quaint enough on the outside, but more like 'an abandoned jumble sale' inside, with its ghastly vases, tatty lampshades, varieties of dusty junk and general air of decay. 'Only the mouldering family portraits held the wallpaper in place,' Clifford noted. It came with an upstairs lodger, 'an elderly gentleman, wearing a plaid overcoat thrown over strawberry-coloured serge pyjamas'. Sitting disconsolately in the sombre living room, Clifford and Jenny remembered how Paris had been 'so full of sunshine and happiness and excitement' on the day when the city had been liberated. Number 29 Rue de Cambray was from a different, more austere Paris, one still overhung with German grey. Jenny's first reaction was that they could not possibly live there.

Nonetheless, when the sun came out, Paris recovered some of its charm and even the house looked better – so the Cliffords decided to take it after all. They began the process of doing it up, a process which seemed to symbolise a widespread wish to 'hoist life back on the familiar track from which war had derailed it'. They left the two Spanish servants José and Estelle to preside over the building changes and supervise the decorators, while they left Paris for Greece to cover the elections there. José and Estelle still kept their money in a sock for safe keeping and so the Cliffords were unsure what would await them when they returned. Heading south on the Rome express, on a train with no dining car, they began to see what Estelle's qualities might include: she had prepared them hard-boiled eggs and sandwiches for the journey. Moreover, when they returned, the house in Rue de Cambray was much improved, and both the sun and the lilac in the garden were out. The Spanish couple were still capable of crass errors – Estelle damaged Jenny's precious and delicate wedding dress by plunging it unceremoniously into boiling water, while a shirt of Clifford's was summarily dispatched to the laundry with its gold cufflinks still gleaming in the sleeves. The household accounts were kept in 'phonetic Andalusian'. Clifford and Jenny would shake their heads in disbelief, but they had after all now embarked on peacetime life with a degree of certainty, even if it was 'in a too-large, out-of-date house, with two ultra-reactionary servants and a conservative old gentleman living under the roof'.[2] It was to become a household which lingered in people's memories: more than twenty years later, when events had conspired to change so much, Kathleen Liddell Hart recalled that it was Clifford who 'did all the housekeeping' and produced such 'marvellous meals'.[3]

*　*　*　*

In the middle of 1946 the Trio finally received official recognition for their war service – but there were to be no knighthoods, unlike those awarded to war correspondents at the conclusion of the Great War. Instead each of them received the OBE. It had been enough of a surprise when the New Year's Honours list was published with no recognition for the likes of Moorehead, Clifford and Buckley that the *Express* editor Arthur Christiansen led a delegation of editors to Downing

Street to ask why they had been ignored. It seemed that the newly formed Labour government was not prepared to give knighthoods to the correspondents of three Tory papers.

The Trio took the news stoically, caught up in their new lives and none of them permanently in the UK. Moorehead was in Australia and Clifford was based in France for the time being, while Christopher Buckley spent much of 1946 travelling widely, 'zig-zagging about up and down the Iron Curtain', as well as visiting the Cliffords in Paris.[4] In Poland, he had been shocked by the Polish security police who he felt had little to learn from the Gestapo and the Russian secret police. He reflected on the implications of that, given that it was the violation of Poland's independence in September 1939 which had started the war. Despite the Trio's OBEs, there was something of a sustained public outcry about the absence of adequate recognition, exemplified by the letter to Moorehead from Major Alan Simpson of the War Office Directorate of Public Relations, based in York: 'You should have had a CBE at least. Preferably a KBE. But the work of War Correspondents was not, apparently, fully appreciated.'[5] The issue did not readily go away: when Jenny was in the USA the following year, she interviewed an American who was convinced that the king was on the point of knighting her husband.

When Moorehead returned from Australia he was no nearer determining what his future career might be – he had, as yet, 'no clear design for living'.[6] He spent a weekend at Lord Beaverbrook's house at Cherkley Court in Surrey, where the press baron made a concerted effort to retain the correspondent's services. Moorehead was 'received royally – food, drink, talk, flattery,'[7] but it made no difference since he remained resolute about wishing to cut himself free from the *Express*, and newspapers generally. Once he had made his position clear, Moorehead noted, Beaverbrook acted as if his star reporter no longer existed.

When the Mooreheads exchanged the cottage in a leafy, narrow lane in Jevington, Sussex, for an art deco semi-detached town house, 3 Wells Rise in Primrose Hill, near London's Regent's Park, it was a clear indication that Moorehead recognised the importance of being close to the city's literary world. He had become a highly regarded writer: his biography of Montgomery was published in November to critical acclaim and he was much sought after socially, beyond even journalists and publishers, with invitations from prominent people in the worlds of politics, theatre and finance. It was a far cry from a slit trench in the desert.

*   *   *   *

One day in June 1946 Alexander Clifford left Paris to return to Bayeux on the Normandy coast, wanting to be there on the second anniversary of the D-Day landings. He found the experience poignant: 'Outside the cafe window the old grey square is as dead as a doornail. Only an old woman shuffles across it, wearing British army socks.'[8] There were neglected festoons of signal wire still draped over the convent walls. Somehow it seemed to symbolise a widespread post-war pessimism. Europe was yet to recover, and Clifford felt a 'bitter sense of frustration and disappointment' at the outcome of all that wartime sacrifice. He saw a 'Europe pulling its fragments wretchedly together, fretfully cobbling up new reconciliations, new fears, new hates, new loyalties, new follies' and the result was a world dark with quarrels, starvation and division.[9] Christopher Buckley had felt much the same when he had been in Saigon just after the war, fearing for the country's future because of what he saw as the 'truculent and overbearing' attitude of the French. He foresaw major problems there, 'somewhat along the lines of the Irish troubles of 1919–1922'.[10] To his intense irritation too, despite the war being over, censorship remained, evident in what he called 'the tendency to perpetuate military censorship by means of political censorship'. The Foreign Office's pressure on correspondents, he believed, was 'considerable and sinister'.

Clifford's travels often reminded him of the contrast between Northern Europe's austere greyness and the blue warmth of the south. Covering the elections in Greece had reminded him of the beautiful clarity of the Mediterranean light and the distinctive smell of the Greek air, an exotic blend of tobacco, pine trees, herbs and spring flowers, the very dust of the city. He and Jenny had checked into the Grande Bretagne Hotel where six years before he had bumped uneasily into Alan Moorehead in the lift. The hotel was 'still in a state of depressed requisition', its sheets needing to be hired as well as the room itself, and semolina was served for lunch.[11] There were men in uniforms everywhere, the vast army of post-war administrators, observers and advisers. But it was unquestionably, gloriously, beautiful. He and Jenny walked to the Parthenon which 'gleamed honey-coloured in the spring sunlight' and, not for the first time, he contemplated living closer to the sea, and not just any sea, but the Mediterranean, on the Spanish or Italian coast.

Later, Clifford made plans to visit Spain, obtaining a visa 'with the greatest alacrity,' only to be stunned when it was inexplicably withdrawn. 'I was already half way to Spain when it happened', he wrote to Robert Graves. He had become, it seemed, *persona non grata* and suspected that it was 'because Alan Moorehead was coming with us and … he is regarded by Madrid as little short of anti-Christ'.[12] The Spanish government's decision shocked him, not least because he had never written about the country or, to his knowledge, given any kind of offence to Franco's government. So they turned their backs on Spain and went to Rome instead, motoring down as two families. For both Clifford and Moorehead the trip offered an antidote to the cold and damp of Northern Europe; instead Italian sun, light and tranquillity! As they motored deeper into Italy, the villages, the coast and the pace of life all seemed increasingly attractive. Finally they drew up in the square at Portofino and 'realised at once that we had reached the journey's end'.[13] It was a picturesque fishing port situated on a wooded and hilly promontory on the west coast of Italy, not far from Genoa. For Clifford, who had contemplated buying a vineyard on the island of Capri during the war, the small town was everything he had been subconsciously searching for. He bought a house there very cheaply and he and Jenny worked hard to restore it. It had been 'a ruin at the end of the war' and had 'views of the sea below on three sides'.[14] Later he wrote to Moorehead that 'Portofino was a dream … I am certain you will be mad about it.'[15] Moorehead came to love it too and rented a cottage nearby for a time, his eyes drawn by the 'hills (which) rose up from the sea in sparkling terraces of vines and bright rocks' and the sumptuous views down the Ligurian coastline. He long remembered the way he and Clifford worked, painted in oils, swam and danced as the light faded on the terrace high above the harbour.

In February 1947 the Cliffords were driving through Rome's moonlit streets in a car whose wheezing and groaning had worried them ever since they left Pisa. They were sufficiently short of petrol to indulge in some judicious freewheeling. Worse, 'Jenny had left her bag, with her passport and money and our marriage lines and everything, on a chair in a bar in Grosseto'.[16] In Rome there were two telegrams waiting for them – echoes perhaps of the 'Follow Moorehead, Follow Clifford' orders early in the war? The *Mail's* instructions to him were: 'essential return London immediately to complete formalities for going Moscow early March with British Delegation to Foreign Ministers' Conference.' Jenny's, from the *Sunday Dispatch*, was similar: 'Vital return London instantly to complete arrangements for going America for couple months to write personal articles stop have booked you Queen Elizabeth February 28th'.

They travelled together on the next available train to Paris and flew from there to London. Soon after, at Waterloo Station, with Jenny booked on the boat train south, they parted – Clifford 'for Red Square', as Jenny wrote in her first letter to her husband, 'and me for Times Square'.[17]

NOTES

1   *Enter Citizens*, op. cit., p.13.
2   Ibid., p.27.
3   Letter from Kathleen Liddell Hart to Alan Moorehead, 10 February 1971. Moorehead papers, NLA, MS 5654.
4   Liddell Hart papers, letter of 9 November 1946.
5   Moorehead papers, NLA, letter dated 26 June 1946.
6   Pocock, p.210. Pocock is quoting from a letter to David Woodward from Paul Holt.

7   Ibid., p.210.

8   *Daily Mail*, 6 June 1946.

9   James Cameron in *The New York Times*, 2 May 1971.

10   Letter from Christopher Buckley to Basil Liddell Hart, 23 September 1945.
     Liddell Hart Archives, LH 1/125/9.

11   *Enter Citizens*, op. cit., p.93.

12   Clifford papers (16727), IWM, file AGC/2/5; letter of 22 February 1947.

13   *A Late Education*, op. cit., p.143.

14   E-mail to the author from Lyndall Passerini, 24 March 2013.

15   Pocock, p.212.

16   Clifford and Nicholson, p.5.

17   Ibid., p.9. Jenny's letter is dated 1 March 1947.

21. 'Why In Hell Don't We Fight Them?'

Jenny sailed for America aboard the *Queen Elizabeth*, sharing a cabin with 'the pale, sympathetic wife of *The Daily Telegraph* correspondent in New York, Tom Steele'.[1] The ship's rolling movement made Jenny feel sick and reluctant to eat, writing to Clifford at one point that she had 'only two limp lettuce leaves' in her stomach. Invitations to the Captain's table she was loath to accept, given her continuing queasiness and the fact that 'the captain has no control over the rolling of his ship'. Clifford telephoned her from England on 3 March, with the great liner in mid-ocean, insisting that, 'We'll have to talk fast because it's very expensive.' His parsimony amused her, not least because the call was to pass on the news that the purchase of the house they had found in Portofino had finally gone through: 'we have bought the little castle in Italy!'

Jenny arrived in New York on 5 March after a five-day crossing. As the ship lay alongside the dock, Maurice Chevalier was on the top deck being given the royal treatment by the New York press photographers. After the 'nightmare' of the three-hour immigration 'formalities', conducted in an echoing, brightly painted hall with long queues staring resentfully ahead at the unwelcoming man at the desk, she was met by Bill Parsons, the *Dispatch*'s New York correspondent. The city was very cold, with dirt-stained snow on the sidewalks. Rooming on the nineteenth floor of the St Regis Hotel, Jenny felt very lonely, depressed by the size and strangeness of the great city, a feeling that eased once she moved in with Tom Matthews's family in Park Avenue. He was the managing editor of *Time* magazine. Jenny saw two musical shows – *Oklahoma* and *Annie Get Your Gun* – but was disconcerted to see people collecting money outside the theatres and protesting 'Against the British Terror in Palestine'.

Alex Clifford's journey through Germany was slow and raised many ghosts. He wrote to his wife from Grunewald station, Berlin, on 5 March, having spent the whole of that day travelling across a country that seemed 'dead and broken and dreary' and in the grip of an icy winter. The Cliffords had been in Germany the previous summer when, despite fine weather, the sun making the green landscape look pleasantly verdant, they could not rid themselves of an obsession with the 'moral degradation, the hopelessness, the brokenness of spirits' amongst the German people.[2] In early March even the weather was bleak and it was all too clear that this remained a defeated nation. Clifford was unsure of what to expect once they reached Russia and kept remembering things he should have brought with him, as well as returning anxiously to pore over the Foreign Office's detailed instructions. They had been issued with 'an extravagantly bizarre set of ice-proof garments', and he had been warned to take items like toothpaste and soap. Taking a camera would be 'as much as our life was worth'.

After Berlin the train continued its journey east, stopping for a while in Warsaw where Clifford looked out at the ruins and destruction 'softened by snow', before the train continued its rhythmic clatter across Poland, during which a number of delegates tried to stave off boredom with bottles of vodka. At Brest-Litovsk they changed to a Russian train which reminded Clifford of Tolstoy's *Anna Karenina* – the *fin de siècle* dining car, the Cyrillic script, the plush and brass-work 'cosily lit with pink-shaded lamps in the windows'. Outside on the platform, bemedalled Red Army officers strode through the snow in leather boots. The heat in the carriage was unbearable, stifling each of the four delegates, but anyone unwise enough to open a window would have been frozen by a blast of viciously cold air. One had to sit back and endure as the train rumbled on through the endless Russian plains where 'the snow-bound earth was the same colour as the sky'.[3] They arrived in Moscow dead on time into a city whose destruction echoed that of Warsaw. Clifford moved into a room on the tenth floor of the Moskva Hotel. It was small and clean but sparsely furnished and stuffy, with its windows cemented in to discourage guests from opening them in search of fresh air. There was no plug in the sink. It was a sobering thought that the Moskva would be his base for most of the next month or so.

Jenny, by contrast, had embarked on a whistle-stop journey across America, leaving New York for Washington D.C. on 14 March and staying at the city's Shoreham Hotel. She visited the Senate building and lunched at the Embassy where 'the Bowes-Lyons turned up to stay as guests'.[4] Driving around Washington in an embassy car, Jenny thought the city seemed more like Cheltenham than the capital of a great nation. Three days later she took the night Pullman from Washington to Charleston, South Carolina, bewitched by the impact of the floodlit Lincoln and Jefferson memorials and the dome of the Capitol, and occasionally where 'a cherry tree waved its silhouette with Chinese delicacy against the light'. The Pullman rolled through 'good train country' then, as dawn broke, Jenny looked sleepily out at 'the worn out landscape of South Carolina'.

They drew into Charleston before breakfast. The talk in Charleston's drawing rooms was of the coming war with Russia.

In Moscow meanwhile, Clifford, in a moment of minor rebellion, had 'hacked the cement off' his windows so that he could escape the soporific heat. The resulting cold, however, was enough 'to whip your face with steel wires and freeze the brain'. Undeterred he went for a long walk, crossing Red Square and its piles of dirty snow to queue at Lenin's tomb, before witnessing Stalin's motorcade sweeping out of the Kremlin, in a flurry of ringing bells and flashing lights. The Four Power Conference, by contrast, was low-key and dreary, held at 'an airmen's club on the outskirts'. On 14 March he wrote again to say that he had received a letter from Rome 'saying that your bag has been found intact at Grosseto'.[5] Five days later he had heard from Estelle and José in Paris, but José's letter was in Andalusian, and 'his grammar and spelling got all snarled in all the most important passages'. 'It is clear', Clifford wrote, 'that something terrible has happened to the heating.' But beyond the fact that there was heavy snow in Paris and they had run out of coffee, it was difficult to tell.

The day before, Jenny had been in Palm Beach where, at the hairdressers 'the women looked rich even with their hair wet'. She went bowling with David O. Selznick, who the year before had produced *Gone With the Wind*, together with his son. They went back to her hotel for a drink but the film producer took exception to the anti-Semitism of the hotel staff, a judgement with which Jenny agreed. She ended the letter by telling Clifford that former war correspondent Eve Curie was to speak to the people of Palm Beach that day to 'a gushing crush of women in hats' who would, Jenny thought, feel good 'having spent an hour or so having their minds "done" instead of their toenails'.[6]

Alex Clifford's letters were invariably sober, political and 'sombrely on one theme', while Jenny's were energetic, gossipy and youthful. He frequently spent lengthy paragraphs trying to analyse the essence of Communist Russia, in contrast to her scattergun, whimsical impressionism, her warm evocations of people and places. In a way, that difference of writing symbolised 'the difference between the two halves of the world'. In Russia, Clifford wrote, 'theory is the thing'; in the USA 'only practice counts'.[7]

The weather in Moscow that spring was profoundly gloomy with few breaks in the grey cloud above the city, and Clifford found it 'a leaden drag on the soul'.[8] He pined for Italy, for some colour and sunlight, some sign that life could be frivolous. On 23 March he wrote to Jenny describing the 'ostentatious austerity' of a recent party put on by Molotov, the Russian foreign minister. Alex likened it to a reception they had been to the previous winter in Albania, the female guests in unfashionable evening dresses dating from the mid 1920s, and hungry partygoers consuming iced cakes with 'terrifying speed'. As for the conference on which Clifford must report, each day fell into a similar pattern: ministers and officials jousting with words till 8 p.m., before a few hours of attempting to summarise the unreportable to make it readable, before embarking on the arcane procedures to get the latest story dispatched home. That done, it was time for a drink before dinner which would duly begin at 11 p.m. and then drift on past 1 a.m. The lack of progress and the monotony were increasingly frustrating. On 27 March Clifford complained of 'a day of abysmal melancholy', provoked by the 'flatness and greyness and dullness' of Russia generally, and the down-at-heel ugliness of Moscow in particular. Just occasionally there was a glimmer of hope, for example, when he thought about his future with Jenny: 'When I crawled home from my miserable walk I looked at my diary' – it proved to be the anniversary of the day they had first seen their house in Paris, a building that had initially appeared so unsuitable and scruffy, but that was now loved by them both.

For day after day Clifford continued to be trapped in Moscow, while Jenny progressed across America: a flight from Miami to New Orleans (23 March), a greyhound bus to Natchez (Mississippi) a week later, then on to Dallas with its 'glaring white clusters of skyscrapers'. Her distaste for American food had made her 'gratifyingly slimmer'. She questioned the Americans she met closely, fascinated by their perceptions; she noted that when southerners talked about 'the war' they were more likely to mean the civil war against the north, rather than the struggle against Germany and Japan. She was disturbed by the race problem, noting that 'the plight of the American Indian is said to be worse than that of the American negro'.[9] She warmed to the energy and vitality of Texas, typified by the bookshop that was still open at midnight. She was aware of a widespread resentment directed at the British and a prevailing view of the 'Russos as barbarians',[10] usually followed by a bullish 'Why in hell don't we fight them?' – get it over with now! She travelled on from Dallas, arriving in Rockdale, Texas on 3 April, then El Paso next day and on to San Antonio. Heading further south, she savoured the 'strong smell of spring' and the proximity of Mexico, across the nearby border, with its 'strong whiffs of Spain'.

By then Clifford was in Leningrad where he enjoyed 'a day of delirious Northern springtime, with sunshine so thin and fresh and tender that you felt it would shatter if you moved in it'.[11] He had travelled to Leningrad on the all-night sleeper – the Red Arrow – which proved 'cosily Anna Karenina'. He explored the picture galleries of Leningrad with *Express* foreign affairs reporter Sefton (Tom) Delmer, liking its atmosphere and imperial grandeur. It was a brief stay, however, and once back in Moscow, a cold wind whirled the snow down the icy streets, while 'the conference stumbles foolishly on, pretending to be a conference'.[12] There was a nostalgic meeting-up with Alec Gatehouse, now the military attaché in Moscow whom he had met, the soldier dressed in sheepskin jacket and rug, in the western desert in 1941. Then it had been a bitterly cold dawn, a time imbued with that typical desert feeling 'of being alone and unprotected in the middle of a vast empty stage which was just going to be lighted up'.[13] One Moscow morning Clifford was woken by a phone call from a whore, or a spy, or both, seeking a meeting – somehow it summed up the seamy, dark side of the Russian city. By contrast, a letter from Estelle in Paris describing the springtime glories of the lilacs in their garden reminded him of a more normal existence.

Jenny arrived in Phoenix, Arizona on 6 April, travelling through a 'country of date ranches, Palomino ponies and Indian reservations'. In Los Angeles, the film director Alfred Hitchcock sent her six red roses, with a card which declared: 'Welcome to our six suburbs in search of a city'. In Beverly Hills she crashed her hired car, having forgotten momentarily to steer, no doubt distracted by her celebratory trips around film studios and frequent encounters with Michael Redgrave and his wife Rachel, Gregory Peck ('my favourite film star, is even more attractive eating sandwiches'[14]), and Evelyn Waugh. She drove the glorious coast road from San Francisco with Rachel Redgrave, stirred by the magnificence of Big Sur and the way the road sometimes sliced right through the broad trunk of a giant redwood. She caught the essence of small-town America, the 'hedgeless gardens, little white wooden blow-away houses'; and its isolationist state of mind: 'One gets the impression that history has just arrived or just left,' she wrote, while the American people themselves, she felt, were unsettled, 'like a cat trying to discover the most comfortable position in which to relax'.[15]

Clifford did not warm to the America portrayed in Jenny's letters. 'Your description of Palm Beach made my blood run cold,' he wrote on 12 April, but Russia was chilling too in its totalitarian way. Clifford was disturbed, for example, by a flight to Stalingrad, given the rumours 'about Russian aeroplane engines never being warmed up, and the pilots being dumpy little ex-schoolmistresses'.[16] Despite his fears, the aircraft made a safe landing at Stalingrad 'on a bright, bare, greenish, slightly undulating plain' which reminded him of the Libyan Desert, the parallel prompted by the sun's brightness, the empty horizon and 'the rhythm of the naked contours'.[17] The rusting grey remains of German military hardware was strewn far and wide, while makeshift homes had been built from dismembered aircraft wings, mud, broken lorries and other discarded army junk. Clifford stayed at the city's Intourist Hotel with Sefton Delmer and Giles Romilly; from the window of the room they shared they could look down on a family 'living in a roofless cellar beneath an intricate edifice of old machine-gun belts'.[18] Lulled into near-optimism by the flight from Moscow, the return flight caught Clifford unawares – it proved terrifying thanks to the pilot's insistence on hedgehopping for the full 600 miles. The close-up views of an empty flat landscape further convinced him that he could never like Russia, no matter what the future held.

Jenny, meanwhile, was on the night train from Salt Lake City to Denver where, thanks to the good offices of an acquaintance she had made earlier in the trip, she was allotted the Brown Palace Hotel's Presidential Suite. The two previous occupants, she was told, were General Eisenhower and Ginger Rogers ('I trusted not together'). After visits to Chicago ('huge, tall, noisy') and Lexington, her American safari was over. She flew back by BOAC Constellation on 25 April, writing to Clifford that, at 19,000ft, 'my Old World fountain-pen has burst, so has the Old World mechanism of the baby in the next seat!'[19] After a brief stopover at Shannon airport, she landed at Heathrow wondering when she would be reunited with her husband. He too was contemplating a return home, since the conference was due to end any day, and, given its tedious irresolution, not before time. The journalists' principal entertainment by then was the planning of exotic trips home (Delmer by train via Sofia, Romilly by air to Prague, someone else via Vladivostok). The practical, earnest Clifford opted for the cheapest and quickest which he concluded would be via Leningrad, Helsingfors (Helsinki) and Stockholm by air. While Jenny looked back on her time in America with a degree of optimism, warming to the American spirit – 'the truly great qualities of exuberance and kindliness'[20] – Alex's mood post-Russia was heavily despondent, believing that the human race was on the point of entering 'another dark age'. He was convinced too that, in the struggle ahead, 'Communism is going to win'. The darkness ahead was cloaked in uncertainty: 'When history is rounding a hairpin bend on two wheels,' he wrote in his last letter from Moscow, 'no one can see very clearly.'[21]

NOTES

1   Clifford and Nicholson, p.12.
2   Ibid., p.15.
3   Ibid., p.31.
4   Ibid., p.39.
5   Ibid., p.46.
6   Ibid., p.78.
7   Ibid., p.121.
8   Ibid., p.83.
9   Ibid., p.111.
10   Ibid., p.128.
11   Ibid., p.112.

12   Ibid., p.120.
13   Ibid., p.151.
14   Ibid., p.165.
15   Ibid., p.184.
16   Ibid., p.174.
17   Ibid., p.196.
18   Ibid., p.197. Giles Romilly had been a POW of the Germans and was the brother of the poet Esmond Romilly, who had died in Spain's civil war; he was Winston Churchill's nephew.
19   Ibid., p.243.
20   Ibid., p.251.
21   Ibid., p.240.

22. The Trio Divided

Within two years of the war ending, the Trio was effectively disbanded, its purpose gone and the future too impenetrable for the wartime 'bond of trust and comradeship' to hold firm.[1] Buckley continued to see Moorehead fairly often, but saw less of Clifford, partly because he did not warm to Jenny. John Moorehead, Alan's son, who as a baby had been so close to his godfather Alex in Cairo, has only one vivid memory of him, on New Year's Eve in 1946 or 1947 when, in deference to an old tradition, 'a tall, dark man with a bit of coal' was the first to knock on the Moorehead front door. It was Clifford, hoping to be the bringer of good luck.

Those years immediately after the war were a time of exploration for each of them – but of separate journeying and with different ends in mind. Moorehead thought his parting of the ways with Alex Clifford 'was something more than a physical separation'.[2] Already, by the time they were living as neighbours in Portofino, it was clear to Moorehead that their lives had drifted apart and that he and Clifford had 'never quite resumed the long conversation' which they had sustained – and which had sustained them – during the war years. The passage of time had changed them both: Clifford had become a political journalist of considerable standing, comfortable in a world of high-level conferences and sleek dinner parties, while Moorehead regarded himself now as 'more or less sedentary, isolated and egocentric',[3] the lonely, gifted writer. It was clear to Moorehead that potentially great things lay in store for Clifford – 'an editorship of one of the national newspapers, (or) a career in politics.'[4] At one point, in 1949, Clifford was asked to act as the *Mail*'s foreign editor. But it was evident too by that year that all was not well. In late April he wrote to his brother, 'I am longing to get back to Portofino myself – I have suddenly become terribly tired.'[5] He had moved, he calculated, seventy-six times in seven months. Portofino attracted many visitors – too many: 'I only hope,' Clifford wrote, 'most of them won't have the energy to climb our garden path – which is a quarter of a mile long and consists mostly of steps.'[6]

As for Christopher Buckley, he was eagerly pursuing a career in journalism and writing detective novels as well as commissioned histories of the war.[7] He had, he believed, seven years of experience to draw on and enough material to occupy him fully for the next four; moreover he was mulling over what he called a 'spiritual autobiography', as well as a book of essays. Once Cecilia's divorce from her American husband, Lincoln Brown, had gone through, she and Christopher Buckley were free to marry. The ceremony took place at the Caxton Hall, Westminster on 6 August 1947, with, like Clifford before him, a reception at the Savoy. Buckley was 42 and Cecilia four years his junior. He gave his address as 'The National Liberal Club' in Whitehall. They lived together at 46 Mount Sion in Tunbridge Wells – Cecilia's house – where Buckley would work upstairs ('always writing while Cecilia brought him coffee and stopped for little chats').[8] They were evidently very much in love. Above all things, he wanted to spend time with Cecilia: 'I would give up the rest of my life,' he declared, 'for ten years of peace to spend with my wife.'[9] His first novel, *Rain Before Seven*, duly came out in 1947 and Basil Liddell Hart for one was impressed, writing to Buckley that he 'couldn't put it down'. By November, Buckley was busily organising visas for a tour of Eastern Europe, departing from Finland and heading for Greece and Turkey. The plan was for both he and Cecilia to travel to Finland, leaving on 31 December 1947, but circumstances dictated otherwise and he began the trip in Greece instead, before moving on to Prague, Trieste and Rome. He might have longed for ten years of peace, but he was frequently 'preparing to buckle on my armour for my next "sweep"'. Gradually he was banned from various countries, the result of being 'never afraid to speak if he disliked what he saw'.[10] His marriage certainly made him very happy, but the state of the world profoundly disturbed him. Jean Nichol, who worked as a public relations officer at the Savoy at the time, remembered him 'standing by my office window one grey wet afternoon and repeating the lines from Barrie: "Do not stand aloof, despising, disbelieving, but come in and help – insist on coming in and helping."'[11]

Some months before, in early October 1947, Alan Moorehead travelled to India on behalf of *The Observer* to report on the country post-independence. He went by BOAC flying boat to Karachi, spent a week in Delhi, met Field Marshal Auchinleck, the Supreme Commander of British Forces in India, and was invited to an 'At Home' on 30 October 1947 at the governor general's residence in New Delhi by Lord Mountbatten, the country's last Viceroy. It was the first week of the last month of 1947 when his flying boat returned to Poole.

Alex Clifford's travels continued into 1948.[12] He went to Miami to meet up with the Rothermeres and accompanied the electioneering Senator Taft on a

46 Mount Sion, Tunbridge Wells, where Buckley would work upstairs – 'always writing while Cecilia brought him coffee and stopped for little chats'. (Author's Collection)

train tour of the American mid–West. He went to British Honduras (anticipating an invasion), San Salvador and Berlin. However, 'I want nothing,' he wrote, 'but to live in Portofino.'

* * * *

In the late summer of 1948, Moorehead rented a villa in the hills above Florence. It lay 'at the end of an old Etruscan road that winds among olive groves and lines of cypresses'.[13] He was working on a novel, as well as socialising with a galaxy of the great and good: Freya Stark, Ernest Hemingway, George Bernard Shaw, and Martha Gellhorn, amongst others. He was in correspondence with Nevil Shute who had proposed the two of them embarking on a joint expedition. He bred boxer dogs and goats. For once, however, perhaps for the first time, Moorehead tasted failure: his novel was turned down (one publisher damned it out of hand – 'it just stinks'). Moreover there were tensions between the Cliffords and the Mooreheads, partly because Lucy and Jenny did not always get on: Jenny, Lucy wrote, 'now has marmalade-coloured hair but is immensely full of herself and successful. I must get my strength up before I see her.'[14] Dispirited by a continuing lack of success, Moorehead accepted a job in London at the Ministry of Defence as a senior public relations officer – he had been asked to set up an information department. It rankled that he was no longer the undisputed star of the Trio. Then, just before he left Florence for London, he received a disturbing letter from Clifford who had been taken ill with an unexplained lump under his arm.

*   *   *   *

Christopher Buckley was to enjoy just three years of peace with Cecilia. Husband and wife travelled together widely in that period, often in the folds of the Iron Curtain; Buckley wrote a second murder story (*Royal Chase*) and he was offered the editorship of the magazine *Time and Tide*. It looked as if there was not a blemish in a cloudless sky. In 1950 he had visited Noel Monks in Pretoria

Christopher Buckley and his stepdaughter, Chloe. (Genista Toland)

who later described Buckley's 'last words as he climbed into his car to the airport: "I've done with wandering. I'm going to settle down in England. No more war for me'.[15]

But then the fragile peace broke, not perhaps where those bellicose Americans whom Jenny Nicholson had met in 1947 expected, but in the Far East, in a conflict between communist North Korea and the western-backed South. The Korean War began on 25 June 1950 and *The Daily Telegraph*'s foreign editor was soon on the telephone to Buckley pressing him to fly east and report on the conflict for the paper. Buckley was torn between his loyalty to Cecilia and the sense of obligation he felt – the need to report to the wider world on this most dangerous of confrontations. Initially, his instinct was to remain in the UK: 'I'm not going. I can't leave you,' he said, but Cecilia made accepting the commission easier: 'If you do go, I'm coming too,' she told him. She became accredited to cover the war for *Time and Tide*, a decision which meant that Buckley could head out east with a clear conscience. So the two of them duly travelled to Japan.

Once in Tokyo, they were greeted with bad news: the North Korean army was in the ascendancy, moving south rapidly and already threatening the vital port of Pusan. So uncertain was the situation that Buckley headed for Korea on his own, leaving Cecilia behind in Tokyo. He was in Korea for the next six weeks, missing his old friends from the Trio, but compensating to an extent by establishing a working relationship and friendship with Ian Morrison of *The Times*. Buckley's reporting was consistently honest, accurate and evocative. He had lost none of his brilliance in this new conflict, nor his diligence – he visited the front on a daily basis. Indeed, he stood out above the rest. 'In appalling conditions (he) worked tirelessly for 18 hours a day'. On Sunday 13 August, Buckley and Morrison, together with Colonel M.K. Unni Nayar and a South Korean lieutenant, set out from headquarters in the early afternoon, heading again for the front. The Indian colonel was a journalist and diplomat seconded to the United Nations who, at one point in his career, had been in Washington as a public relations officer. He was driving the jeep. North of Waegwan, they were within 9 miles of the front, when they were obliged to edge their way through six separate swathes of mines. It was the kind of situation that Buckley had faced many times, always harbouring deep anxieties about the potential for a catastrophic explosion should the vehicle trigger a mine. Clifford and Moorehead had known this and it added to their respect and admiration for his great courage. This time, however, Buckley's luck had run out: the jeep did not make it past the sixth set of mines, exploding instead and scattering debris over a wide area. All but Christopher Buckley were killed outright.

Buckley had survived the blast, albeit severely wounded and unconscious. He was rushed to the American field hospital at Taegu, arriving sometime before 7.15 p.m., but died soon after. He and the others were buried with military

Ian Morrison of *The Times* who died with Buckley.

honours at a ceremony attended by twenty-five war correspondents. Buckley and Morrison were placed in neighbouring graves in a small tree-shaded cemetery attached to the Presbyterian mission in Taegu at noon on 14 August 1950. A Union Jack was draped over his coffin which was carried by some of his war correspondent colleagues; American troops fired a trio of rifle shots into the air, and the Last Post was sounded.[16] Ian Morrison's body was subsequently removed to Singapore, leaving Christopher Buckley 'alone, beneath a little mound of Korean earth'.[17]

Cecilia heard the news in Tokyo and faced the prospect of a long and lonely flight home, returning to their empty house in Tunbridge Wells. Cruelly, Buckley died within a week of their third wedding anniversary. Moorehead heard the news on the island of Ischia off the Naples coast, where he had been holidaying. There was an immediate exchange of letters with Alex Clifford who was in Yugoslavia, with the latter expressing what they both must have thought – 'it could have been us'. Both were deeply shocked by the loss of the third member of the Trio. Clifford wrote that he had tried to express his condolences to Cecilia in a letter but couldn't find the words: 'How can one say anything that can help her?' For his own part, he knew that he could not contemplate facing another war, 'at least, not as a war correspondent'.[18] Those days were now truly over.

*   *   *   *

It had been evident to Buckley before he died that Alexander Clifford had begun to behave out of character. As early as January 1949 Christopher had written to Alan Moorehead asking what the matter was with their mutual friend. Both Cecilia and he had 'found him quite curiously cold and distant and he almost pointedly avoids us when he is in London. Why?'[19] Friends were also anxious about the Clifford marriage, which did not seem very harmonious; there was a view that it stemmed from the clash between Clifford's 'retiring nature' and Jenny's 'social aspirations'. Clifford had also become desperately disillusioned with England, whose post-war condition 'horrified' him: the country was 'down the drain – the last gurgle before the bath-plug spiral into the dark ages'.[20] His letters to Jenny often displayed a hurt, disappointed irritation: 'It was wicked of you to order another dress from Horrocks, and then lie about it at the air terminal. It is not the sort of thing I thought you would ever do.'[21] He told her, 'I am going to stop our joint account'. In another, later letter Clifford added a postscript which revealed another festering grievance: 'I don't want to be depressing about the motor bicycle,' Alex wrote, '(but) I am very surprised and mortified that you should even think it possible.'[22]

By September he was describing a worrying medical condition: there was 'a bad gland lurking behind (his) heart' and a lot of fluid in his lung. He pleaded with Jenny not to make him worry about money or 'other mischief' since the doctors worried about him worrying. In early 1950, Clifford wrote to Moorehead revealing the fact that he was suffering from 'an incurable disease'. He had told his brother at the end of the previous year: his swollen glands indicated a disease which was 'incurable and potentially fatal … it was very rare and obscure and boring'.[23] Clifford had been in Germany when he had first felt the lump, although he had been feeling unwell. He went to London for a second opinion. The diagnosis was that he was suffering from Hodgkin's Disease, a form of leukaemia, and the prognosis was not good – he probably had only two years left to live. To Buckley and Moorehead it all seemed so unfair: 'Alex never smoked, scarcely drank, lived the most healthy of lives.' Moorehead wrote years later. 'Why pick on him?'[24] Nonetheless there was hope: in the summer of 1950, with the lumps gone, he and Jenny went to Cairo and drove across North Africa in a nostalgic reprise of the war years' journey, finally crossing back to Gibraltar from Tangier.

While Clifford's health deteriorated through the winter of 1950 and spring of 1951, Moorehead was working as a civil servant, travelling abroad, often with Manny Shinwell, the Labour government's minister for defence. For a while it seemed as if Clifford's condition was stabilising, although he was thinner in the face, unnervingly more gaunt. He kept working, turning out pieces for the *Mail*, and being pressed for more short stories following his success in winning a competition in *The Observer*. Jenny was freelancing, 'working too hard for *Picture Post*'. Her business card proudly boasted 'Roving Correspondent, London Sunday Dispatch and Continental Daily Mail'. Alex went to America to see specialists 'about myself and about what I might do about myself', hoping that the cancer could be stemmed. He went to John Hopkins and two other hospitals in New York, but discovered that there was no sign of a new cure; indeed nothing had replaced the use of nitrogen mustard, whose properties beyond its use in chemical warfare had been discovered during the war. He was told that London's Middlesex hospital was probably the best in the world for radiotherapy; America could give him nothing. There had been lots of research, Clifford wrote to Jenny, but 'they haven't yet found anything worth having'.

In September 1951 Jenny wrote to Mrs Clifford in a state of 'passionate melancholy', distraught by Clifford's illness and his evident wish not to let his employers down. Through the intercession of her brother-in-law Gordon, she received a phone call from the editor of the *Mail* who 'was charming and awfully relieved to hear what was really wrong with Alex because Alex has never told him'.[25] Clifford was angry at Jenny's perceived interference.

Through it all, Clifford rarely complained, but the illness closed in on him inexorably. His decline was made cruelly obvious when he realised that he could no longer climb the steep steps from the harbour in Portofino to his house on the promontory high above the sea. It was a stark warning that now was the time to move away and settle back in Rome. His nights were plagued by night sweats and he increasingly relied on sleeping pills to help him through the darkness until morning. By now, he was finding it harder to write and was growing weary of the time the doctors spent 'conducting long exhausting experiments'.

In January 1952 the Cliffords and the Mooreheads met up in Switzerland for some skiing. Alan and Lucy took the train from London to the Swiss Alps and the two couples rendezvoused at the White Horse Inn in Kitzbühel, arriving on the 18th of the month. Alex's condition seemed to have stabilised and the prospect of a few days on the slopes, visiting an old haunt from the 1930s, cheered him. It started well enough: they enjoyed days of picnic lunches on the mountain peaks before skiing down to hot baths, dinner and some hands of bridge. For a while it was possible to remember how things had once been.

One bright, cold morning Clifford suggested that he and Moorehead should make for the highest ski run on the mountain and ski down into the valley next door, returning by train to Kitzbühel. The idea appealed to both of them and they set out from the top of the run before the sun was fully up and the shadowed cold was still biting.

The conditions were unsettling: it was very icy and the descent was steep. Neither factor seemed to disconcert Clifford who launched himself down the run, wearing a black ski-jacket and a brightly coloured hat, at breakneck speed, leaving his friend to follow behind, occasionally losing his balance and ending up flat out in the snow. Clifford, however, 'skimmed away into the milky space like some great black bird on the wing'.[26] They stopped halfway down and then continued together, racing in tandem across the crisp snow. To Moorehead 'it felt like flying'. Eventually they returned to the slushy lower slopes and civilisation, both exhausted by their headlong descent. They walked to the station and sat in the fug of the waiting room drinking hot wine before climbing on board the Kitzbühel train where they sat on wooden slatted seats in a carriage loud with fit young Austrian skiers high on mountain air. Moorehead looked at Clifford and his heart sank: his friend's face was deathly pale, his eyes staring blankly ahead; he was sitting stock-still and on his lips a pool of spittle had gathered. The train journey, and then the sleigh ride back to the hotel, were conducted in desperate silence and that night Clifford suffered a relapse.

It was clear the holiday was over and that Clifford must return to his doctors in London, but, hoping against hope, they waited a couple more days before finally beginning the long trek home. It was a nightmare journey with Clifford in considerable, growing pain. By the time they reached the French coast snow was falling, and it was still tumbling from a sombre sky when they reached Dover. The London train, predictably, was unheated. By the time Clifford reached the flat at the Albany, Piccadilly, he was so cold that he could do little else but kneel for hours in front of the fire, still in his overcoat. His temperature was sky high. In a letter to Jenny he reported that one diagnosis was that 'the Hodgkins has got into the bone in my lumbar region'. He wondered whether it was his stomach glands that were to blame or perhaps it was both? Whatever the actual situation was, by now he was fearful of the nitrogen mustard treatment. He had lost his appetite and resented the fact that he had to receive so many visitors. In a letter to Jenny early in February he wrote that, 'It is a horrid day *and the King has died*.'[27] He was undergoing hourly barium X-rays and felt 'somehow rather low and weakened'. On 4 February he sent a cable: 'nothing developed so far still investigating but staying hospital. Anyway while fever sweats continue quite comfortable thanks letter love Alex.'

He was near the end and Jenny, Lucy and Alan took it in turns to sit beside his bed. The three of them, deeply upset by his deteriorating condition, talked in the hospital corridor about how he might be released from his torment, but the hospital consultant was evidently unwilling to contemplate anything other than a continuing and desperate attempt to keep him alive. It was time for the nitrogen mustard, a last treatment that produced an unexpected reaction. Alex had been uncommunicative for days, but now 'his eyes were open and there was a bright feverish light in them'.[28] He was thankful for the treatment of which he had been so fearful, declaring it 'wonderful'. Moorehead thought that it had 'conjured up in his mind an ecstasy which had filled him with an inexpressible joy'.[29] Clifford talked incoherently while his friend tried to make sense of what he was saying and watched him drift away, only too aware that Lucy and Jenny were out of the room. Alex's sister arrived and, moments later, 'a dry rattle' emerged from Clifford's throat. A nurse whispered to Alan that if there was anything he wanted to say, it would be as well not to delay. Moorehead found the words: 'What was there to say except that I loved him?' Clifford did not reply, and, soon after Lucy and Jenny slipped back into the room, he stopped breathing. It was 13 March 1952 and he was just 42 years old.

Clifford was buried in Walstead Cemetery near Lindfield in Sussex and a service was held at the Church of St James on Monday 17 March. It ended with 'Abide with Me' and included Psalm 23 and a reading from Revelations 21 verses 1–7. Alan and Lucy Moorehead, Eddie Ward, Richard McMillan, James Cameron, Lord Rothermere and the cartoonist Osbert Lancaster were among those attending. Clifford's father-in-law Robert Graves wrote a moving obituary for *The Times* which noted Clifford's 'staggering talent' and declared that he could easily have been 'a first-class swimmer, golfer, skier, musician, designer, gardener, historian, or mechanic'. It also noted the fact that 'he carried an encyclopaedia in his head', and described him as 'the perfect correspondent … (and) cook and oracle to a famous group of war correspondents'.[30] Graves also wrote the words on the headstone:

ALEXANDER CLIFFORD OBE
Foreign Correspondent 13 March 1952
'Of those charged to witness violence and misery, few have left so truthful
and compassionate a record'

Alexander Clifford's grave.
(Author's Collection)

A number of journalists, including Moorehead, wrote a joint letter to *The Times* suggesting the establishment of an 'Alexander Clifford Award' to mark the fact that he had done so much 'to uphold the highest standards of British journalism'.[31]

A fortnight after Clifford died, his mother wrote to Moorehead. She had visited the grave that weekend with her son Tony and his wife and took comfort from the 'flowers (which) are still lovely' while the rural cemetery was peaceful and full of birdsong. Moorehead had written to her a few days before and she had found that 'a great help'. She knew that 'Alex counted you as his greatest friend' and told him how glad she was that he had been there with Clifford at the end. She wanted Moorehead to read the letters Clifford had sent home from North Africa and asked him to stay in touch since 'there is so much you can tell me, and so much I want to know'.[32]

One of the many letters of condolence to Jenny was from his marquesa in Spain: 'He was the most truthful, honest, fair and altogether reliable and intelligent friend I ever had.'[33]

*   *   *   *

As for Jenny, she was sufficiently hurt by the death of her husband to sign a letter sent to her father that April: 'Jenny Lose Heart (almost)'.[34] Indeed she was ill: her doctor had prescribed a series of injections and early nights, and advised her not to drive. It was a shock for her parents when, within six months, she had married Patrick Crosse, war correspondent and head of Reuters in Rome. On 3 January 1953 she wrote to Mrs Clifford about Alex and about her new husband: Clifford had 'travel fever', she wrote, 'and was always happiest in the kitchen'. She hopes that Mrs Clifford would meet Patrick Crosse who was not 'a great man like Alex', but was decent and full of integrity.[35] Jenny was still corresponding with Alex's mother as late as 1957: 'It's five years and the sense of loss is just as sharp'.[36]

NOTES

1   The phrase is Freddie de Guingand's in a letter to Alan Moorehead, 25 May 1945.

2   *A Late Education*, op. cit., p.144.

3   Ibid., p.145.

4   Ibid.

5   Clifford papers (16727), IWM, file AGC/2/3; letter of 25 April 1949.

6   Ibid., file AGC/2/1/10; letter of 12 June 1946.

7   There were three such books: *Five Ventures*, *Greece and Crete 1941* and *Norway, The Commandos, Dieppe* – all published in the early 1950s.

8   Interview with Genista Toland, 18 December 2013.
9   Pocock, p.212.
10   Oakeshott, op. cit. Clifford was banned too – from Yugoslavia and Hungary.
11   *Meet Me at the Savoy* by Jean Nichol, pp.152–3.
12   Ironically his father – also Alexander – was reluctant to travel anywhere. Frequent pleas by Jenny for him to come to Portofino were always anticipating refusal.
13   *The Villa Diana* by Alan Moorehead, p.7.
14   Pocock, p.236.
15   Monks, p.314.
16   Buckley was the eighth war correspondent to be killed in Korea. See *The Christian Science Monitor*, 14 August 1950.
17   Monks, p.332.
18   Pocock, p.239.
19   Ibid., p.237.
20   Clifford papers (16727), IWM, file AGC/2/3, an undated letter, presumably 1949.
21   Ibid., file AGC/2/4, letter of 9 August, year unknown.
22   Ibid., 21 September 1951 (or possibly 1950).
23   Clifford papers (16727), IWM, file AGC/2/3; letter to Tony Clifford, 15 December 1949.
24   *A Late Education*, op. cit., p.166.
25   Clifford papers (16727), IWM, AGC/2/5, letter dated 24 September 1951.
26   *A Late Education*, op. cit., p.170.
27   Clifford papers (16727), IWM: letter undated, but written in early February 1952 since King George VI died on 6 February 1952.
28   *A Late Education*, op. cit., p.172.
29   Ibid., p.173.
30   *The Times*, 28 March 1952.
31   Ibid., 27 March 1952. The signatories were James Cameron, Brian Connell, Alastair Forbes, Alan Moorehead, Edward Ward and Chester Wilmot.
32   Letter from Mrs Marian Clifford, 26 March 1952.
33   Clifford papers (16727), IWM, file AGC/2/2.
34   *Robert Graves* by Miranda Seymour, p.341.
35   Clifford papers (16727), IWM, file AGC/2/8, letter of 3 January 1953.
36   Ibid., letter of 13 March 1957.

23. A Loss for Words

By October 1951 Alan Moorehead had resumed his writing career to the gratification of those who thought his talent fitted him for greater things than public relations work for the Civil Service. One such friend, writing from the United States, was unequivocal in her view: 'How much longer are you going on rotting in Whitehall when you could be writing books?'[1] Another friend wrote: 'I am delighted to hear that you are writing again'. Moreover, for some his fiction did not match the quality of his other work and he would be well advised to shun it: 'You just are not a novelist and never can be. You have such supreme gifts in other directions. It makes me a bit mad that you *will* write novels!'[2] So began a sequence of non-fiction books – about Gallipoli, Australia, Africa and so on – which drew on his roots, his experience and his prodigious talent for selecting material and writing with great clarity, elegance and power.

With the other members of the Trio dead, Alan contemplated emigrating to Australia: after all, what was there to keep him and the family in Europe? After Clifford's death, in 1952, he travelled to his home country, intent on writing a series of articles. He met up with the novelist Nevil Shute in Alice Springs, having driven there from Adelaide, struck by the way two weeks of rain had transformed the landscape after three months of drought, the brown dust turning green again. He and Shute drove for three days to Darwin, before flying on to Townsville so that Moorehead could see the Great Barrier Reef and write another article. It was clear that his idea of moving to Australia was a serious one: in a letter, Shute offered to help him find a house: 'I do not think you would regret it if you spent a few years in Australia.'[3]

By now Alan's post-war writing career was flourishing: there were two novels and a series of non-fiction books which won considerable recognition as well as good sales figures. Gratifyingly he received praise from friends and the wider world: Freya Stark wrote congratulating him; so too did Bernard Berenson. He went deep sea fishing with Ernest Hemingway. Angela du Maurier, Daphne's sister, suggested he might dramatise *A Summer Night* which she had read with enormous pleasure in a single sitting. It was, she wrote, 'a "real" story'. The world of newspapers was changing and he did not appear to hanker after his old life; Osbert Lancaster was not alone in thinking that newspapers had not changed for the better. Writing to Lucy, he observed that the decline of the *Daily Express* would hit its former editor hard: 'poor old Chris must be turning in his grave.'[4]

In 1956 Moorehead was awarded the Duff Cooper Prize for his account of the Gallipoli campaign. Winston Churchill presented him with the award, observing that Moorehead, as the first recipient of the prize, must feel greatly honoured and proud that he had been unanimously nominated by three such celebrated and eminent writers as Sir Maurice Bowra, Sir Harold Nicholson and Lord David Cecil.

As for the memory of Alexander Clifford, there was talk of a biography written by Jenny Nicholson (Crosse as she had become). An aunt of Clifford's wrote to Jenny on 9 February 1958: 'I am of course delighted to know "THE LIFE" is to BE! And your father will help you.' A fortnight later a further letter indicated that the family had been talking over the writing of Alex's life 'and we do feel as Alan Moorehead *promised* to write it, *he should be kept to it*'. Jenny wrote back several months later with the news that Alan had only just returned from a trip on the

Alan deep-sea fishing with Ernest and Mary Hemingway. (John Moorehead)

Nile and revealed that Alan had, at home in a trunk in the cellar, 40,000 words he had already written about his old and dear friend.

For a while, though, the trunk remained unopened. Moorehead continued writing and travelling for the next decade until, in December 1966, his own health began to give cause for concern. He had had a series of headaches and these were followed by other, more disturbing symptoms: occasional numbness, garbled words, pain in his neck and arms. Lucy prevailed on him to go to the doctor's and he duly underwent a series of tests.

Soon after, he suffered a major stroke which left his prognosis in doubt. He had an operation after which he was in a coma for a week when it became clear that it had not been entirely successful. The man who lived by words could no longer speak, read or write; indeed he could hardly move. A course of physiotherapy followed but progress was slow. It was cruel: 'His brain was active, his memory was clear, but he could not communicate'.[5] He was essentially a prisoner in his own body.

Strangely he could still play bridge, doing so once a week, the family having devised a strategy for ensuring that he could manage the cards. His writing days, however, were conclusively over. Lucy worked hard to define a workable structure for Moorehead's memoir *A Late Education* about Alex Clifford and this came out four years after Moorehead had ceased writing. After it was published, Lucy threatened to sue anyone who suggested that Alan had not written it, writing to his publisher, 'I can only imagine what you, as a publisher, must feel when anyone even infers that A LATE EDUCATION, published by you as an autobiographical book written by Alan Moorehead, has been in any way written by anyone else but him.'[6] The book was greeted with great enthusiasm by the critics, although *The New Yorker* turned it down: 'Mr Moorehead's writing is so good – so elegant, really that we wish we could see our way clear to publishing his memoir of Alexander Clifford.' But the magazine sniffily declined, declaring that it was 'outside the scope of what we do'.[7]

After Moorehead's stroke he and his son John drew very close. They lived next door to each other and John would always remember his father's 'grace and courage' as he faced death.[8] While *A Late Education* marked an ending to his writing life, his domestic certainties were to be thrown into deep confusion in 1979 when Lucy was killed in a crash when her car was hit by a lorry in Italy. Moorehead, who was a passenger in the car, survived.

The last of the Trio lived on for four more years, supported by his children. Then, on 29 September 1983, he suffered a second, fatal stroke, some seventeen years after the first. The Trio's lone survivor was gone.

NOTES

1   Moorehead papers, NLA, MS 5654. Letter dated 15 March 1951 from Marianne (surname illegible) in New Jersey.

2   Ibid., letter dated 19 October 1954 from Lionel (surname illegible).

3   Ibid., letter from Nevil Shute Norway, dated 9 July 1952. Follow-up letter dated 17 July with similar sentiments.

4   Ibid., letter to Lucy from Osbert Lancaster.

5   Pocock, p.281.

6   Moorehead papers, NLA, MS 5654. Letter dated 23 October 1970.

7   Ibid., letter to Lucy Moorehead from William Shawn, 24 February 1970.

8   Interview with John Moorehead.

24. A Final Dispatch

I t was only thirty years from the time Clifford and Moorehead first met in the Bar Basque in Saint-Jean-de-Luz to the day when the only surviving member of the Trio suffered his catastrophic stroke. Over that period, three of the greatest war correspondents of the last century travelled the world, wrote dispatches from deserts, battlefields, army headquarters and bomb-scarred airfields. The three of them bore witness to a turbulent time and, in so doing, their lives became crossed or entangled, however briefly, with those of many others – wives and lovers, fellow newspapermen, soldiers, family and friends.

Of the wives and lovers, Jenny Nicholson, who had married the Reuters man Patrick Crosse so soon after Alex Clifford's death, continued to work as a journalist based in Rome and died in 1964 of a brain haemorrhage at the age of 45. Cecilia Buckley married twice more, the second time to a successful brewer in East Anglia, and died as Cecilia Russell-Smith in 1996.

Of the journalists, Kim Philby, who had worked in Spain with Clifford during the Civil War, was a double agent and defected to Russia in 1963. He died in 1988. Geoffrey Cox, the head of the *Express*'s Paris office before the war, where he had crossed swords with Moorehead, became a broadcasting executive and the second editor of ITN. He died in 2008 at the age of 97. Richard Dimbleby became the BBC's lead news reporter and the sonorous voice covering major royal ceremonies and public events. He was one of a number of war correspondents who died young, in his case in 1965 at the age of 52. Chester Wilmot, for example, was killed in 1954 when the Comet air liner in which he was returning to London plunged into the Mediterranean. Philip Jordan, who had worked closely with Moorehead in North Africa in 1943, later became a press adviser to Prime Minister Clement Atlee, but died in 1951. Moorehead made all the arrangements for his memorial service, as he did with Wilmot's.

Arthur Christiansen, Moorehead's editor at the *Daily Express*, held that post from 1933 to 1957, dying just six years later at the age of 59.

Patrick Crosse worked for Reuters for thirty-six years, becoming deputy general manager, then Latin American manager. Jenny's death was a bitter blow to him and remained painful until he died, nearly thirty years later, in 1993. Edward Ward, a BBC man who worked with Moorehead and Clifford in North Africa and who became a POW, inherited the title Lord Bangor in 1950 and continued working as a foreign correspondent for many years. He was also an author, writing amongst other things three volumes of autobiography. Like Patrick Crosse, he died in 1993. Clare Hollingworth, who had lived with Christopher Buckley in Cairo, continued to work as a war correspondent and journalist for many years. She celebrated her 100th birthday in 2011. Richard McMillan was similarly long-living, dying in 2007 at the age of 99. In old age he had returned his OBE in protest at the Poll Tax, appearing in court for non-payment when he was 90. Russell Hill, who as a reporter for the *New York Herald Tribune* worked – and played bridge – with Moorehead and Clifford, remained in Europe after the war, working for Radio Free Europe. He later became a senior reporter in Washington in 1963 and died in 2007. Geoffrey Keating became a Public Relations Officer with British Petroleum. Ronald Monson returned to Australia, working for the *Sydney Daily* and *Sunday Telegraph* covering amongst other things, the war in Korea, the Suez Crisis and the Arab/Israeli conflict. A stroke in 1972 prompted his retirement and he died the following year.

Of the soldiers with whom the Trio had dealings, Field Marshal Archibald Wavell became Viceroy of India until his retirement in 1947. He became Earl Wavell and died in 1950. Field Marshal Sir Claude Auchinleck became commander-in-chief in India until 1947, retired to the UK in 1948, emigrated to Morocco at the age of 84 and died in 1981 at the age of 96. Field Marshal Bernard Montgomery was ennobled as Viscount Montgomery of Alamein in 1946 and ended his military career as Chief of the Imperial General Staff. He died in 1976, aged 88. Freddie de Guingand, Montgomery's chief of staff, retired in 1947 and emigrated to Southern Rhodesia where he became a successful businessman. He died in Cannes in 1979, aged 79.

Both John and Caroline Moorehead, Alan's two elder children, became journalists, and Caroline is an acclaimed writer and biographer of, among others, Martha Gellhorn.

25. A Return to the Bar Basque

In any story there are decisive moments when, if another road had been taken, things would have turned out differently. What would have been the consequence for each member of the Trio, for example, if Alexander Clifford had not been in the Bar Basque on that day in 1938 when a travel-stained Alan Moorehead wandered in, anxious about his schoolboy French, but full of youthful energy? Or if Christopher Buckley and the rest had not been in Greece in the war's early days and shared ouzo and conversation? Or if cables had come back from London, saying 'Don't follow Moorehead (or Clifford) stop European theatre clear priority'? It was happenstance that threw all three together, and the shared experience of life in Cairo, and desert hardship which cemented the relationship. For Clifford and Moorehead, in particular, the friendship was life-changing – transforming – and deeply felt: few friends, after all, share so much time together, or travel in partnership through such a high octane life. The three correspondents were bound together by a hundred conversations under the stars, bullets and bombs aimed indiscriminately at them, journeys together to the back of beyond, and a never-ending balancing act between rivalry and mutual regard. The war gave them the need for a kind of friendship that most of us can never know.

They may have been fortunate to share such a friendship, but their post-war lives were all cruelly cut short, with only Alan Moorehead surviving more than a decade after the war had ended. For a man of words to lose the very quality which set him apart was – is – heartbreaking. What might they have achieved, the three of them, given kinder gods? Weighty academic Christopher Buckley, content in his Oxford college, researching military strategy; Alexander Clifford anchoring a politics programme for the BBC with suave assurance; Alan Moorehead casting an eye on a Nobel prize for literature? It was not to be: Buckley was killed by the very thing he had always feared in the field of battle; Clifford succumbing to cancer after a war in which he had been beset by a worsening series of minor illnesses; and Moorehead's last book being a eulogy for his old friend, a book which had lain unregarded in the cellar in Primrose Hill and which Lucy had been enlisted to help shape.

What made these special correspondents so special? To begin with, they understood what constituted genuine news. Moreover, all three could write with clarity, insight and economy. They were able to describe events in such a way that readers could see the Caspian Sea, or the mountains of Italy, or the flashes of gunfire at night, or the limitless desert; could smell the cordite, taste the heat, feel the danger. They travelled relentlessly, driven on by inquisitiveness and a sense of responsibility. They could identify the wider significance of events – it was Moorehead who was particularly adept at sensing the 'turn of the tide'. Their reports from war zones could easily have been placed in each other's papers: through the war years there was little, if any, difference in the quality of war reporting amongst the three newspapers, broadsheet or tabloid. It was all writing of genuine quality. They all kicked against the desire of the authorities to restrict and censor, sought to avoid the trap of propaganda, and reached the war's end exhausted and war-weary.

In my mind's eye I prefer to see them when their world was young, when as novice reporters they froze in Spanish winter, or later, wide-eyed on first entering the North African desert, and stunned by its silence, or choked by sandstorms, or clinging on to the seat as a dusty jeep bounced over mountain tracks, or laughing and drinking in the evening light at Shepheards, playing fiercely competitive bridge in a haze of cigarette smoke, hunched up against the cold in the rattling fuselage of some Cairo-bound aircraft, poised over typewriters in the light of a hurricane lamp, or squinting against the sun's unforgiving light and the vivid bright blue of the Mediterranean on the cliffs of Taormina, enjoying a respite from the war, before its last remorseless and oh-so-slow denouement.

In the early days, when the three of them were in Spain, before marriage and before careers that had taken their final unalterable course, before the bombing of Guernica was surpassed in horror by hundreds of war-torn cities from Warsaw to Nagasaki, the future must have seemed so uncomplicated, life so long-lasting, and hope largely unblemished. Imagine the three of them – Buckley too, why not? – back at the Bar Basque all those years ago, three young tyros, and map out for them a different story, where the careers of these three special correspondents – fine writers all – led on to lives marked by security, longevity and sustained and recognised achievement. You watch the three of them leave the bar, stepping out into the Basque night arm-in-arm and a voice echoes in your head: 'Follow Clifford, Follow Moorehead, Follow Buckley!'

Appendix: The Trio's Itinerant Years

he table shows the itinerant nature of the Trio's various lives between 1938 and 1945.

In the post-war years the Trio rarely met: the Mooreheads spent their time in London, Australia and Italy, with occasional work trips by Alan – to India for example.

Alexander Clifford travelled widely – Russia, America and the Middle East for example – and was based initially in France and later in Italy.

Christopher Buckley visited the Iron Curtain countries and the Far East, before travelling to Korea to report on that country's conflict. He was based in Tunbridge Wells, Kent.

	Christopher Buckley	Alexander Clifford	Alan Moorehead
Pre-1938	Schoolteacher in Letchworth. Goes to Spain (Friends Ambulance Unit).	Working for Reuters.	Sent to Gibraltar by the *Express* to cover Spain's civil war. At sea (Istanbul to Valencia, Spain).
1938	Hitchhikes around Republican Spain. Writes on the war in Spain for the *Christian Science Monitor*.	To Spain to cover the civil war for Reuters. Meets Moorehead in the Bar Basque, St-Jean-de-Luz. In November, goes to Berlin as chief correspondent for Germany.	Meets Clifford in the Bar Basque, St-Jean-de-Luz.
1939	In Warsaw when the war breaks out. Moves on to the Balkans, Bucharest and Turkey.	Berlin: witnesses the signing of the Pact of Steel and the launch of the *Bismarck*. Leaves Berlin when war seems certain. To Brussels.	Reporting on the end of the Spanish Civil War. Marries Lucy Milner. In Paris when war breaks out, but leaves immediately for Rome.

1940	In the Low Countries during the German attack. The Trio meets up in Greece. Editing a weekly newspaper in Athens.	Based in Amsterdam reporting on the 'Phoney War'. Joins the *Daily Mail* from the beginning of May. Meets Moorehead in Athens. Travels by flying boat to Cairo with Moorehead. To Jerusalem (June). To Libya with Moorehead. Operational flight in a Sunderland flying boat (July). At Wavell's briefing (9 December). To the desert. Contracts sand-fly fever and jaundice.	In May stays in the Grande Bretagne Hotel in Athens and meets with Clifford. Travels by flying boat to Cairo with Clifford. To Libya with Clifford. Goes to the Sudan with Richard Dimbleby amongst others (July). Lucy Moorehead arrives in Cairo. John Moorehead born (December). At Wavell's briefing (9 December). To the desert.
1941	Working for *The Daily Telegraph* in Athens. Escapes from Greece, then Crete (April–May). Travels to Cairo, sharing a flat with Clare Hollingworth. Christmas in Benghazi.	Convalescing in Cairo. Ambushed by Italians and wounded (February). Enters captured Benghazi (February). Travels to Athens to cover the war in Greece. Escapes from Greece, then Crete. Returns to Cairo (May). Near Tobruk having had 'too much of the desert'. Back in Cairo (July). Decides to go to Persia (August). With Moorehead overlooking the Caspian Sea. Travels from Cairo to the Belgian Congo (October). Christmas in Benghazi.	Leaves Cairo (4 January). Ambushed by Italians (February). Libya. Enters captured Benghazi (February) Sent to Addis Ababa, arriving too late; eventually returns to Cairo. Travels to Haifa and Damascus. Begins writing *Mediterranean Front*. Sent to Persia (August). With Clifford overlooking the Caspian Sea. To the desert with Hill and Jacob, visiting the oasis at Siwa. Christmas in Benghazi.
1942	Cairo. With Clifford and others in Alexandria. Caught up in the 'Flap'. On the desert road with Moorehead (June). Reports on the first battle at Alamein (July). Reports on the Alamein campaign through the summer.	Stays twenty-seven days in the desert. Cairo: begins writing his own book (25 January). To the desert with Russell Hill. Elects not to go to India, but stays in Cairo. To the desert (May). Travels to Siwa with Richard McMillan. Travels to Alexandria with Dimbleby. Caught up in the 'flap'. With Moorehead near Tobruk. At the Alamein front. Takes a flying boat to the UK (August). London, then Glasgow, before sailing back to the Middle East (October). Cairo.	Leaves for Cairo with Jacob over New Year. Skiing with Lucy in the Syrian mountains (February). Travels to India to cover the diplomatic mission of Sir Stafford Cripps (March). Travels to Ceylon and then back to Egypt (May). Alexandria. Caught up in the 'flap'. With Clifford near Tobruk. On the desert road with Buckley (June). At the Alamein front. Sails for America in the *Zola* (August). New York. Made chief correspondent for Africa. Scotland, London, Ireland.

1943	Cairo. Tripoli with 8th Army. Enters Tripoli on 26 January. Meets up with Moorehead and Clifford in Sousse (April) – bridge! The 'Trio enters Tunis (May). Leaves Suez heading for Sicily (June). Invades Sicily. The 'summer school' at Taormina. Over the Messina Straits to Italy (September). Heading north through Italy (autumn). Shared picnic among the oak trees. Christmas at 'Dysentery Hall'.	Cairo. Tripoli with 8th Army and enters the captured city. Meets up with Moorehead and Buckley in Sousse (April) – bridge! The Trio enters Tunis (May). Clifford and Moorehead drive to Algiers. Invades Sicily. The 'summer school' at Taormina. Over the Messina Straits to Italy (September). Heading north through Italy (autumn). Shared picnic among the oak trees. Christmas in Naples.	Arrives in Algiers (January). Attends Casablanca conference (January) Travels with Philip Jordan en route for Tripoli. Meets up with Buckley and Clifford in Sousse (April) – bridge! The Trio enters Tunis (May). Moorehead and Clifford drive to Algiers. Returns to London (end of May). The 'summer school' at Taormina. Over the Messina Straits to Italy (September). Heading north through Italy (autumn). Shared picnic among the oak trees. Christmas in Naples.
1944	Monte Cassino, Italy. England. D-Day: France. Heads for Paris with the Trio (August). At the liberation of Paris and Brussels. Reaches the German border. Christmas in Brussels.	Italy. Back in England travelling in Ike's Flying Fortress. Misses D-Day, but arrives soon after. Heads for Paris with the Trio (August). At the liberation of Paris and Brussels. Falls in love with Jenny Nicholson. Reaches the German border. Christmas in Brussels.	Italy. Back in England travelling in Ike's Flying Fortress. D-Day, France. Heading for Paris with the Trio (August). At the liberation of Paris and Brussels. Reaches the German border. Christmas in Brussels.
1945	Germany. Denmark. London. Far East including Saigon.	Germany. Marries Jenny Nicholson (February). Denmark. Norway. London. Rome.	Germany. Denmark. Norway.

Bibliography

Edward Ardizzone, *Diary of a War Artist*, The Bodley Head, 1974

Rick Atkinson, *The Guns at Last Light*, Little, Brown, 2013

A.B. Austin, *Birth of an Army*, Gollancz, 1943

Cecil Beaton, *Near East*, Batsford, 1943

Cecil Beaton, *The Years Between*, Weidenfeld & Nicholson, 1965

Croswell Bowen, *Back From Tobruk*, Potomac Books, 2013

Christopher Buckley, *Road to Rome*, Hodder & Stoughton, 1945

Christopher Buckley, *Greece and Crete 1941*, HMSO, 1952

Richard Busvine, *Gullible's Travels*, Constable, 1945

Doon Campbell, *Magic Mistress*, Tagman, 2000

Iris Carpenter, *No Woman's World*, Houghton Mifflin, 1946

Arthur Christiansen, *Headlines All My Life*, Heinemann, 1961

Alexander Clifford, *Three Against Rommel*, Harrap, 1943

Alexander Clifford & Jenny Nicholson, *The Sickle and the Stars*, Peter
    Davies, 1949

Alexander Clifford, *Enter Citizens*, Evans, 1950

Julia Kennedy Cochran, *Ed Kennedy's War*, Louisiana State University, 2012

Richard Collier, *Fighting Words*, St Martin's Press, 1989

Artemis Cooper, *Cairo in the War*, Hamish Hamilton, 1989

Geoffrey Cox, *Countdown to War*, William Kimber, 1988

Eve Curie, *Journey Among Warriors*, Heinemann, 1943

John Dancy, *Walter Oakeshott*, Michael Russell, 1995

Francis de Guingand, *Operation Victory*, Hodder & Stoughton, 1947

Jonathan Dimbleby, *Destiny in the Desert*, Profile, 2012

Jonathan Dimbleby, *Richard Dimbleby*, Hodder & Stoughton, 1975

Richard Dimbleby, *The Frontiers Are Green*, Hodder & Stoughton, 1943

Charles Gardner, *A.A.S.F.*, Hutchinson, 1940

Frank Gervasi, *The Violent Decade*, Norton, 1989

William Graves, *Wild Olives*, Pimlico, 2001

Matthew Halton, *Ten Years to Alamein*, Lindsay Drummond, 1944

Mary Welsh Hemingway, *How it Was*, Futura, 1978

Russell Hill, *Desert Conquest*, Jarrolds, 1943

Russell Hill, *Desert War*, Alfred Knopf, 1942

Russell Hill, *Struggle for Germany*, Gollancz, 1947

Wilfrid Hindle (ed.), *Foreign Correspondent*, Harrap, 1939

Clare Hollingworth, *There's a German Just Behind Me*, The Book Club, 1943

Clare Hollingworth, *Front Line*, Jonathan Cape, 1990

Alaric Jacob, *A Traveller's War*, Collins, 1944

Philip Jordan, *Jordan's Tunis Diary*, Collins, 1943

Phillip Knightley, *Philby KGB Masterspy*, HBJ, 1975

Osbert Lancaster, *With An Eye to the Future*, John Murray, 1967

Richard McMillan, *Rendezvous with Rommel*, Jarrolds, 1943

Richard McMillan, *Twenty Angels Over Rome*, Jarrolds, 1944

Richard McMillan, *Miracle before Berlin*, Jarrolds, 1946

Alan Moorehead, *Mediterranean Front*, Hamish Hamilton, 1941

Alan Moorehead, *A Year of Battle*, Hamish Hamilton, 1943

Alan Moorehead, *The End in Africa*, Hamish Hamilton, 1943

Alan Moorehead, *Eclipse*, Hamish Hamilton, 1945

Alan Moorehead, *Montgomery*, Hamish Hamilton, 1946

Alan Moorehead, *The Villa Diana*, Scribners, 1951

Alan Moorehead, *Cooper's Creek*, Hamish Hamilton, 1963

Alan Moorehead, *A Late Education*, Hamish Hamilton, 1970

Caroline Moorehead, *Sidney Bernstein*, Cape, 1984

Michael Moynihan, *War Correspondent*, Leo Cooper, 1994

Jean Nichol, *Meet Me at the Savoy*, Museum Press, 1952

Jenny Nicholson, *Kiss the Girls Goodbye*, Hutchinson, 1944

Barney Oldfield, *Never a Shot in Anger*, Capra Press, 1956

Daphne Phelps, *A House in Sicily*, Virago, 1999

Tom Pocock, *Alan Moorehead*, The Bodley Head, 1990

Miranda Seymour, *Robert Graves*, Doubleday, 1995

I.S.K. Soboleff, *Cossack at Large*, Peter Davies, 1960

Maureen Waller, *London 1945*, John Murray, 2004

Edward Ward, *Give Me Air*, John Lane/Bodley Head, 1946

Edward Ward, *Number One Boy*, Michael Joseph, 1969

Charles Whiting, *Papa Goes to War*, The Crowood Press, 1990

David Woodward, *Front Line and Front Page*, Eyre & Spottiswoode, 1943

Gordon Young, *Outposts of Victory*, Hodder & Stoughton, 1943

Gordon Young, *Outposts of War*, Hodder & Stoughton, 1941

Acknowledgements

A curious side effect of the Second World War was an upsurge in publishing, despite a shortage of paper. Newsmen and newswomen often could not wait to turn ephemeral journalism into memoir, and many of their volumes were a great help to me in researching the story of *The Trio*. It goes without saying that Buckley's, Clifford's and Moorehead's accounts of key campaigns were an inspiration to me, but so were dozens more. Perhaps the most compelling of them were the books by Richard Dimbleby, Eve Curie, Philip Jordan and Richard Busvine, but as my footnotes testify, I could not have written this book without those who went before me, and who endured the discomforts and pain so far removed from my desk in a peaceful Somerset.

The actual starting point for this book was a letter from Alan to Lucy Moorehead describing an idea for his next book 'so fragile and reeking that I scarcely dare to write about it. It's a book about our summer school in Taormina and our winter school in Naples.' I found the quotation in Tom Pocock's readable biography of Moorehead and it prompted me to explore the Trio's long and winding road into and out of Taormina. Initially, I turned to the 'official' sources of information, notably the Imperial War Museum, where I read with mounting admiration and fascination the extensive papers of Alexander Clifford, and the National Library of Australia where the Moorehead papers are kept. I am grateful to the archivists at both institutions. Other sources of material have included The National Archives, the British Library, the Liddell Hart Centre for Military Archives at King's College, University of London, the Bodleian Library, and the *Christian Science Monitor* Library. I am grateful to the trustees of the Liddell Hart Centre for Military Archives for permission to use quotations from their archive.

One of the pleasures of researching this book has been the willing help received from individuals: both Caroline and John Moorehead have been extremely supportive, both in terms of sharing their memories both of their father and the other members of the Trio: their respective godfathers Alexander Clifford (John) and Christopher Buckley (Caroline). Talking to both Mooreheads was a real pleasure. I am grateful too to Mrs Elizabeth Quyke who holds the copyright for Clifford's papers at the Imperial War Museum and who readily gave permission for me to mine and use the extensive documents in Clifford's wonderful archive.

The search for Christopher Buckley's papers preoccupied me throughout the project. I did not want him to be the third mysterious, and therefore less important, member of the threesome. But the obvious ports of call produced nothing. Yet I knew from a reference in *Road to Rome* that he had kept some kind of journal – 'In my diary', he wrote, 'I find the following significant entry for September 6: "The war is over for the Italian people..."'[1] Did the diary still exist and could it be tracked down? I sent tentative enquiries to Oriel College, Oxford University, where Buckley took his degree, for example, as well as the Tunbridge Wells Civic Society – but without luck. I talked to a friend, Judith Bryant, who specialises in locating the real parents of adopted children. She gave me some wise advice about how to proceed: I progressed from Buckley's marriage certificate (Christopher Thomas Rede Buckley, bachelor, aged 42, journalist, resident at the National Liberal Club), to his will (via the London Probate Service), to his wife Cecilia's death certificate (in Suffolk, 1996), and then to her husband's later remarriage and death (John Russell-Smith, Norfolk, 2006). His widow, Gael Russell-Smith, responded to an enquiry from me, kindly suggesting I contact Shirley Tudor-Pole who was able to describe her memories of Buckley and who put me in touch with Genista Toland, the daughter of Cecilia Buckley's brother, Hugh. The conversations I had with both were helpful and confirmed for me Buckley's charm and erudition. They also both took the view, however, that Cecilia's business-like, no-nonsense view of the world was such that Buckley's papers would not have been preserved. 'She would have thrown stuff out', I was told with great certainty. Shirley helped clear Cecilia's house when she died and she confirmed that there were no papers of any significance left.

There are other names I should mention: I wrote to both Jonathan Dimbleby (about his father) and Sir Max Hastings (about *The Daily Telegraph* and Christopher Buckley) and received, in both cases, kind and interested replies. My commissioning editor at The History Press, Jo de Vries, has again been a pleasure to work with and supportive throughout. In addition, I should like to thank Lyndall Passerini, Betsy Connor Bowen, Paul Patterson and Anthony Grey. I am grateful to Ana and Kino Bardaji who explored and photographed the Bar Basque in St-Jean-de-Luz on my behalf from their home across the border in

Spain. I am also grateful to William Lancaster for permitting me to quote from his father's letters to the Mooreheads. Every effort has been made to trace the copyright holders of the material in this book.

Finally I want to thank my wife, Vanessa, who has put up with my obsessive pursuit of these three heroes of mine, provided shrewd and timely advice about the book's structure, and brought me reviving cups of coffee when I was at my desk, just as Cecilia did for Christopher Buckley as he worked away at his writing nearly seventy years ago in that upstairs room at 46 Mount Sion, Tunbridge Wells.

NOTES

1　　　Buckley, p.164.

Index

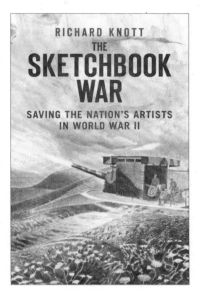

The Sketchbook War

RICHARD KNOTT

978 0 7509 5615 4

During the Second World War, British artists produced over 6,000 works of war art, the result of a government scheme partly designed to prevent the artists being killed. This book tells the story of nine courageous war artists who ventured closer to the front line than any others in their profession. Edward Ardizzone, Edward Bawden, Barnett Freedman, Anthony Gross, Thomas Hennell, Eric Ravilious, Albert Richards, Richard Seddon and John Worsley all travelled abroad into the dangers of war to chronicle events by painting them. They formed a close bond, yet two were torpedoed, two were taken prisoner and three died, two in 1945 when peacetime was at hand. Men who had previously made a comfortable living painting in studios were transformed by military uniforms and experiences that were to shape the rest of their lives, and their work significantly influenced the way in which we view war today.

Portraying how war and art came together in a moving and dramatic way, and incorporating vivid examples of their paintings, this is the true story behind the war artists who fought, lived and died for their art on the front line of the Second World War.

Visit our website and discover thousands of other History Press books.

www.thehistorypress.co.uk

The History Press